Harnett County Public Library

WITHDRAWN

D1307268

Harnett County Public Library

RALEIGH
CITY OF OAKS

RALEIGH
CITY OF OAKS

An Illustrated History

by James Vickers

Picture Research by Jan–Michael Poff

American Historical Press
Sun Valley, California

Raleigh marked the 100th anniversary of the completion of the capitol building and the
Raleigh & Gaston Railroad with a day-long celebration on May 21, 1940. The Centennial Parade of Transportation is
shown making its way down Fayetteville Street. Courtesy, Division of Archives and History (DAH), Raleigh

Harnett County Public Library

Color photographs by Dickson Qualls unless otherwise indicated.

© American Historical Press
All Rights Reserved
Published 1997
Printed in the United States of America

Library of Congress Catalogue Card Number: 97-77099

ISBN: 0-9654754-7-6

For Barth and Hadley

Raleigh's paid fire fighters pose in front of Station Number One in their old and new "fire trucks" circa 1912. Sherwood Brockwell, the nation's first full-time, paid fire chief, is riding in the center car. (DAH)

CONTENTS

Cotton brokers inspect a farmer's crops and await the arrival of other clients in front of the Commercial National Bank building, 14 East Martin Street, around 1913. (DAH)

INTRODUCTION

When I began work on this history of Raleigh, my conception of the capital was no doubt similar to that of many, if not most, North Carolinians. My image of the city consisted almost entirely of a collage of legislative chambers, a natural museum, a pleasant statehouse square, pigeons and statues, and a slow-paced atmosphere. I had gained my very limited insight into Raleigh almost entirely from weekend visits and quick trips through town. I assumed that behind its "official" front Raleigh was a medium-sized North Carolina city pretty much like any other.

John Barth says anything looked at closely enough becomes complex, and in the last year I have given Raleigh a relatively close look. My early impressions are too firmly imprinted to have vanished, but they now occupy a narrow tract of a far larger collage, and Raleigh is a far more complex mesh of institutions, individuals, neighborhoods, and enterprises than I had imagined.

For the first 150 years or more of the city's existence, the great drive was for change, for an expansion of the government-dominated economic and social base. A statewide migration negated any hope for expansion during the capital's adolescent years, and even a new statehouse, the arrival of railroad lines, and the knowledge that the South desperately needed to increase its industrial capacity did little to diversify the local economy. Following the Civil War and Reconstruction, times when physical and fiscal survival was the only hope, civic and commercial leaders achieved some success, and small industries began to thrive. But Raleigh was too far removed from the tobacco belt. High Point became the furniture capital of the region, and textile mills came to Raleigh only sparingly. Raleigh, then, missed out on the major industries of North Carolina, but the consequences were not all negative.

Raleigh weathered the Great Depression, as it has weathered recent recessions, better than most cities in the Piedmont Crescent because of the presence of governmental and educational institutions. But the drive for expansion persisted, and since World War II the city has achieved unprecedented success. That success has accounted for much of Raleigh's current complexity. Without question, the quality of life in Wake County is improving in many aspects, and Raleigh is now as well known in board rooms as in smoke-filled rooms.

In the following pages, hopefully you will enjoy becoming more familiarly acquainted with the Raleigh of old and many of the people—characters, if you will—who helped it along before it became a "megalopolis" of the Piedmont. Some of them—William W. Holden, Josephus Daniels, Walter Hines Page—play roles in state, national, even international histories. Most of them must be content with a more modest stage, but they are often no less interesting than their more famous neighbors. Whether their city as presented in this volume is interesting or not is a matter for which I must assume responsibility; the original was fascinating.

James Vickers

Sir Walter Raleigh was the first Englishman to sponsor a serious effort to establish a permanent colony in the New World. Three exploratory voyages by his agents, beginning in April 1584, preceded his most ambitious expedition in May 1587. The fourth fleet carried the 89 men, 17 women, and 9 children who were to found the ill-fated "Citie of Raleigh in Virginia" on Roanoke Island, which vanished into history as the mysterious "Lost Colony." More than 200 years later, the name of the expedition's short-lived settlement would be resurrected to grace an uninhabited grove of oaks in Wake County that had been newly designated as the permanent capital of North Carolina.

Some 60 years after the disappearance of the Lost Colony, trappers, hunters, and farmers began to drift southward from Virginia into the Albemarle Sound region, reaching sufficient numbers by March 24, 1663, for Charles II to grant a large tract south of Virginia to

I

AN EVENTFUL BIRTH:

TO 1792

eight Lords Proprietors. By 1665 the Lords Proprietors, who were given absolute control over the land, had formed a working government. The Lords Proprietors were predominantly of aristocratic English and Scottish background, and settlers of similar bloodlines soon moved into the Cape Fear Valley from Charleston. By 1729, when North and South Carolina were made separate royal colonies, a spirited political conflict had developed between the older counties in the northeast and the newer counties in the southeast.

Each region naturally wanted to host the General Assembly, and the compromise solution was to allow the General Assembly to "migrate" up and down the coastal area, often meeting at different towns for separate sessions in the same year. In 1766 Governor William Tryon convinced the legislature to build a luxurious executive mansion to serve as the permanent seat of government in centrally located New Bern, but by then another element had entered the sectional conflict.

A different breed of immigrants was settling the Piedmont region, creating counties as far west as Mecklenburg and Rowan. Egalitarian-minded small farmers and merchants for the most part, these Piedmont settlers had little in common with the aristocratic, slave-holding planters of the east. The easterners maintained control over the actions of the General Assembly by creating new eastern counties to offset the votes of entries from the west, relegating the westerners almost to vassal status. They imposed high and corruptly collected taxes on the merchants and farmers, and the western local governments were ruled by governor-appointed officials. When eastern aristocrats began using tax moneys to construct their "Palace" in New Bern, which westerners considered the "enemy camp," the sectional hostilities escalated and finally resulted in action.

Western settlers organized themselves politically under the "Regulator" banner, vowing to pay no more taxes or fees until the government was reformed and treatment of the western counties made more equitable. Negotiations were soon abandoned and Governor Tryon called out the state militia to put down the Regulators. The governor chose recently established Wake County as the militia's initial staging area.

Although Wake County, in 1770, was still sparsely populated, its site had entered history some 70 years before, and isolated settlement had been going on for decades before the county was officially created. The first record of a European visiting what

This portrait of Sir Walter Raleigh (1552?-1618) hangs in the National Gallery, London. Raleigh's desire to establish an English colony probably stemmed from his reading Richard Hakluyt's Divers Voyages Touching the Discoverie of America and the Islands Adjacent. Though his attempts at settling what is now North Carolina failed, the state honors his memory in the name of its capital city. (DAH)

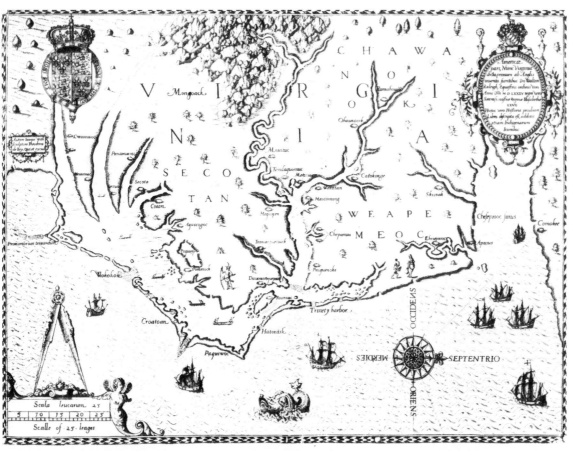

A Theodore De Bry engraving of John White's map, illustrating the destination of the Roanoke voyages, was made in 1590. The chart, which William P. Cummings in North Carolina in Maps called "the most careful delineation made in the 16th century of any considerable part of the North American coastline," features the Outer Banks, Chesapeake Bay (Chesepioc sinus), Cape Lookout (Promontorium tremendum), and the names of extant Indian villages. (DAH)

J. P. Cumming, North Carolina in Maps (Raleigh: State Department of Archives and History, 1966), Plate II.

White - De Bry 1590

Courtesy of State Department of Archives and History, Raleigh

would become Wake County was left by John Lawson in 1701. That year, during an exploration of the interior of the Carolina territory for the Lords Proprietors, he camped the night of February 18 at the "Falls of the Neuse, called *Wee Quo Whom* by the Indians." The Indians referred to by Lawson were the Tuscarora, who were soon to be decimated in the 1711-1714 Tuscarora War. An Iroquois-speaking tribe of hunters and farmers inhabiting the area between the Pamlico and Neuse rivers, the Tuscarora had gotten along peacefully with the settlers until competition for arable land brought on hostilities. Following the war, they no longer represented a threat to the general settlement of their territory, although they still presented dangers to individuals and families. Consequently, the first arrivals in the Wake area around 1740 took care to construct dwellings that could be easily defended. John Hinton, for example, built his house with a door in the roof. It was reached by a rope ladder that could be pulled in after the last entrant. In 1766 the Tuscarora left North Carolina to join related Iroquois tribes in New York, and any menace they had posed left with them.

Both the general westward movement of established Easterners and the southern migration of the Scotch-Irish and Pennsylvania Dutch furnished the first families who settled near the Falls of the Neuse. They purchased large tracts from Lord Granville's agents, and many of the very first families remained to become leading influences for the rest of the 18th century—the Lanes, the Hintons, the Hunters, the Joneses.

Joel, Joseph, and Isaac Lane moved from Halifax in 1741 to holdings that still comprise much of modern Raleigh. About 1760, Joel Lane built his home "Wakefield" near the intersection of the Petersburg-Fayetteville and the Hillsborough-New Bern roads, now the site of Capitol Square. By present standards, the home's most distinctive characteristic is its simplicity, but at the time, Wakefield was the most elegant residence within a 100-mile radius, indicating how isolated it was from the plantations of the east and the villages of the western Piedmont.

In December 1770 the legislature took land from Orange, Johnston, and Cumberland counties to create Wake County, and the law establishing Wake became effective on March 21, 1771. By the following May, Governor Tryon was on his way to engage the Regulators. Tryon camped in the new county at Theophilus Hunter's plantation south of Wakefield, where he appointed John Hinton, the colonel of the new Wake militia. After defeating the Regulators at the Battle of Alamance on May 16, Tryon returned to disband the militia at Hunter's plantation and to spend a night at Wakefield. Then, having dealt with the insurrection, the governor signed the charter officially establishing Wake County, which was entered in superior court at New Bern on May 22.

At the time, what would become Capitol Square was used primarily as a campground, where traveling market men and drovers guarded their herds of sheep, cattle, and hogs for the night. Hunters also knew the area well. A two-foot-thick sassafras near the crossroads was reputed to be an excellent deer stand, and a salt lick just northwest of Christ Church provided another good stalking ground.

After the Wakefield locality had been chosen as the county seat, Joel Lane supervised the construction of a log cabin across the street for a courtroom, as well as a jail, stocks, and whipping post. There is a tradition that he built the Asbury Meeting House—named for Methodist Bishop Francis Asbury—on a path that would now run between the capitol and Mordecai Park. The Lane house area became known variously as Wake Crossroads, Wake Court House, and Bloomsbury. The name was derived from Governor Tryon's address in Bloomsbury Square, London.

The district superior court met in Hillsborough, but beginning on June 4, 1771, the Inferior Court of Pleas and Quarter Sessions convened in the new Wake County Courthouse. Theophilus Hunter and Joel Lane were justices of the first court. The types of cases they decided (and the punishments meted out) indicate the frontier nature of justice in pre-Revolutionary Wake County. The punishment for perjury, for instance, was to cut off a portion of the ear. If someone became "crop-eared" accidentally, he understandably wanted the public to be informed of the manner in which it happened. Consequently, in September 1771, Averington McKelroy appeared before the Inferior Court, calling Mr. Isaac Hunter as a witness to verify that he had lost "the top of his right ear by Jacob Odem's biting it off in battle."

Theophilus Hunter, following his term as a judge, went on to become a Revolutionary War colonel, a senator for Wake in the General Assembly, and one of its five commissioners to oversee the construction of the first capitol in Raleigh. Joel Lane was a legislator from Johnston County when the General Assembly created Wake County and he, too, later served as a colonel in the Revolutionary War. Lane was also a 13-term senator from Wake, one of the first trustees of the University of North Carolina, and a Wake representative to the Committee of Safety, the Provincial Congress, and the Constitutional Conventions.

During the Revolutionary War, Wake County was more unified in support of the rebellion than counties to the east or to the west. Early in the war, Colonel John Hinton and the Wake militia fought under the command of Colonel Richard Caswell in the skirmish at Moore's Creek Bridge on February 27, 1776, which proved to be the most lopsided American victory of the conflict. In the space of three minutes (and at a loss of only one killed and one wounded), the Rebels defeated Brigadier General Donald MacDonald's army of 1,600 Loyalists, killing approximately 50. The Rebels captured some 800 soldiers and large quantities of weapons and supplies, crushing Loyalist hopes of controlling the state.

No major battles occurred in Wake County, but the genuine threat of hostilities was never far removed, and the governmental activity in Wake County made it a tempting target for Tory raiders. The Committee of Safety met at Wakefield in 1776. The General Assembly convened for its first session in 1779 in Smithfield, then for three successive sessions (between June 1781 and January 1782) in the Wake County Courthouse. Wartime inflation deflated currency to such an extent that the legislature appropriated the seemingly astronomical sum of $30,000 for the use of Lane's house and pastures during a single month-long session.

On his retreat from the Battle of Guilford Courthouse to Wilmington in March of 1781 Lord Cornwallis camped four miles south of the Wake County Courthouse. Cornwallis represented no great threat to life and property, but such was not the case with the notorious David Fanning. Later that summer, in July, Fanning and his Loyalist band ambushed Rebel members of a court-martial in Pittsboro, capturing

The Tuscarora Indians captured explorer John Lawson and Baron Christoph von Graffenried in September 1712, as they sailed up the Neuse River into Indian territory. Although both men were acquitted of trespassing charges by an aboriginal tribunal, a post-trial argument between Lawson and a sub-chief cost Lawson his life. The Tuscarora once inhabited the area that now includes Raleigh, Smithfield, Wilson, Rocky Mount, Goldsboro, Tarboro, Greenville, and Kinston. (DAH)

Harnett County Public Library

several officers and three members of the General Assembly. In September, Fanning raided Hillsborough, killing 15 Rebels, wounding 20, and capturing nearly 200—including Governor Thomas Burke. Fanning never struck in Wake County, but his presence nearby added to the apprehensions of the Wake County Lighthorse, which was responsible for protecting the General Assembly during those crucial months.

Although 1783 brought an end to the Revolutionary War and a beginning to the great debates over the shape of the new limited States government, Wake Countians were also concerned about their own local problems of governmental organization. For five years following the war's end, the General Assembly continued to migrate—to New Bern, Hillsborough, Halifax, Smithfield. Growing tired of the inconvenience and fearful for the safety of official records, the legislature finally decided in 1788 to resolve the issue. A convention to consider ratification of the United States Constitution was scheduled to meet in Hillsborough later that summer, and the General Assembly instructed the delegates also to fix an "unalterable seat of government of this state."

The delegates elected a committee "to prepare and bring in an ordinance to establish the seat of government at the place hereafter to be fixed by this Convention." The members of the committee had names that have remained familiar to generations of Raleigh residents as well as to visitors finding their way around the streets of downtown: James Martin, Frederick Hargett, Joseph McDowell, William Dawson, Thomas Person, Thomas Blount, and others. Willie Jones of Halifax, the acknowledged leader of the committee, was also the leading advocate for placing the capital in Wake County.

Jones was an aristocratic sportsman with a devout love of good company, cockfighting, hunting, and horse racing. He was widely read and experienced, and his pleasant demeanor won him friends quickly. Legend has it that he once befriended a young Scotsman named John Paul and that the young man added Jones to his name as a demonstration of his appreciation. Whatever the truth may be, the legend survives in a 1925 historical novel by James Boyd, which centers on the life and adventures of John Paul Jones. Boyd portrays "Wylie" Jones, a leading figure in the first section of the story, as befriending John Paul Jones, conducting cockfights, and attending a horse race.

Later, when Raleigh came into being, Jones moved to a plantation now occupied by St. Augustine's. There he built "Welcome Place," a manor house with rooms 22 feet square and 22 feet high. His wish to be buried in Raleigh was honored, but a visitor will search in vain for the unmarked grave over which a building has been constructed. He ordered that his grave point southeast by southwest as a final expression of his disbelief in a life after death, and his will further directed that "No priest or other person is to insult my corpse by uttering impious observations over my body. Let it be covered snug and warm, and there is an end. My family and friends are not to mourn my death, even with a black rag. On

Above: *The cost and location of the provincial capitol at New Bern—better known as Tryon's Palace—fueled further western outcries of sectional discrimination. Ironically, a Latin inscription over the vestibule door of the new building read, "A free and happy people, opposed to cruel tyrants, has given this edifice to virtue. May the house and its inmates, as examples to future ages, here cultivate the arts, order, justice, and the laws."* (DAH)

Left: *Although this portrait bears the inscription, "Govr. Wm. Tryon of No. Carolina—J. Wollaston, pinxt. New York—Anno D. 1767," some art critics question its authenticity. The controversy lies in the attire of the subject: the uniform the man is wearing in the painting by John Wollaston is not that of the 29th Regiment of Foot, of which Tryon was colonel.* (DAH)

The Regulator movement withered away following the Battle of the Alamance, May 16, 1771, in which Governor Tryon and the militia defeated armed insurgents. This illustration rather fancifully depicts the governor confronting a group of Regulators, circa 1771. (DAH)

the contrary, I give my wife and three daughters colored silk to make their habits on this occasion."

The fascination with Jones stems not just from his larger-than-life personality, but also from his importance to Raleigh's origins and future course. His leadership at the 1788 convention would prove invaluable. The convention accepted nominations for seven localities: Smithfield, Tarboro, Fayetteville, New Bern, Hillsborough, the fork of the Haw and Deep rivers, and "Mr. Isaac Hunter's in Wake County." The suggestions reveal a continuation of the old sectional struggle to possess the state capital, but the preponderance of inland sites also attests to the realization that a centrally located tract was the only viable political alternative.

During its deliberations, the committee visited Isaac Hunter's Tavern twice, but at the Saturday morning session of August 2, they had not yet reached a decision and requested a delay. At four o'clock that afternoon, the committee reported that a majority agreed on Isaac Hunter's, but Cumberland County delegate Barry Grove objected forcefully on the grounds that Wake County had no commercial future and, consequently, the capital would never "rise above the degree of a village." Grove argued that placing the capital in Fayetteville would act to unite the state commercially (as well as politically) by channeling "tobacco and other valuable articles of export" from the west through North Carolina ports and away

from Virginia and South Carolina markets. Ultimately, 119 of the 268 delegates present agreed with Grove, but the majority voted for Wake County, and the convention forwarded that recommendation to the General Assembly. Following a suggestion by Willie Jones, the delegates voted to leave the exact location of the capital up to the legislators. This was done to forestall land speculation and to allow further consideration of such matters as water supply, access, and the contour of the land, "provided always that it shall be within ten miles of the plantation whereon Isaac Hunter now resides, in the County at Wake."

Even though the Hillsborough Convention had recommended that Wake County become the site of a permanent state capital, Fayetteville advocates kept the issue alive in the General Assembly, mostly through delaying tactics. When the proposal finally came to a vote on November 29, 1790, the outcome could hardly have been more dramatic. Both the house and the senate split evenly, with the speaker of the house voting in favor of Wake County and the speaker of the senate voting in opposition. Nevertheless, on December 5 of the following year, the legislature finally agreed to approve the Hillsborough recommendation. The close vote was 27 to 24 in the senate, 58 to 53 in the house.

The General Assembly then appointed a nine-member commission to purchase an appropriate tract of 640 to 1,000

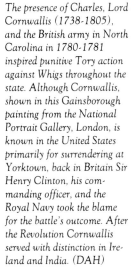

Thomas Burke (1744?-1783), governor of North Carolina, asked General Horatio Gates to increase the Whig military presence in central North Carolina, since "governmental activity" in the area surrounding Wake County provided many opportunities for Tory disruption. The governor was right: in October 1781, five months after Burke was elected, Tory raider David Fanning captured him in Hillsborough. (DAH)

Alexander Martin (1740-1807), six times governor of North Carolina, suggested the name "Raleigh" for the new state capital. (DAH)

acres on which a town of 400 or more acres could be laid out. On March 20, 1792, five of the commissioners—Frederick Hargett, William Dawson, Joseph McDowell, James Martin, and Thomas Blount—assembled at Isaac Hunter's Tavern, moving to Joel Lane's house the next day to begin their search for a townsite. On March 22, they were joined by Willie Jones, and for eight days they leisurely looked over a total of 17 tracts, which included land owned by Nathaniel Jones, Theophilus Hunter, Sr., Theophilus Hunter, Jr., Isaac Hunter, Henry Lane, John Hinton, and Joel Lane.

On March 29, the six commissioners unanimously elected Frederick Hargett chairman, and he conducted the voting procedure. The first ballot revealed three votes for Colonel John Hinton's property across the Neuse River, two votes for Joel Lane's holding in Bloomsbury, and one vote for Nathaniel Jones' land near Cary. They adjourned to Joel Lane's for the night. The next day—reportedly after an evening enlivened with more than adequate food and spirits—the vote was five for the Lane property, and one for the Hinton.

The Lane and Hinton families were very close. In fact, John Hinton, the old Revolutionary War colonel, was Joel Lane's father-in-law and grandfather to his 12 children. Many years before, Joel Lane had married one of John Hinton's daughters,

The presence of Charles, Lord Cornwallis (1738-1805), and the British army in North Carolina in 1780-1781 inspired punitive Tory action against Whigs throughout the state. Although Cornwallis, shown in this Gainsborough painting from the National Portrait Gallery, London, is known in the United States primarily for surrendering at Yorktown, back in Britain Sir Henry Clinton, his commanding officer, and the Royal Navy took the blame for the battle's outcome. After the Revolution Cornwallis served with distinction in Ireland and India. (DAH)

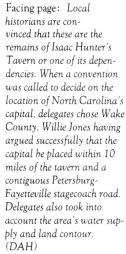

Facing page: *Local historians are convinced that these are the remains of Isaac Hunter's Tavern or one of its dependencies. When a convention was called to decide on the location of North Carolina's capital, delegates chose Wake County, Willie Jones having argued successfully that the capital be placed within 10 miles of the tavern and a contiguous Petersburg-Fayetteville stagecoach road. Delegates also took into account the area's water supply and land contour. (DAH)*

Martha, who bore them three sons before her death in September 1771. In 1772 Lane married another of Hinton's daughters, Mary, and they had nine more children. But the Lane and Hinton families apparently became estranged over the manner in which the capital site had been chosen. Public opinion seems to have sided with Hinton. Joel Lane had been elected 10 times in succession as senator for Wake County, but in the next election Hinton challenged him and won.

In any event, Lane and the commissioners agreed on a purchase price of 1,378 pounds ($2,756) for 756 acres of "woodland and fresh ground" and 244 acres of "old field." Lane deeded the 1,000 acres to the state on April 5, 1792. Governor Alexander Martin is credited by most historians with suggesting that the new capital be named "Raleigh," to honor the man who had first attempted to plant a town in North Carolina.

Later in the month William Christmas, with Lane's assistance, was contracted to plan and mark off the new town. A planter and state senator, Christmas had served as a colonel under General Washington at Valley Forge, and had previously laid out new towns in four states. Christmas fashioned Raleigh in a rectangle 11 blocks by 10, leaving small rectangles vacant at each corner. Slightly to the north of the town's center, on the high ground at the old drovers' camp, he placed a six-acre square intended for the capitol. One diagonal block from each corner of the six-acre square, he left four-acre squares. The remainder of the land was divided into 276 one-acre lots, 20 of which were reserved for state use and two for brickyards. Following instructions from the General Assembly, Christmas made the streets issuing from and bordering the central square 99 feet wide, and the others streets 66 feet wide.

The commissioners enjoyed the task of choosing names for the squares and streets. They designated the capitol site "Union Square." The smaller squares were named Moore, Nash, Caswell, and Burke—honoring the current attorney general and the first three governors following North Carolina's declaration of independence from England. Streets emanating from and bordering Union Square were named after the judicial districts toward which they pointed, and boundary streets after the cardinal points of the compass. The remaining streets were named after dignitaries, including Joel Lane and—exercising the pleasures of prerogative—each of the commissioners themselves.

The "City of Oaks" was now ready for occupation.

Raleigh, alone among North Carolina towns at the time, resulted from a political decision. Hillsborough, Warrenton, Salisbury, Statesville, Charlotte, and other existing inland towns had grown up around the juncture of trails or trade routes. The first significant intersection of roads in Raleigh, however, occurred after it was formed and the town was not even near a navigable watercourse. Raleigh's sole reason for existence was to serve as a governmental center; it would continue to be a "political" city for decades to come. The state put up no money for internal improvements before 1815, which meant that the trade routes in Piedmont and western North Carolina developed toward tidewater Virginia and coastal South Carolina rather than through central North Carolina and Raleigh. Prior to the Civil War, when cotton was king, there was little industrial development in the South and almost none in Raleigh. Raleigh was, additionally, west of the cotton-producing and naval-stores region of the state and south of North Carolina's tobacco-growing region.

II

A PLANNED CITY:

1792 - 1820

Despite these seemingly serious impediments to Raleigh's future growth, plans for the new capital proceeded enthusiastically. The legislature ordered an auction to be held on June 4-5, 1792, which would raise money to build a new statehouse by selling residential and commercial property in Raleigh. Of the 234 lots offered at auction, 192 were sold at prices ranging from $60 to $263. Willie Jones bought 15 lots, and four past, present, or future governors all bought property. James Bloodworth and Theophilus Hunter acquired lots on Fayetteville Street, which they would later donate as the site of the Wake County Courthouse.

The General Assembly set a limit of 10,000 pounds for the cost of the capitol, and a commission selected Massachusetts architect Rhoddam Atkins to design the building and to oversee its construction. Using brick from the original brickyards at the corners of Harrington and Hargett streets, and following the custom of "orienting" important buildings toward Jerusalem, Atkins began work in 1792. Construction was advanced enough by December of 1794 for the legislature to meet for the first time in Raleigh proper. Completed in 1796, the capitol contained offices on the first floor for the governor, treasurer, secretary of state, comptroller, and their clerks. Facilities for General Assembly members and functions were located on the second floor. The finished structure was not aesthetically pleasing and it was popularly described as a "misshapened pile." (Later, in 1819, the General Assembly would sell more lots to raise money for remodeling, renovation, and beautification. Captain William Nichols, state architect, supervised the addition of a new dome, the construction of false porticos to relieve the original starkness, and the attachment of a coat of yellow stucco to most of the original brick.)

Two popular state art purchases later improved the aesthetic appeal of the capitol. Governor William Miller in 1816 had Philadelphia artist Thomas Sully commissioned to paint a portrait of George Washington. Sully had almost completed a work entitled *Washington at the Passage of the Delaware*, which depicted a heroic Washington on horseback, when he discovered that it was far too large for the space allotted in the State House. He then copied his *Portrait of Washington* from a Gilbert Stuart likeness of the President (now housed in the Boston Museum of Fine Arts) and sent it to Raleigh in November 1818. The other acquisition created a greater sensation. In 1816, following the recommendation of Thomas Jefferson, the legislature commis-

This oil painting of the remodeled first State House was made by Jacob Marling sometime between 1819 and 1831. Marling came to Raleigh about 1813, opened a reading room and museum, and sold rare coins and books, drawings, and paintings. As a painter he was most prolific between 1825 and 1831, specializing in portraits of state legislators. (DAH)

Above: *One of the first works of art commissioned by a state legislature, Canova's statue of George Washington was unveiled December 24, 1821, under the capitol dome. The likeness of the general, dressed in the garb of a Roman soldier to indicate "simplicity, strength of character and various heroic qualities," cost North Carolina taxpayers $10,000. (DAH)*

Right: *Italian sculptor Antonio Canova (1757-1822) was commissioned by the state legislature in 1815 to create a "full-length statue" of George Washington. Thomas Jefferson recommended Canova to Governor William Miller, remarking that the artist was unrivaled in Europe. Canova felt "a desire. . .to send some specimine of his powers to this country." Courtesy, North Carolina Collection, University of North Carolina Library, Chapel Hill*

sioned the Italian master Antonio Canova to carve a statue of Washington, and the finished product was awaited with anxious anticipation. Raleigh citizens were ill-prepared, however, when on November 9, 1821, they flocked to witness the arrival of a pure white, Carrara marble rendition of a pensive, larger-than-life, bare-armed Washington dressed in a thigh-length Roman martial uniform. They soon recovered from their initial amazement and came to cherish the statue, described by David L. Swain as "a noble specimen of a noble art, commemorative of the noblest of men."

On February 7, 1795, the General Assembly passed an act establishing a Raleigh city government. The town would be governed by seven resident, landowning commissioners. Appointed for terms of three years, these commissioners would choose from among their number an "intendant of police" (i.e., mayor) and a treasurer. The legislature empowered the commissioners to "make such rules, orders and regulations and ordinances, as to them shall seem meat for repairing the streets, appointing a Constable or Constables, City watches or patrols, and making proper allowances by fees or otherwise for such services, and for all such other necessary ordinances, rules and orders which may tend to the advantage, improvement and good government of the said city." The commissioners could exact fines and other penalities for crimes, including sentencing slaves to a maximum of 39 lashes, and they progressively gained other regulatory powers.

The General Assembly renewed the charter in 1797 and again in 1801, at which time the commissioners were instructed to fine "any merchant or shopkeepers" 10 pounds per offense for selling goods on the Sabbath. An 1803 renewal extended voting rights to all free male residents owning lots in the town. Article XIX of the 1803 renewal further declared: "*Be it enacted*, That the Commissioners shall have power to make regulations for preventing hogs running at large in the City," an ordinance that would remain loosely enforced, at best, five decades later.

In 1815 the state legislature granted the Raleigh commissioners "power to bind their successors or to borrow money" to build a municipal water system, essential in providing the town with fire protection. In 1816 a destructive fire spurred these efforts, and two years later Raleigh had completed the system. It consisted of three underground reservoirs with a total capacity of 8,000 gallons, strategically spaced hydrants, and one and a half miles of wooden pipes conveying water from distant springs. Constantly plagued by rotting pipes, the system was maintained for several years by the commissioners. In 1821 the state gave them authority to run pipes through private property, to exempt from military duty up to 40 citizens to form a fire-fighting company, and to assess a fine of $10 to anyone who "wantonly" damaged the waterworks. The legislature also gave the commissioners authority to control a surplus dog population, to fine anyone elected to a city office who refused to serve, and to force owners to maintain sidewalks bordering their property.

While some of the first town ordinances had singled out pigs and dogs for closer scrutiny, the 1820s saw a drive to regulate the less delicate activities of Raleigh's human residents. On February 1, 1822, the *Raleigh Register* applauded the commissioners: "We are glad to find that the Board has determined to use a greater degree of energy than heretofore in maintaining good order in the city. For this purpose several Ordinances have been passed, which direct the apprehension and punishment of vagrants, gamblers, swindlers, prostitute women, and disorderly negroes." In 1825 the legislature authorized the city police "to take such precautionary measures . . . as . . . may seem necessary" to prevent the introduction and spread of contagious and infectious diseases.

This increasing concern for public order and health derived, in no small part, from the fact that Raleigh was home to North Carolina's governors. A General Assembly act of 1794 had required the governor to live in the capital for a minimum of six months each year, and a later act required

Above: *Completed in 1816, the Executive Mansion, also called the "Governor's Mansion," was first occupied by Governor William Miller. Featuring an Ionic portico, paneled foyer, and skylight, it was inhabited by the state's chief executives until 1865, when General Sherman commandeered the structure as his headquarters. (DAH)*

Left: *Willie Jones (1741?-1801) diligently persuaded fellow commissioners to choose Joel Lane's property as the site for the capitol of North Carolina. Jones, a congressman, constitutional expert, state legislator, and trustee of the University of North Carolina, moved in 1799 from Halifax to Raleigh and built "Welcome Place" plantation on the current site of St. Augustine's College. Courtesy, North Carolina Collection, UNC Library*

permanent residency. Some early governors had lived in a two-story frame house on the corner of Fayetteville and Hargett streets, but general embarrassment over its modesty led the legislature, in 1813, to name a commission of state officials and townspeople to raise $10,000 through the sale of lots for the erection of a governor's mansion. The commission chose James Calder of Washington, North Carolina, to build a brick, two-story, Ionic-columned "Palace" at the end of Fayetteville Street where the Memorial Auditorium now stands. When finished in 1816, the "Palace" was imposing, but its inhabitants unanimously agreed that it was an uncomfortable dwelling.

Richard Dobbs Spaight, the first native-born North Carolina governor, was also the first to occupy offices in the new capitol. A Federalist while governor, he later became a Republican representative in the U.S. Congress. In 1802 his fellow Republican John Stanley accused him of voting with the Federalist party, and Spaight challenged Stanley to a duel. At Spaight's insistence, Stanley published an apology, but he also published "verification" of his original charge. After further exchanges of printed denunciations, the men met for a duel outside New Bern. Neither demonstrated much ability as a marksman, and it was not until the fourth exchange of shots that Stanley mortally wounded Spaight, who died after 23 hours of extreme suffering.

As important as the capitol was to the political life of the town and state, it proved not to be the focus of Raleigh's commercial and social activities. When William Christmas had laid out the town, he had assumed that business would accumulate on New Bern Avenue in front of the capitol. But the laws of commerce prevailed and Raleigh's first inns arose on Fayetteville Street, because it had become a part of the main road running from Fayetteville to Petersburg, the closest centers of trade. Since the inns attracted legislators and affluent travelers, they soon acted as magnets for other enterprises. Peter Casso built the first inn in Raleigh around 1795 at the southeast corner of Fayetteville and Morgan streets, and his establishment quickly became the social center of Raleigh, instituting an enduring tradition perpetuated by several later inns and hotels. Casso operated the inn continuously until his death in 1811, at which time the Casso family continued to operate it. The inn became an even greater focus of activity in 1808 when the town bell was installed on the sidewalk in front of the main building.

It was also in 1808, in a small house within the courtyard at Casso's Inn, that one of the truly momentous events in early Raleigh history occurred, although no one could have predicted a noteworthy consequence at the time. Jacob Johnson, who had migrated from Northumberland, England, to Boston in 1795, moved to Raleigh to work for Peter Casso as a hostler and a porter. Johnson became a popular figure and the town's official bell ringer. On the evening of December 29, 1808, Jacob's wife Mary McDonough Johnson, known as "Polly the Weaver" after her occupation at Casso's Inn, gave birth to a

Richard Dobbs Spaight (1758-1802) of New Bern was a representative in congress and the state's first native-born governor. He was mortally wounded in a duel with his Federalist rival John Stanly, prompting the legislature to pass "An Act to Prevent the Vile Practice of Duelling within this State" a month later. Courtesy, North Carolina Collection, UNC Library

John Stanly (1774-1834), state legislator, congressman, and speaker of the North Carolina house, was known to possess a quick temper and a penchant for trouble. Escaping death himself (after fatally wounding Richard Dobbs Spaight in a duel), a decade later Stanly goaded his brother Edward into a duel with Lewis Henry in Virginia, resulting in Edward's death. Courtesy, North Carolina Collection, UNC Library

hierarchy refused to elect him an elder, Glendenning adopted Unitarianism, but he soon became distraught over lingering atheistic concepts. He attempted suicide and journeyed to North Carolina to convalesce. In mid-January 1785 he saw the devil, "black as any coal—his eyes and mouth as red as blood, and long white teeth gnashing together." Further distracted by the severe headaches brought on by Lucifer's repeated visitations, he again attempted suicide. He recovered and regained a degree of stability, but even a series of visions of God failed to alleviate his persistent headaches. He returned to preaching on a Methodist circuit, but his vivid references to his past experiences once again disenchanted his church superiors.

He moved to Philadelphia in the mid-1790s and published religious tracts and books, and he finally settled in Raleigh where he opened a book and stationery store on New Bern Avenue in 1799. Although he was successful as a businessman, he maintained his eccentric behavior. Glendenning published collections of sermons after arriving in Raleigh, and about 1806 he built a nondenominational church near the intersection of Morgan and Blount that he named Bethel and in which he preached without pay. However, when his erratic behavior failed to abate, William Boylan was named his guardian. David L. Swain reports that Glendenning, upon hearing of the appointment, invited Boylan to his house. He showed his guest a $50 bill inserted in a Bible as an amulet against the devil, and he then asked if he retained control over who could visit his house. When Boylan answered in the affirmative, Glendenning replied, "Then, sir, get out of my house, get out of my house this instant." Glendenning remained a curiosity until his death in 1816.

For the first several years, Raleigh citizens conducted their church services in the Conference Chamber of the State House, services that included funerals and revival meetings. In 1802 citizens petitioned the legislature for money to purchase a plot of land and to build a church. Although refusing to finance the building costs, the legislators did grant the city a lot for a church, provided that it be "free and open to all ministers of every denomination." However, Glendenning's church building remained the only one in Raleigh until 1811.

In general, early Raleigh citizens were suspicious of the fervent enthusiasm associated with the Methodist religion then gaining popularity throughout the South. A *Raleigh Star* account of an 1811 conference of Methodist ministers in the city clearly reveals the writer's surprise that the participating ministers were "a highly respectable body of men, and possessed a degree of talent, and liberality of sentiment that many were not prepared to expect." The suspicion of "enthusiastic" religion was by no means universal, however, and the "Great Revival" that swept the nation during the first two decades of the 19th century visited Raleigh and Wake County on several occasions. Large camp meetings assembled in 1802 and 1804, and in 1811 the powerful Methodist Bishop Francis Asbury led a revival in Raleigh that converted more than 50 people, including James Glasgow's former clerk

son. According to some accounts, Hannah Casso was at a party at the inn; according to others, she was attending her prenuptial celebration in the State House. The differing accounts agree, however, that "Polly" called for Hannah Casso to name the child and that Hannah suggested Andrew Jackson Johnson. The family dropped the middle name, and Andrew Johnson went on to become the 17th President of the United States—two days after the city of his birth had surrendered to General William Tecumseh Sherman.

Early Raleigh had its characters, and without doubt the most eccentric of them all was William Glendenning. Born in Moffatt, Scotland, in 1747, he became a tailor's apprentice at 13. Shortly thereafter, he began to have apocalyptic visions— "The earth and all the elements appeared, to my view, as all in a flame of fire," he remembered in his privately printed 1795 autobiography. He sailed to the United States in 1767 and eventually became a Methodist circuit preacher in Virginia, Maryland, and Pennsylvania. In 1784, after the Methodist

William Hill, who helped found and build the United Methodist Church on Edenton Street in the same year.

The Reverend McPheeters organized a Presbyterian congregation in 1806 and conducted services on special occasions in his capacity as "Pastor of the City," including establishing the custom of holding sunrise services on the Fourth of July. The Presbyterians built their first church in 1818 at Salisbury and Morgan, the same year the Baptists built their first church at South Person Street. It was moved to Moore Square (Baptist Grove) in 1822 and used for various purposes.

Patriotic celebrations afforded social observances of a different sort for townspeople and nearby countryfolk. Following George Washington's death in December 1799, over 1,000 people gathered in Raleigh on his next birthday. The militia fired cannons and a solemn procession slowly marched up Fayetteville Street to the State House, accompanied by the sounds of "the bell tolling and minute-guns firing." The Fourth of July was another customary day of festivity. The Reverend Mcpheeters traditionally began the day with a sunrise service; small arms and cannon fire echoed through the morning hours; speeches, toasts, barbecues, and picnics punctuated the afternoons, with social and governmental leaders dining apart; and elite subscription balls brought the day to a close for those fortunates who could afford to attend.

During its early years, however, the only area outside government in which Raleigh enjoyed larger recognition was the newspaper business, and that business was decidedly influenced by partisan politics. William Boylan, originally from New Jersey, and Abraham Hodge had published the *Minerva* in Fayetteville before they moved to Raleigh in 1799. On May 7 of that year, Boylan and Hodge, both ardent Federalists, began publishing the *North Carolina Minerva and Raleigh Advertiser*—a title soon simplified to the *Minerva*. Several anti-Federalist leaders, led by Nathaniel Macon, sought a Jeffersonian Republican editor who would move to Raleigh to counter the *Minerva*. They found their man in Joseph Gales.

Gales had previously published the *Sheffield Register* in his native England, but the British government's objection to his sympathy for the French Revolution, the writings of Thomas Paine, and the English workers' reform movement had forced Gales and his family to flee first to Germany and later to Philadelphia, where he began publishing an anti-Federalist paper. Gales accepted the invitation of the Raleigh Republicans, and on November 22, 1799, he printed the inaugural issue of the weekly *Raleigh Register*. The paper became known throughout the state, and an intense rivalry quickly developed between Gales and Boylan, inspired not only by their political opposition but also by their competition for the job of state printer.

In 1799 the General Assembly chose Boylan and Hodge to be the state printers, but Gales won the contract the next year and remained the official printer for a decade. Boylan refused to accept his defeat quietly, however. He criticized Gales repeatedly, both in print and privately. Gales responded in

Nathaniel Macon (1758-1837) of Warren County, state legislator, representative in congress, and president of the 1835 state constitutional convention, invited Joseph Gales to publish a newspaper to counter the Boylan-Hodge Minerva. (DAH)

William Boylan (1777-1861), publisher of the Raleigh Minerva, devoted much of his life to public service. A state legislator and councilor of state, he was a founder of Wake County's first almshouse. During the "big snow of '57" he sent wagonloads of wood from his estate to warm Raleigh's poor. (DAH)

kind, even insinuating that Boylan may have been responsible for a fire that had damaged the *Register* press. Finally, in November of 1804, Boylan attacked Gales with a cane on the streets of Raleigh and beat him ferociously. However, Gales did not cower; on December 10, he renewed the attack in print: "The cold-blooded assassinator of private character, the secret plotter against his neighbor's fame, is at length dragged before the public and stands forth that literary wonder, that scientific desperado, that butcher of good names—*William Boylan*. Why, Sir, your very name is antidote to the calumnies you so industriously, so honestly, and with such consummate art have circulated."

In spite of their animosity, professional ethics prompted Boylan to allow Gales the use of the *Minerva* press while Gales' equipment was being repaired. Also, when the Superior Court of Hillsborough ordered Boylan to pay Gales 100 pounds in damages, Gales magnanimously—and publicly—donated the money to the Raleigh Academy.

Both Boylan and Gales became highly respected, conscientious citizens who contributed immeasurably to the quality of life in early Raleigh. Boylan published an almanac, operated a bookstore, became president of the State Bank and president of the Raleigh & Gaston Railroad. He helped found and served as a trustee of the Raleigh Academy, promoted a state deaf-and-dumb institute, and served as a commissioner for the construction of a new statehouse in the 1830s. His demeanor was unambiguously aristocratic. In *Early Times in Raleigh*, David L. Swain quotes merchant Joseph Peace's account of an election meeting he and Boylan attended at Brasstown. The rowdy crowd became offended by Boylan's aloofness and reluctance to join them in a dance. To stave off trouble, Peace told their leader, "My friends be careful how you act. Bless your life, that is Mr. Boylan, the man who made the almanac and can foretell eclipses and thunder storms." Peace reported that the resentful crowd instantly became respectfully deferential to the awe-inspiring Boylan.

Gales, who knew shorthand and printed transcripts of General Assembly debates, also published an almanac and ran a bookstore. He owned a paper-producing factory on the Neuse, was elected intendant of police for many years, and served on the board of two societies seeking to emancipate and to colonize slaves. He helped organize the North Carolina Agriculture Society in 1819, serving as its first secretary. Like Boylan, Gales helped found the Raleigh Academy and the North Carolina Institute for the Education of the Deaf and Dumb. Gales opposed dueling in his editorials, and he consistently supported law, order, and anti-Federalist political principles. Thomas Henderson, Jr., and Dr. Calvin Jones began publishing Raleigh's third newspaper, the *Star*, on November 3, 1808. The *Star* promoted agricultural interests, however, and seldom took sides in political disputes.

Other forms of communication were also undergoing expansion during this period. As late as 1796, the road running from Fayetteville to Petersburg remained the only postal route through town. But the importance of the meeting place of the General Assembly, and a growing population, had boosted the number of direct postal connections by 1804 to six: Chapel Hill, Chatham County, Fayetteville, Smithfield, Warrenton, and Oxford. These "roads," however, were in reality little more than paths that became impassable for vehicles during periods of bad weather. The landed gentry of the east, which had navigable waterways, still dominated the General Assembly. They declined to participate in voting for, and consequently paying a majority of, the taxes necessary to build and maintain a road system chiefly benefiting the west. The legislature refused to appropriate a single dollar to build roads prior to 1815, a policy that encouraged the western part of the state to establish trade routes bypassing central North Carolina and thereby relegating Raleigh to relative isolation.

But Raleigh was, by no means, totally isolated. On October 2, 1799, the *Register* reported the appropriation of 298 pounds to build a marketplace to serve farmers and townspeople. The market was "to be of an Octagon form, 30 feet in diameter, with a Cupola on the top for a bell; to be set upon eight posts; to have four gates; to be banistered around three feet high; the floor to be laid with brick; the whole to be neatly painted." Incredible as it may seem, considering the condition of the road network, farmers sent produce to the Raleigh market from distances up to 200 miles. Slaves drove most of the wagons arriving from outlying areas. During harvesting season, large camps assembled outside of the city, with audible celebrations extending into the late hours.

Tobacco arrived from the counties to the north, cotton and naval stores (tar, pitch, turpentine, rosin) from the east, and rice from the southeast. Local and western producers furnished hay, corn, wheat, potatoes, yams, peas, beans, and other foodstuffs. In deference to the peaceful repose of the townspeople and late-working government officials, the commissioners forbade the hawking of produce in the streets prior to noon. The Raleigh market was noted for commanding good prices during the city's formative years, especially in the years of prosperity following the War of 1812, but prices fell markedly after the Panic of 1819.

In its beginning, Raleigh had offered little commercial challenge to the established cities of Virginia, South Carolina, and eastern North Carolina. Merchants concentrated on serving the local population, visiting legislators, and transients attracted by state government. Nevertheless, several early merchants became respected community leaders and developed prosperous and lasting businesses. One of the most noteworthy was William Peace. Born wealthy, Peace had attended the University of North Carolina briefly before he and his brother, Joseph, opened a general store on Fayetteville Street just prior to 1800. Alone among early Raleigh merchants, Peace was accepted into the highest level of society. He became a leading churchman, business leader, a member of the commission that built the "Palace," and a bank director. A patron of education, he later founded Peace

Raleigh Academy opened on July 2, 1804, to educate young men and women alike. One student, Fetney I. Price, daughter of Thomas and Rebecca Robertson Price, received this medal from the school in 1827. (DAH)

Students at Raleigh Academy learned reading, writing and advanced English, classical languages and literature, the Bible, and mathematics. The school building shown here was erected on Burke Square around 1804 and demolished around 1889. (DAH)

College.

Prior to the initiation of a statewide public school system in 1839, all secondary education was purely a local and a private responsibility. Raleigh citizens took early measures to provide quality training for their youth. Joseph Gales, William Boylan, John Craven, State Treasurer John Haywood, and others had founded the Raleigh Academy shortly after the turn of the century. When a new two-story building on Burke Square was nearing completion in 1804, Gales announced in the *Register* that the trustees were seeking a "fit Person to superintend the Institution. If they could meet with a Clergyman of liberal Education and Principles, who would take charge of the Academy . . . such an one would be preferred, and for such a Character, it is believed, a handsome Salary would be provided."

Although three ministers would precede him in the post, it was not until 1810, when John Haywood brought the Reverend William McPheeters to Raleigh, that the Academy received a man who could answer the ad in all its particulars. In the dual capacity of principal of the Academy and "Pastor of the City," McPheeters soon became an influential figure in Raleigh. Assisted by Alexander Wilson and James Grant, he taught and supervised an Academy curriculum that included Latin, Greek, English grammar, mathematics, geography, chemistry, and the Bible. The Reverend McPheeters was also a moving force in the creation of the North Carolina Institute for the Deaf and Dumb. Contributions from the Raleigh Thespian Society, which was formed to raise money for the

Academy, helped finance a separate building for the "Female Department" in 1807. Although it never gained permanent relief from its financing problems, the Raleigh Academy endured during a period when most schools expired after a few trying years.

Prior to 1808, John Chavis, a free black, opened another secondary school, which taught white and black children together for some time. Chavis was probably born in Granville County about 1763, but differing accounts also record his birthplace as unknown and as in the West Indies. He probably attended Washington Academy (later Washington and Lee University) and may have even attended Princeton University. Whatever his background, on April 26, 1808, Chavis announced in the *Register* that his school would henceforth be segregated and that he would "open an Evening School for the purpose of instructing children of color, as he intends for the accommodation of some of his employers to exclude all children of color from his day school. . . . When the white children leave the house, those of color will take their places and continue until 10 o'clock." The tuition was $1.50 per quarter for whites, $1.75 for blacks. Chavis continued the school intermittently until 1838.

In 1823 Mr. and Mrs. J.A. Lunsden started yet another school in their home. Although the private schools by no means offered universal secondary education, Raleigh was still an advanced locality in a state woefully lacking in educational facilities. Raleigh could hardly be called progressive in its early cultural offerings, but the demand for intellectual and artistic pursuits was high, especially among the city's elite.

Long before Raleigh could truly be called a "city," in fact, its citizens exhibited a taste for culture—although that taste tended to be decidedly pedestrian. The Conference Chamber in the capitol itself was put to use by "drama" groups, dancers, puppeteers, magicians, singers, speakers, and other entertainers. Over the course of time, such a maze of theatrical paraphernalia accumulated that the General Assembly was forced to take drastic measures. On December 6, 1810, it instructed the capitol caretakers "immediately after the adjournment of the house this day to remove from the Conference Hall, any rope or wires, or other apparatus there found for the purpose of rope or wire dancing, or any hook or staple attached to the wall of said Hall for such purpose, and to prevent in the future the introduction for any such purpose."

The Raleigh Thespian Society, organized in 1807 mainly as a venture to raise money for the Raleigh Academy, enjoyed such success that it continued on after the fund-raising drive ended. In 1814 the Raleigh Thespian Society moved into the "New Theatre" at Morgan and Dawson on the ground floor of the newly constructed Grand Lodge of the North Carolina Masons. In January 1815 they inaugurated their new facility with an all-male cast performing Thomas Morton's *Secrets Worth Knowing* and a farce entitled *The Bee Hive*. Soon Raleigh developed a reputation as a supportive "theater" town, and Northern companies made it a regular stop on their tours. As elsewhere in North Carolina, however, Shakespeare and other serious dramatists were anathema. Even the liberal *Raleigh Register* looked askance at such strong fare, warning that theatergoers "run the risque of giving nature a victory over conscience."

Facilities for more restrained and intellectual forms of culture and entertainment were pursued by some Raleigh citizens. Winifred Marshall Gales became the author of the first novel published in North Carolina by a native when her husband, Joseph, printed her *Matilda Berkeley, or Family Anecdotes* in 1804. Set in England and Russia, the novel reflected little of Mrs. Gales' American experiences. While Raleigh had its first novelist, it still did not have a library. In November 1813 the *Star* described the reading rooms of New Bern, Wilmington, and Fayetteville and suggested that Raleigh citizens could also benefit from a repository "where intelligent citizens and strangers can meet daily and enjoy the pleasure of reading and conversation." The Polemic Society had operated a circulating library out of the Raleigh Academy since 1808, and in 1815 it merged with other concerned citizens to form the Raleigh Library Company, whose 40 members contributed a $10 initiation fee and $5 per year in dues for operating expenses. The Library Company opened a reading room to members and "respectable" strangers. Its subscriptions and holdings included 67 newspapers representing every state and three foreign languages, four magazines, maps, gazetteers, public documents, and some museum pieces contributed by General Calvin Jones. When hard times hit Raleigh following the Panic of 1819, the Library Company ran short of funds and closed the reading room.

When Raleigh was in the process of emerging as a viable young capital, not all was enlightenment and entertainment. Scandal played its role as well—most notably in the James Glasgow affair. Glasgow had served as the Secretary of State of North Carolina since independence in 1776, and during the course of his long tenure he had engineered a scheme to issue fraudulent land grants in western North Carolina and eastern Tennessee, then North Carolina territory. In the winter of 1797, two Tennessee judges sent a secret message to Governor Samuel Ashe informing him that the State House and its records were in danger of being burned to eliminate evidence incriminating Glasgow and other officials. Ashe placed a guard on the capitol, and one evening, while several state officials were attending a party at Casso's Inn, the guard caught Phill—a slave of William Terrell, one of the suspected conspirators—attempting to break into the state comptroller's office. With suspicious urgency, Phill was tried, convicted, and hanged on an oak tree between South and Lenoir streets.

In spite of the seriousness of the allegations, the General Assembly ordered the Superior Court justices to investigate Glasgow on a "misdemeanor" charge, and Judge John Haywood (not to be confused with State Treasurer John Haywood) created a sensation when he resigned to accept a $1,000 retainer to defend Glasgow. The court convicted Glasgow, who moved to Tennessee soon after the trial . . . followed in 1806 by Judge Haywood. Demonstrating the need for the location of a state supreme court in the capital, the case prompted the legislature in 1801 to create the Court of Conference—the forerunner to the North Carolina Supreme Court.

In 1810 the General Assembly enacted legislation making Raleigh the center of banking—the only enterprise outside government that the city would dominate in the 19th century. Commercial banking had begun in North Carolina in 1804, when the General Assembly had chartered the Bank of New Bern and the Bank of Cape Fear at Wilmington, which became Raleigh's first bank when it opened a branch in the city in 1807. Both banks had the authority to issue notes, but poor management and the issuance of an excess of paper money quickly created a general reluctance by merchants and workers to trade in the depreciated currency. After a long debate, the legislature chartered the State Bank of North Carolina in 1810 in the hope that it would both absorb the existing banks and establish a sound currency. The charter called for the central office to be located in Raleigh, and many of Raleigh's most prominent citizens would manage the bank during the coming decades.

During the War of 1812, when the British threatened coastal North Carolina, officials moved the specie from the branch banks in Edenton, Wilmington, Fayetteville, and New Bern inland to a branch bank at Tarboro and to the central bank in Raleigh. The accumulation of so much money pro-

The Bank of the State of North Carolina issued its own currency. This $10 bill is decorated with an engraving of the capitol and two views of the Canova statue. (DAH)

Possessing an "unusually powerful and logical mind," John Haywood (1762-1826), jurist and historian, was first cousin to the state treasurer of the same name. When Haywood resigned from the North Carolina superior court, he claimed that his decision to step down resulted from the meager salary the post afforded. Courtesy, North Carolina Collection, UNC Library

vided the impetus to construct a more formidable central office, resulting in the building at 11 New Bern Avenue, which contains the oldest brick of any structure in the city.

When Admiral Sir George Cockburn landed troops on Ocracoke Island on July 13, 1813, Raleigh citizens hurriedly formed the City Corps to protect the capital, naming Colonel William Polk as captain and William Peace, William Boylan, and Judge Henry Seawell as lieutenants. Governor William Hawkins personally led the Wake Dragoons, commanded by Major Thomas Henderson, to reinforce defenses at New Bern. By the time they left Raleigh on July 19, however, Cockburn had withdrawn his landing force and his fleet of over a hundred ships, and the Wake Dragoons were spared the ordeal of active combat. When word reached Raleigh that the state and the city were again secure, the commissioners set September 9 aside as a day of thankful prayer and fasting.

Although Raleigh enjoyed a lengthy period of consistent growth and prosperity prior to the economic decline of the 1820s, like other towns that matured quickly, it experienced problems associated with the perverse side of human nature. In the *Register* Joseph Gales followed a liberal editorial policy supporting law and order and the humane treatment of prisoners that applied pressure to reform and reflected the thinking of many Raleigh citizens. In May of 1802 he questioned why the town commission had failed to appoint "a sufficient number of patrollers so as to patrol the streets every night, in order to discover and suppress fire and robbery." But law-enforcement officials had more to contend with than simply apprehending criminals and suspicious characters. They were reluctant to condemn petty violators to damp, filthy, and unheated jails, and they realized that their "prisons" were too ramshackle to hold inmates intent upon escape or prisoners with determined friends. In fact, jail breaks assisted from without became routine throughout the state, leading Gales to lament on July 7, 1806: "Thus you catch and perhaps convict the small fry; but your sharks and great offenders will always escape your net."

Conditions in the Wake County jail had become so abhorrent by November 1818 that Wake Superior Court Chief Justice Taylor appointed a grand jury to investigate claims that prisoners were being chained in cells during all seasons without heat or toilet facilities. After its inquiry, the grand jury recommended that "some provision should be made against the Cold of Winter, which is sometimes so excessive as to endanger the lives of the prisoners thus confined there." Reforms followed in the Wake County jail, and in 1822 the General Assembly passed a bill forcing all jailers to provide prisoners with blankets.

There were punishments other than penal confinement for noncapital crimes, however. For specific offenses, judges could sentence convicted criminals to a maximum of 39 lashes on the bare back, to pillory, to branding, to the loss of one or both ears, to dismemberment, or to a combination of the preceding.

The large population of state government officials, many of them in town temporarily, attracted transients, who in turn attracted another sort of camp follower. As a result, Raleigh commissioners and citizens alike fought an unremitting battle to control vice. In 1815 the voluntary formation of the "Raleigh Association for the suppression of vice and for the preservation of morality and good order" was announced. Its declared purpose was to halt "Drunkenness, Profanity, Gambling, Straining Horses, Negro dances and frolicks, Keeping disorderly houses and dram-shops, and Sabbath-breaking." The Association's efforts failed to vanquish the wicked, however, and in January 1822 the commission issued ordinances instructing the police to use greater vigilance to apprehend and to punish "vagrants, gamblers, swindlers, prostitute women, and disorderly negroes."

Those convicted of capital crimes (which included everything from burglary to murder) were usually condemned to the public ritual of death by hanging. Dressed in a shroud, the prisoner rode to the execution site sitting atop a coffin drawn in a wagon, accompanied by a preacher also dressed in a shroud. On occasion, the procedure included a detour to a church, where the condemned and the curious were

John Marshall (1755-1835), justice of the U.S. Supreme Court, visited Raleigh in June 1805 to hear the case of the Granville heirs against William R. Davie, Nathaniel Allen, and Josiah Collins. Circuit-riding brought Marshall to the city on many occasions. He preferred staying at Cook's Tavern and was a great favorite of the townspeople, with whom he played quoits in the street after court adjourned for the day. (DAH)

John Haywood (1755-1827), Raleigh's first "intendant of police" (mayor) and member of the first board of trustees of the University of North Carolina, was state treasurer from 1787 until his death. A legislative committee auditing Haywood's official records discovered that he had embezzled over $68,000 in state funds, nearly half the amount of the government's annual expenditures from 1813 to 1835. Courtesy, North Carolina Collection, UNC Library

His notoriety as a cemetery despoiler (from when he plowed up Joel Lane's grave) aside, Peter Browne (1766?-1833) was considered one of the foremost attorneys of the era, and as a Wake County court judge he acquired a reputation "for deciding cases with unprecedented facility and dispatch." A chief stockholder of the Bank of North Carolina, in 1831 Browne succeeded Duncan Cameron as president of the bank, holding that post until his death. Courtesy, North Carolina Collection, UNC Library

enlightened with a full service. Notices of hangings usually attracted large and festive crowds composed of all ages and both sexes. Drinking, gambling, and sporting events contributed to the holiday atmosphere, but once the procession reached the place of execution, solemnity ensued. The audience wanted the condemned to deliver an exhortation announcing the remission of his sins and sorrow over his crime. Often the prisoner obliged, but in many instances that sad duty fell to the minister when the prisoner's composure succumbed to emotion. The condemned then mounted the wagon, the executioner applied a rope suspended from a crossbar between the branches of a tree or between two trees, the minister offered a final prayer, and the wagon was pulled from beneath the central figure in the gruesome spectacle.

Other crimes went undetected, let alone punished, including one of the most shocking of the period, considering who had committed it. Upon the death of State Treasurer and longtime city resident John Haywood, it became evident that he had embezzled a considerable fortune during his 40-year tenure (1787-1827) in office. Nevertheless, the reputation he

had earned over many years of selfless civic contributions caused his descendents and fellow citizens to continue to respect his memory even after his malefactions had been exposed. Born on an Edgecombe County plantation, Haywood had come to Raleigh in 1794 in compliance with the new law requiring state officials to live in the capital. He engaged Rhoddam Atkins to build the house still occupying 211 New Bern Avenue. He was the first intendant of police for Raleigh and a trustee of the University of North Carolina, had helped found the Raleigh Academy, and was chiefly responsible for bringing the Reverend McPheeters to Raleigh.

When rumors circulated in 1820 that he had misused his office, he called for a complete investigation, and the General Assembly consented by appointing a joint select committee chaired by Willis Alston. The committee scrutinized Haywood's records all the way back to 1787 and found them "to have been regularly balanced and settled." The committee dismissed the charges against Haywood as "base and calumnies," and "*Resolved*, That John Haywood, public treasurer of North-Carolina, had during the 33 years in which he has been in office invariably acted as became an intelligent, honest, useful and faithful public officer; and that he is entitled to the gratitude of the good People of this state for his public services, and to their respect and esteem for his virtues." So complete was his exoneration that after Haywood's death, Governor Hutchins G. Burton told the General Assembly, "to attempt to recount his many virtues would far exceed the limits of this communication," and the legislature showed its own appreciation by passing a memorial resolution honoring "the long, tried, and faithful Treasurer of the State."

But within a month of a formal state funeral conducted by the Reverend McPheeters, another joint select committee went over Haywood's records again. This time their findings were decidedly different: "Your committee laments that this investigation has resulted in the painful discovery that there is a balance due from the late Treasurer of sixty-eight thousand, six hundred and thirty-one dollars, eighty and three-eighths cents." To place the shortfall in perspective, total state expenditures between 1813 and 1835 averaged only $132,000 per year.

The revelation of Haywood's misdeeds roughly coincided with a turning point that marked the end of Raleigh's early "boom" and signaled the beginning of a decline that would significantly diminish the economic base of the capital city. Following the Panic of 1819 and the depression that followed, cotton prices fell 50 percent, land values declined 20 percent, and the western migration intensified to the extent that Raleigh's population fell from 2,674 in 1820 to exactly 1,700 in 1830. Nevertheless, the state's largest expenditure remained the cost of running the General Assembly, and the presence of the General Assembly both guaranteed a consistent minimum level of commercial activity in Raleigh and promised recovery for the capital whenever state government expanded.

I n February of 1825, the Marquis de Lafayette visited Raleigh for two days during an extended tour of the United States. Both the state and the city were unreserved in efforts to make the reception lavish and memorable, and an observer of the proceedings might well have thought that Raleigh was enjoying unbounded prosperity. Governor Hutchins G. Burton sent Colonel William Polk, a Revolutionary War comrade of Lafayette, to command the cavalry corps that accompanied the old general from the Virginia border to the capital. Captain John J.S. Ruffin, in command of the Raleigh Blues, escorted the procession through town to a formal reception at the "Palace." Cannons were fired, the governor delivered a formal speech, and Lafayette spoke briefly—all to the immense pleasure of a wildly cheering crowd. Lafayette then rode to the State House to view the Canova statue of Washington. Officials and guests partook of a bountiful dinner and a stately ball concluded the

III

THE CITY OF OAKS GROWS:

1820-1850

day-long festivities. Lafayette retired for the night at the governor's "Palace." But the opulence manifested was anything but indicative of the true disposition of the economy of either North Carolina or its capital.

Several factors—including the General Assembly's refusal to appropriate money for internal improvements and public education, the state's depleted pine forests and exhausted farmlands, and the general migration to the West and to the cotton belt— had all combined to start an exodus from Raleigh and much of North Carolina that would continue at alarming rates for decades to come. As early as 1818 Governor John Branch had pleaded with the legislature to initiate programs to make "our citizens contented and happy to remain at home," but the eastern-dominated legislature had opted to maintain the status quo. A lengthy drought in 1826 contributed further to the capital's agonies. But once more the legislature refused to intervene, voting down an 1827 bill to contribute $500 each to Wake and the seven other counties most affected by the dry weather.

Raleigh's population fell by more than 35 percent in the 1820s, an emigration that continued into the next decade. The February 16, 1834, *Register* declared, "North Carolina must do something NOW or be content to take a position lower and lower in the Confederacy, until she becomes without weight in the National Scale." The 1860 U.S. Census would reveal that 272,606 native North Carolinians were living in other states, a remarkable figure considering that the state's population was 638,829 in 1820 and only 737,987 in 1830. Between 1830 and 1840, when the population of North Carolina increased a miserly 2.1 percent, Mississippi (in the cotton belt) increased 174.9 percent and Indiana (in the grain belt) grew 99.9 percent.

The 1840 census would show that 9 out of 10 working North Carolinians were still employed in agriculture. Cheap goods from the North had also altered traditional domestic manufacturing practices, causing once self-sufficient families to become increasingly dependent on outside sources for many common household articles. As one example, antebellum Raleigh residents purchased between 40,000 and 70,000 pounds of tallow candles per year from a single Fayetteville factory.

In the absence of state-financed improvements, county courts continued to maintain roads, bridges, and ferries by collecting local taxes and by appointing annual overseers who had the authority to conscript white males between the ages of 18 and 45 and free blacks or slaves between 16 and 50 for work on the roads. By the mid-

Director of Archives and History Christopher Crittenden inspects the Henry Clay Oak on North Street, circa 1955. It was under this tree that Clay, convinced that the Texas question was not an issue to be decided in a Presidential campaign, wrote a letter to the National Intelligencer *claiming that annexation was unpopular among voters and would cause a war with Mexico, endanger national unity, and plunge the government into debt. Unfortunately he misread public sentiment. (DAH)*

The Marquis de Lafayette (1757-1834) visited Raleigh in 1825 during his tour of the United States. He was entertained by Governor Hutchins G. Burton and other Raleigh citizens. Lafayette continued his trip southward starting at Fayetteville, the first town in the nation named for him. (DAH)

1830s Raleigh had mail contact by stagecoach daily both north and south; thrice-weekly to New Bern, Tarboro, Greensboro, and points west; twice-weekly to Oxford; and weekly to Roxboro and Haywood. The general situation was still so bad, however, that in 1833 Governor Swain officially branded North Carolina the "Rip Van Winkle State," a cognomen that has lingered to the delight of some and to the dismay of others. Relief would finally become possible in 1837, when the state received over $1.4 million from the federal government's distrubution of a surplus resulting from the sale of land. The inflationary boom created by the land sales and the closure of the Second U.S. Bank would also bring on a deep national depression that lasted well into the 1840s. Nevertheless, despite generally unfavorable conditions, the newly dominant Whigs would use the federal money to launch North Carolina's first well-financed movement to improve transportation and education.

Statewide and national trends, as unsettling as they were, were overshadowed in 1831, when the State House burned to the ground, a disaster that threatened the very foundation of Raleigh's existence. The fire also destroyed the Canova statue of Washington, which Lafayette had so admired, and reawakened efforts to move the capital to Fayetteville. David L. Swain was present and describes the scene poignantly: "It was my lot on the 21st of June, 1831, to stand a helpless spectator, when that noble edifice adorned with the Statue of the father of his country, was a sheet of blinding, hissing flame, and to hear admidst the almost breathless silence of the stupified multitude around it, the piteous exclamation of a child, 'poor Statehouse, poor Statue, I so sorry.' There were thousands of adults present as sorrowful and as powerless as that child."

For several years, western North Carolinians had been calling for a convention to amend the state constitution in order to make it more democratic and rectify the imbalance favoring the eastern counties. Following the State House fire, some easterners consented, hoping to use an open convention to relocate the capital. So dominant was the issue in the east that Craven County Senator Richard Dobbs predicted that Cape Fear representatives would "give up everything else" in the next session of the General Assembly in exchange for fixing the seat of government at Fayetteville.

Raleigh residents reacted vehemently and even the normally subdued *Star* (August 11, 1831) was indignant: "The mere supposition that North Carolina would be willing, upon any plea of expediency, to remove her seat of government from the city, which she had pledged herself should remain *permanently* and unalterably the Capital of the State, for the purpose of building up and enriching another town, is too humiliating even for contemplation." Judge Henry Seawell, senator from Wake County, vigorously opposed a constitutional convention and introduced a bill in December 1831 to appropriate $50,000 for a new capitol in Raleigh. The General Assembly delayed action for a year, however, before voting 73-60 in the house and 35-28 in the senate in favor of Seawell's bill. Many Cumberland County constituents were upset over their house member Louis D. Henry's unenthusiastic efforts to fix the capital in Fayetteville. However, according to Kemp P. Battle, they were aided in restraining their criticism by the knowledge that Henry had already killed one man in a duel for offending him.

The General Assembly named a commission, including Raleigh citizens Joseph Gales, William Boylan, Duncan Cameron, and Judge Seawell, to oversee construction of the new capitol. Governor Swain laid the cornerstone on July 4, 1833, and the commissioners chose W.S. Drummond and Colonel Thomas Bragg to supervise the project. Ithiel Town and Alexander Jackson Davis of New York were the architects. Drummond and Bragg resigned when available funds had been expended entirely on the construction of the foundation, and David Paton of Edinburgh took over, employing several skilled stonemasons from his native Scotland. By the time the capitol was completed in 1840, total costs had run to $530,684.15—a welcome expenditure in depressed Raleigh.

To transport the stone from a quarry 1.25 miles to the southeast of Union Square, Mrs. Sarah Hawkins Polk, who led the Raleigh Female Benevolent Society in charity work in the 1840s, financed the construction of the Raleigh Rock Quarry Experimental Railroad. The first "railroad" in North Carolina, it consisted entirely of a horse-drawn car that traversed wooden rails on a route via New Bern Avenue. Rides on the "railroad" became a popular Sunday pastime, predating a full-fledged streetcar system by a half-century.

The year 1840 saw not only the completion of the new State House, but also the completion of the first genuine railroad line to link Raleigh to the outside world. The General Assembly had chartered the Raleigh & Gaston Railroad Company in 1835 with an allowed sale of $800,000 in stock and provision for an increase to one million dollars. Following the new Whig policy of supporting internal improvements, the legislature backed $500,000 in bonds in January 1839 and approved an additional $500,000 in stock to meet construction costs; in 1840, as the line neared completion, the legislature endorsed another $300,000 in bonds. Several Raleigh citizens, including William Boylan and Duncan Cameron, were on the board of directors.

In 1835 engineers had begun construction of the Raleigh & Gaston Railroad by bridging the Roanoke River at a place they named Gaston, in honor of Judge William Gaston of Raleigh. Work progressed at a steady pace and the tracks had reached Littleton in May of 1838, when advance surveyors encountered their first problem. An armed group of Warrenton citizens, opposed to a railroad in their area, confronted the surveyors and ran them out of the area. The engineers judiciously bypassed Warrenton on their way through Ridgeway, Henderson, and Franklinton. The directors contracted D.J. Bur & Company of Richmond to build locomotives. They ordered iron strips from England to attach to the wooden rails, but since delivery was delayed, the first locomotive entered Raleigh gingerly riding on bare wooden rails. Another order of rails from Philadelphia arrived shortly, and the 86-mile Raleigh & Gaston Railroad was ready for full operation.

At about six p.m. on a Saturday, March 21, 1840, "the first Steam Locomotive that ever snorted amongst the hills of Crabtree" arrived to the cheers of an excited crowd. The locomotive pulling the inaugural train was named the *Tornado*, and later engines — *Volcano, Whirlwind, Spitfire* — would also bear appellations inspired by turbulent natural upheavals. Within a week the Raleigh & Gaston, as the *Register* reported, had "cars arriving from, and departing to the North, daily, with Passengers and Mails. The Passenger Cars are entirely new, of very handsome construction, and possessing comforts and conveniences not always found in them. The Northern Train left for the first time on Wednesday last, about 2 o'clock, P.M. and notwithstanding a driving snow, that turned the noses of the most resolute *blue*, a large Company collected to witness their departure."

City and state officials decided to honor the completion of

Lafayette (1757-1834) was a friend of George Washington from the days of the Revolutionary War. This lithograph shows the Frenchman gazing at Canova's statue of his comrade-in-arms in the State House. The young lady at his left, Miss Betsey John Haywood (daughter of the state treasurer), escorted him around the city. (DAH)

David Paton (1801-1881), a 33-year-old architect from Scotland, had been in the United States less than a year when he was asked to supervise the completion of the new capitol. Its exterior walls were largely in place by the time he arrived in Raleigh in 1835. Paton added a number of personal touches to the interior that were not included in the original plan, like the internal arrangement of the east and west wings and the cantilevered gallery in the rotunda. (DAH)

Raleigh's new capitol and railroad with one gigantic festival, setting June 10 as the start for three days of the most jubilant celebration in Raleigh's history. The grand events included a stately procession, band performances, excursions on the new railway, a dinner for 700 in the railroad warehouse (catered by the former Hannah Casso), and a series of balls in the capitol. In recounting the celebration a week later, the *Standard* editor congratulated dignitaries and citizens alike for their meritorious conduct, but he was most impressed by the absence of partisan political activities, having heard "no reference to political topics . . . in any part of the City during the three festive days."

Raleigh's love affair with its new railroad would prove short-lived, however, as mounting expenses and disappointing income kept the Raleigh & Gaston in almost constant financial straits, despite state assistance. In January of 1846 the state bought the company for only $300,000 in a bankruptcy auction, installing Wesley Hollester as its new president and superintendent. But the company's problems continued to worsen. In February of 1848 the Raleigh machine shops burned, destroying one engine and damaging four others. By that time, too, the tracks had dangerously deteriorated, but the managers persevered.

Between 1849 and 1860, the General Assembly granted charters to 84 companies authorizing them to build plank roads. More than 500 miles would be completed before the late 1850s (when interest began to flag), including the world's longest plank road, which ran from Fayetteville to west of Salem. But since the planned road from Greenville to Raleigh never reached west of Wilson, the capital continued to be served by often-delayed trains, coaches that operated at the mercy of the weather, and mail carriers on horseback. Raleigh's Postmaster William White complained in 1851 that North Carolina was more poorly served by the mails than any of the original 13 states.

Except for the initial boosts to the Raleigh economy resulting from the construction of the new capitol and the building of the Raleigh & Gaston Railroad, increased business and trade during the 1830s resulted almost entirely from the establishment of a few extremely modest firms. John H. DeCarteret started the Raleigh Book-Bindery in 1833, for instance, and Henry J. Brown moved from Petersburg to open a business known as the H.J. Brown Coffin House. But the capital's economy remained lethargic. Guion Griffis Johnson, whose *Ante-Bellum North Carolina* is the most respected study of the period, states flatly, "Raleigh, legislated into existence in 1792, had become the fourth largest town in the State by 1860, not from its advantageous situation, but from the fact that it was the State capital." During the 1840s most new residents still came to the city because of the activities of the state government, but their very presence laid the foundation upon which Raleigh would begin to build a more diversified commercial community in the mid-1850s.

Buffeted though they were by economic hardships, or

According to tradition, this Neoclassical frame building served as Raleigh's post office in the mid-19th century. Later, Dr. Fabius J. Haywood purchased the structure, hitched some horses to it, and (it is thought) had it pulled down muddy Fayetteville Street to South Street, where he used it as his office. The Raleigh Historic Properties Commission moved it to Mordecai Historic Park and restored it as a post office. (DAH)

Governor David L. Swain (1801-1868) laid the cornerstone of the second State House on July 4, 1833. Although one writer described him as "tall and heavy with a grotesquely ugly figure and ungraceful carriage," Swain was eminently successful as a lawyer, judge, state legislator, and president of the University of North Carolina. Courtesy, North Carolina Collection, UNC Library

perhaps because of them, Raleigh citizens were constant in their enthusiasm for religion. The popularity of revivals remained high throughout the lean years, as evidenced by an item in the September 10, 1829, *Star:* "A considerable revival has taken place in the Methodist Church in this town, within the last ten days. The preachers and leading members exert themselves in a surprising degree. The church is scarcely

Under construction since 1833, the capitol cost $532,682.34 by the time it was completed and furnished in 1840. The structure features such classical Greek architectural motifs as the Doric columns on the porticoes. (DAH)

perance Society, organized in Raleigh in 1828, engaged the Reverend Thomas P. Hunt in 1831 to form auxiliary units statewide. He recorded his inauspicious beginning in his memoirs: "At the first efforts to organize a temperance society in Raleigh, we could not get a sufficient number to fill the offices. Indifference, hesitation, opposition, and ridicule met us on every hand." In a three-month campaign to raise funds, he collected only $3.50. But when Hunt focused his attention beyond the borders of Wake County, his success was phenomenal. Sympathetic adherents to the precepts of temperance formed branches in 27 counties with a total membership exceeding 4,700.

The New York Sons of Temperance opened a branch in Raleigh in 1843, although it too aroused scant enthusiasm initially, accumulating only 139 dues-paying members statewide by 1846. But, in 1851, the Sons employed a proven organizer in Philip S. White, who in a single tour of the state collected more than 12,000 new members organized into 281 local chapters. The Sons adopted Alexander M. Gormon's Raleigh-based *The Spirit of the Age* as their official publication, and it grew to become the most widely circulated and longest-lasting of the many temperance sheets of antebellum North Carolina.

The Daughters of Temperance followed their male counterparts in 1849, establishing their Grand Union in Raleigh and forming 29 local orders within three years. But success proved fatal to the North Carolina temperance movement. Encouraged by the rapid increase in membership, temperance leaders entered politics. Their rigid advocacy of prohibition and other controversial issues offended large segments of their own following, as well as the public at large, and most local chapters quietly expired.

Despite all the energy that proponents of temperance poured into their cause, they were no more successful than the earlier Association for the Suppression of Vice had been at eradicating objectionable activity. Seldom, however, have crusaders had more formidable obstacles to overcome. Kemp P. Battle recalls drinking habits among the antebellum elite: "Our forefathers . . . thought they were drinking down health and long life. In fact, even when they did not become drunkards and die the drunkard's death, they were gathering to themselves all such evils as gout, disease of the liver, of the heart, of the kidneys. It was the fashion to offer spirits on all occasions. My father told me when he was in the Legislature in 1833-1834, the members, as a rule, kept a jug in their rooms and offered a glass to every visitor." Excessive drinking was by no means the exclusive prerogative of the elite and the wealthy. Grog shops, also known as "doggeries," were to the wage earner and the slave what the tavern was to the gentleman and the merchant. North Carolina law may have forbade the sale of liquor to slaves, but they frequented Raleigh grog shops with consistent regularity. During the late antebellum period, it seemed to some, the entire city was on a collective binge. A correspondent to the *Standard,* in January 1856, observed: "It

closed from morning to midnight, and sometimes even later, and the short intervals they allow themselves there, are filled up by prayer and exhortation in private dwellings." The Reverend John W. Childs led equally zealous Methodist revivals throughout the Piedmont area in 1833, and the next year the Baptists conducted lengthy revivals statewide. Fervent religious services often attracted detractors, however, who fired guns, laughed, whooped, and even stoned churches. To protect worshipers from malicious ridicule, the North Carolina Supreme Court in 1833 ruled it a misdemeanor to disturb "a congregation assembled for the purposes of religious worship, by laughing and talking, and indecent acts and grimaces."

Lay religious activity was also plentiful in the capital. The North Carolina Bible Society centered its functions in Raleigh in 1830, at which time it promised to provide a Bible for every "destitute family" in North Carolina. On May 28, 1847, when local volunteers in Company L of the 12th Infantry Regiment left Raleigh to join the expedition invading Mexico, Bible Society President Duncan Cameron gave each officer a complete Bible; for reason unknown, the enlisted men received copies of the New Testament only. The Reverend Melville Cox, pastor of the Methodist Church, achieved distinction in 1833 by becoming the first American missionary to serve in Africa, but he succumbed to disease five months after his arrival. The Reverend Thomas Meredith, who founded the *Baptist Interpreter* in Edenton in 1832 and changed its title to the *Biblical Recorder* in 1834, moved in 1838 to Raleigh—where the *Biblical Recorder* is still published.

A significant portion of Raleigh society, at one time or another with varying degrees of zeal, also supported the quasi-religious temperance movement. The North Carolina Tem-

Above: *Designed and crafted by the English firm C. Tayleur and Company, the locomotive* Raleigh *was one of the first trains in service on the Raleigh & Gaston Railroad. (DAH)*

Left: *William Gaston (1778-1844), civil rights advocate and prosecutor in the Granville lands-confiscation case, served in the state legislature from 1800-1832, was elected twice to Congress, and was justice of the state supreme court from 1833 to 1844. His office originally stood at the southwest corner of West Hargett and Salisbury streets. Courtesy, North Carolina Collection, UNC Library*

is notorious that more ardent spirits are consumed here than at any former period."

Gambling was also a popular activity, which many found as offensive as intemperate drinking. Cockfights had attracted large crowds in North Carolina ever since the first settlers crossed the Virginia border, and they retained their popularity in an age that provided the bettor a greater selection. Establishments from the grand tavern to the common grog shop could purchase licenses to house billiard, backgammon, and shuffleboard tables. In 1838 a jockey club built a racetrack near Raleigh and claimed to offer the highest purses between Mobile and Baltimore. Like cockfights, horse races attracted truly democratic gatherings, where slaves and gentlemen alike placed wagers different only in denomination and where one "authority's" assessment of horseflesh was pretty much equal to the next. The sport became so popular that during the 1840 racing season, the *Register* began printing something resembling a sports page.

capitol. The legislature appropriated $500 yearly to purchase books and to preserve North Carolina newspapers, and by 1860 the library's holdings exceeded 1,000 volumes. But intellectual and cultural life generally suffered throughout the period of economic decline. Nowhere was this more evident than in the area of education. Literally scores of special schools operated for varying lengths of time between 1820 and 1850. Most taught a few subjects at best, and merely served to underscore the lack of a comprehensive educational system in Raleigh.

Beginning in 1815 the Raleigh Academy had accepted poor children without tuition, but the experiment was abandoned in the early 1820s. In 1828 the trustees of the financially troubled school took another fateful step when they announced that they could no longer guarantee teachers any pay in excess of tuition. In 1830 the trustees finally dissolved the corporation. They sold Academy property on West Jones Street for $1,000 to Henry W. Mills and property on Burke Square for $600 to William Peace, who had already contributed $900 in a vain effort to keep the school solvent. However, teachers continued to operate the school, and the situation improved in 1841 when Jefferson Madison Lovejoy—dubbed "Yankee Lovejoy" because of his Northern heritage—opened his Lovejoy Academy in the old Raleigh Academy building and operated it continuously until his health declined in 1876.

The Episcopal Classical School for boys, under its principal George W. Freeman, was also in trouble in 1830. The Episcopal Church accepted responsibility for running the school and purchased a 159.5-acre campus site on Hillsborough Street from Colonel William Polk three years later. An Episcopal Convention meeting in Hillsborough provided funds to complete three buildings (now called Smedes Hall, East Rock House, and West Rock House), and a special convention in Raleigh in November 1837 allotted money to relieve the school of all debts. Nevertheless, insufficient income forced the directors to close the school permanently in 1840. The property was bought by Duncan Cameron, who lived across the street.

Duncan Cameron had practiced law, built a plantation that employed the labor of more than 1,000 slaves, and served in the House of Commons and the Senate before becoming a Raleigh resident. Afterwards he accumulated an incredible list of accomplishments: he became a trustee of the University of North Carolina, a superior court judge, president of the state bank, longtime clerk of the North Carolina Supreme Court, a member of the board for internal improvements, a founder of Christ Church, president of the Colonization Society, chairman of the commission to build the new capitol, and a director of the Raleigh & Gaston Railroad. In 1833, across Hillsborough Street from the Episcopal School, he built a large, colonnaded house said to have inspired the setting for Thomas Dixon's *The Clansman,* a poor novel that has gained a modicum of fame as the basis for D.W. Griffith's film, *The*

Birth of a Nation.

When Cameron bought the Episcopal School property, he donated it and some seed money to found St. Mary's School for Girls. In the spring of 1842, area newspapers carried the following announcement: "The Rev. Aldert Smedes, of the City of New York, designs to open a school for Young Ladies, in the City of Raleigh, N.C., on the 12th day of May next. This institution is to furnish a thorough and elegant Education, equal to the best that can be obtained in the City of New York, or in any Northern School." Thus, Raleigh's oldest educational institution had its birth during a time when the city's educational fortunes were at their lowest.

In 1844 the decades-long effort to establish a school for the deaf and dumb finally came to fruition with a General Assembly appropriation of $5,000. In May 1845 William D. Cooke accepted the first seven deaf-mute students in a residence on Hillsborough Street. (Blind students began attending in 1851.) By 1848 a beautiful, spacious instruction and dormitory building on Caswell Square was in use, and the school officially became the North Carolina Institute for the Education of the Deaf, Dumb, and Blind in 1852.

In 1817 Archibald De Bow Murphey had chaired a committee which drew up plans to implement a public school system funded jointly by the localities and the state. The legislature did not approve Murphey's ambitious innovations, but in 1825 it did create a Literary Fund to finance schools, although the Fund remained inadequate until 1837, when it received over $1.1 million from the state's share of surplus money distributed by the federal government. In an 1839 referendum to decide whether citizens were willing to match every two dollars in Literary Fund money to operate the schools with one dollar in local taxes to build the schools, Raleigh voters approved the school tax, 311-45. Wake County voters passed it by a smaller margin of 848-656.

In 1841 Raleigh opened two schools, the Eastern Schoolhouse in the old church building in Moore Square, and the temporary Western Schoolhouse on land owned by William Boylan. In 1843 the latter was replaced by the Gum Spring School at Cabarrus and McDowell, and in 1848 a school for girls was erected at New Bern and East, next to the city cemetery. The early public schools concentrated on reading aloud, writing, and arithmetic, during annual sessions of about three and a half months in the coldest period of winter.

Even though Raleigh was North Carolina's fourth largest city and the home of many of the "important" people of the state for at least a portion of the year, its citizens could expect little from enlightened medical education when illness struck. Wake County had a total of 10 doctors in 1823, but few doctors anywhere in North Carolina were college trained. Low income prompted the well-educated doctor to seek practices in other states, and even as late as 1856 the average annual income of North Carolina doctors was only $300. General practitioners usually pulled teeth, but patients with special problems had to wait for the arrival of itinerant dentists.

Left: A founder of the Baptist State Convention of North Carolina, author of its constitution, and editor and originator of the Biblical Recorder, *Thomas Meredith (1795-1850) was also a member of the three-man team that organized Wake Forest College in 1833. His advocacy of higher education for women prompted the change of the name of the Baptist University for Women to Meredith College in 1909. (DAH)*

Below: Godey's Lady's Book *was widely read in antebellum Raleigh; thus during their autumn strolls along Fayetteville Street, Raleigh women probably wore fashions similar to these from the September 1843 edition. Raleighites could subscribe to the magazine or buy it issue by issue from Henry D. Turner at the North Carolina Book Store. (DAH)*

Right: *Stone and McCollum's Great Western Circus was to perform in Raleigh on September 7 and 8, 1849. The advertisement in the August 29* North Carolina Standard *promised entertainment for the entire family. Courtesy, North Carolina Collection, UNC Library*

Left: *The May 1857 issue of* Harper's New Monthly Magazine *featured this drawing of a cockfight (by "Porte Crayon") in the series "North Carolina Illustrated." Watching the bloody antics of feathered gladiators was one way Raleighites entertained themselves at mid-century.* (DAH)

But modern health care in Raleigh had its beginning at this time — in the provisions of John Rex's will. A wealthy landowner, tanner, and moneylender, John Rex was described as "a grave, quiet, retiring, modest man." When he died in January 1839, his will revealed two interesting provisions. Rex left 25 acres and $8,000 "for the erection and endowment of an infirmary or hospital for the sick and afflicted poor of the city of Raleigh." After the fund had grown to over $40,000 in 1861, patriotic trustees purchased Confederate bonds, leaving the fund worth less than $1,000 at the end of the Civil War. But after it had grown once again to over $30,000, the first department of Rex Hospital finally opened in 1894. Rex had also manumitted his 18 slaves in his will, setting aside enough money to pay the passage to Africa for any who wished to return — 17 accepted.

Even though Raleigh endured to the end of the Civil War without experiencing violent racial strife, apprehension over the possibility of a slave revolt intensified around 1830. The General Assembly attempted to defuse the situation by placing further restrictions on slaves in the spring of 1831, motivating the *Register* to seek a more lasting solution: "It is admitted that slavery is a curse to the Southern States. Would it not be better to think of some means of getting rid of it, rather than thus fly in the face of humanity and the constitution." However, as sectional attitudes became increasingly encrusted and reflexive, even the *Register* abandoned its humane approach.

Following the bloody Nat Turner rebellion of August 1831, all able-bodied white men of Raleigh formed four companies to alternate a night watch. The elderly called their company the "Silver Grays." The State House bell was to signal trouble, in which event women and children were to take refuge in the Presbyterian Church. While the tension was at its highest, John O'Rorke's blacksmith shop burned one night, causing much alarm. In eastern North Carolina, the panic caused two slaves to be hanged and scores punished, even though the Fayetteville *Observer* insisted that "not a single party of negroes, nay, not a single individual, has been found in arms or in rebellion, in any of the counties." The most painful symptoms of a lingering malady were erupting.

Principal of the Episcopal Classical School for Boys, the Reverend George W. Freeman (1789-1858) spent two years as a missionary in the diocese of North Carolina before becoming rector of Christ Church in 1829. Leaving Raleigh in 1840, Freeman's last ecclesiastical post was as missionary bishop to Arkansas and the Indian Territory. (DAH)

Raleigh attitudes regarding free blacks became generally more intolerant as sectional differences over the slavery issue drove both sides to extreme positions. Lunsford Lane was an industrious slave who had earned enough money by growing, curing, and selling high-quality tobacco to buy his freedom from Sherwood Haywood of Raleigh in 1836. He then made pipes, ran a store, and sold firewood to supplement his income further, and in 1839 he was able to make a down payment toward purchasing his wife and six children. Since Lane had legalized his freedom with a three-month visit to New York, he could no longer remain legally in North Carolina and was forced to leave the state. Weston Gales, Governor Edward B. Dudley, and C.C. Battle all assisted Lane after he moved to Massachusetts, but when he returned to get his family, capital citizens who were angered over abolition lectures Lane had delivered in the North tarred and feathered him.

Slave shoemaker Isaac Hunter also bought his freedom and legalized it with a stay in New York. When he returned to Raleigh to purchase his family, authorities ordered him to leave the state. When he then pleaded for time to earn sufficient money, "the most intelligent and respectable persons of the City" signed his petition. Responding to another petition seeking his immediate expulsion, the General Assembly ordered him to leave the state within 20 days.

When a group of vigilantes dragged a free Negro blacksmith from his home in Raleigh and beat him, however, the *Register* rushed to protest the action and the violation of the sanctity of the blacksmith's home: "If a man's house—his castle, as the law defines it—is to be forced at midnight, the locks broken and he taken out and butchered to gratify the vindictive feelings of any set of individuals, it is worse than idle to talk about the security which the law gives, for its boasted supremacy is but a farce, and Courts of Justice, ridiculous mockery."

As dominant as the slavery issue may have been, there were other popular political interests. On the state level, the old contention between east and west was as divisive as ever. The January 14, 1834, *Register* warned the legislature "that unless the grievances complained of be speedily redressed, the yeomanry of the West will take the remedy in their own hands." The western rebellion did not occur, in large measure because the Whigs began to appropriate money for projects in

transportation and education that pleased the west and because the 1835 amendments to the constitution gave the west a near-equal voice in government. True to tradition, the once-progressive Whigs grew protective of the status quo as their tenure in power lengthened, and it was the democratic candidate David S. Reid who first ran on a platform of free manhood suffrage in 1848. Charles Manly, the first Wake County resident to serve as governor, defeated Reid, but his majority of only 854 votes signaled the end of Whig domination. Once in power, the Democrats supported increased expenditures for internal improvements and education that, perhaps only briefy, broke the "Rip Van Winkle" syndrome and would benefit Raleigh in particular during the decade of the 1850s.

On the national level, local and state interest ran consistent-

Right: *Duncan Cameron (1777-1853), recognized as one of 19th-century North Carolina's best legal minds, was defense counselor in the Granville land-confiscation case of 1805 and taught law to future governor Willie P. Mangum. He was also a founder of Christ Episcopal Church and made possible the establishment of St. Mary's School for Girls—now St. Mary's College. Courtesy, North Carolina Collection, UNC Library*

Below: *Designed by architect Thomas Wiatt and completed in 1835, the Duncan Cameron house allegedly provided the setting for Thomas Dixon's The Clansman, the novel upon which D.W. Griffith's epic silent film Birth of a Nation was based. The mansion was razed in 1938 to make way for an apartment complex. Courtesy, North Carolina Collection, UNC Library*

The North Carolina Institute for the Education of the Deaf, Dumb, and Blind is shown as it appeared in 1874. Enlarged and renovated in 1898, it remained in use until 1923, when the Governor Morehead School was completed. (DAH)

ly high, although North Carolina in fact exerted little influence on national affairs. When Whig William Henry Harrison ran as the "log-cabin-and-hard-cider" candidate in 1840, the Tippecanoe Club of Raleigh built Harrison Hall out of logs to serve as Whig Party campaign headquarters, and the Whig Ladies campaigned actively. The Tippecanoe Club may have played an insignificant role in the election of Harrison, but an event that occurred in Raleigh became the central issue in the next Presidential election. While visiting Congressman Kenneth Rayner, announced Whig candidate Henry Clay sat beneath a 500-year-old oak tree on North Blount Street on April 17, 1844, and wrote a letter to the *National Intelligencer* in Washington, D.C. Clay opposed the admission of Texas into the Union, which cost him votes in the South. He hedged on the slavery issue, which cost him votes in the North. In no small part because of the Raleigh letter, North Carolinian James Knox Polk defeated Clay by only 38,681 popular votes in the 1844 election.

When President Zachary Taylor died in office in July 1850, Raleigh citizens of all political persuasions mourned his pass-

Because of a bronchial ailment, Aldert Smedes (1810-1877) left New York for Raleigh's milder climate. Shortly after his arrival in 1842, he established St. Mary's School for Girls, of which he was rector until his death. Courtesy, North Carolina Collection, UNC Library

ing. A full-dress military parade, a symbolic funeral hearse drawn by six white horses, eight pallbearers, and hundreds of officials and private citizens walking and on horseback formed a procession nearly one-half mile long. They marched past black-draped government buildings, businesses, and residences on the way from the "Palace" to the capitol. At the Presbyterian Church, Wake County Whig leader Henry W. Miller delivered a eulogy. On July 24 the *Register* described, "The measured tread of men and horses—the beat of muffled drums—the loud lamentations of cannon—the woful peal of bells—the closed stores and the mourning Statues on the sidewalks . . . all these things spoke, in eloquent terms the sorrowful tribute of a no ordinary admiration for the living Hero, a no common grief for the departed Patriot."

On the municipal level, the town commissioners strove to improve the quality of urban life, prodded by an increasingly active constituency. They experimented with streetlights in 1830 and installed permanent lamps in 1835. The *Register* congratulated the commissioners for their work and rejoiced that "the nocturnal traveller, in his perambulations through the town, can no longer say Silence how dear! Darkness how profound!" A new brick courthouse was built in 1837, complete with a jail, a whipping post, and sheriff's quarters. A new city hall and market was erected in 1840. When the commissioners denied use of the new hall to the Mechanic's Association in 1841, the July 7 *Standard* proclaimed "Of all the tyrannies in the world, that of a city police is the most ridiculous and absurd." After public pressure had mounted for three weeks, the commissioners capitulated and directed "That the City Hall be hereafter used for the following purposes, to wit: Public Meetings of the Citizens; meetings of the Commissioners of the City; Fire Company; Uniform Military Company; City Watch; and Private Associations or Societies of the City." A prototype of later unions, the Mechanic's Association of the 1840s was primarily concerned with competition from skilled slave labor and with the difficulty of collecting bills.

Above: *This two-inch sterling silver medal, made by F.B. Smith of New York, was awarded at North Carolina's first annual state fair in October 1853. (DAH)*

Top: *Henry Clay is featured in this Whig Party poster from the 1844 Presidential campaign. While the Kentuckian misjudged popular support for the annexation of Texas, the electorate misinterpreted his reluctance to make the topic a major election issue. The misunderstanding cost Clay the Presidency. (DAH)*

1839 when he retired to Washington, D.C., to live with his son, Joseph, Jr. (The elder Gales eventually returned to Raleigh, where he died in 1841.)

As politically opposed organs, the *Standard* and the *Register* each freely attacked the other, and one of Weston Gales' last editorials (June 10, 1848) exhibits the flavor of the exchange: "We never feel so certain that we are in the discharge of our duty, as when we are assailed with the filth and venom of the *Standard.*" Six weeks later (July 26), Holden ended one phase of the warfare in his obituary to Weston: "Let the past be forgotten; let it sleep evermore beneath the clod that rests upon the bosom of our lamented fellow-citizen." In an age that had no elaborate nominating machinery, editors often possessed decisive power in determining which candidates would become serious challengers for office, and Holden skillfully used the *Standard* to launch himself into the most remarkable political career in the history of North Carolina and to become the dominant figure in Raleigh during the crucial 1860s.

Newspapers other than the *Standard* and the *Register* were published in Raleigh, some representing specific interests, such as agriculture. Joseph Gales and others had formed a North Carolina Agriculture Society in 1819, and Thomas J. Lemay had published the *North Carolina Farmer* in Raleigh from August 1845 to July 1850. When Thomas Ruffin, Robert Hamilton, Frederick Hill, and J.W. Norwood organized the new State Agriculture Society in 1852, they made Raleigh the center of agricultural research and education in North Carolina. An immediate manifestation of the new status was the first annual State Fair held in 1853 on an 8.5-acre field bordered by East Hargett, East Davie, and Haywood streets. Soon thereafter, William D. Cooke and Company purchased Dr. John Tompkins' *Farmer's Journal* and moved it from Bath to Raleigh. Thomas J. Lemay began publishing the *Arator* in 1855, and A.M. Gorman, editor of the temperance paper *Spirit of the Age*, added still another farm journal, the *North Carolina Planter*, in 1858.

Imaginative innovators in the field of agriculture brought a new kind of attention to the capital in the 1850s. In that decade Raleigh continued to progress in educational theory and institutions, transportation facilities, and commercial development, but overall the years are chiefly memorable for the consolidation of commercial and population advances of previous years. By the end of the decade, Raleigh seemed poised to break out of the "legislated capital" syndrome, boosted by a new railroad line linking Raleigh to the markets and resources to the west.

But disaster struck to delay the transition for a quarter of a century. Raleighites had yet to endure a long period of reflection and debate over the matter of secession, ending in unified support for the Confederacy; they would have to outlive the humiliation of surrender and occupation and the hardship of Reconstruction and depression before they could once again look hopefully to the future.

When the telegraph came to Raleigh in 1848, for the first time the capital enjoyed up-to-date information from political and commercial centers, especially in the North. The *Register* remained the most influential Raleigh publication until the mid-1840s, when William Holden turned the *Standard* into a formidable political "institution." Joseph Gales, Sr., left Weston Gales the sole owner and editor of the *Register* in

Attracted by the completion of the Raleigh & Gaston Railroad, by the economic opportunities following recovery from depression, and by assurances that the permanent site of state government had been reinforced by the construction of an expensive new capitol, people had flocked to Raleigh in unprecedented numbers during the 1840s, swelling its population by 101 percent. But during the decade of the 1850s, Raleigh's population increased by only 6 percent, from 4,518 to 4,780, as consolidation took precedence over growth. When New York journalist Frederick Law Olmstead visited the capital in 1856, he saw "a pleasing town—the streets wide and lined with trees, and many white wooden mansions, all having little courtyards of flowers and shrubbery around them. The State-House is, in every way, a noble building, constructed of brownish-gray granite, in the Grecian style." But Olmstead also saw hogs using Union Square as a wallow, and he observed that the

IV

YANKEES COME AND GO:

1850 - 1880

commerce of the city was undeveloped and that the "industry is almost entirely rural." To at least one cosmopolitan observer, Raleigh was still a provincial town exhibiting greater influence from its rustic surroundings than from its supposedly more sophisticated functions.

The area's small farmers were self-sufficient, growing corn, peas, potatoes, melons and other fruits, making their own cheese and butter, and usually producing surplus pork to finance purchases of coffee, sugar, and salt. Plantation owners concentrated more on money-making crops and depended on purchases to clothe and feed their families and slaves. Throughout the region, poor whites had to compete with slave labor, and many followed the age-old custom of migrating to the city when conditions grew difficult in the country. The August 1855 issue of the Raleigh agriculture magazine, the *Arator,* notes the problem: "There are many in this city, whose wives and children are suffering for the want of food and raiment, who, if they remain here, are doomed to drag out a miserable and useless existence."

But Raleigh was by no means regressive. The legislature had chartered the North Carolina Railroad Company in 1848. In 1856 the completion of its 223 miles of track, running between Goldsboro and Charlotte via what would later become the "Piedmont Crescent," made Raleigh an important railway junction. The trains, however, brought far more products to the capital than they carried out. As late as 1861, North Carolinians manufactured less than 50 percent of their cotton goods, 10 percent of their shoes, 10 percent of their woolens, and 5 percent of their iron implements.

New businesses continued to be modest endeavors, but a new hotel soon evolved into one of the city's most enduring institutions. The son of a North Carolina chief justice and the former owner of the Guion Hotel, Edwin Marshall Yarborough headed a group of stockholders who financed the construction of the Yarborough House on Fayetteville Street in the early 1850s. Under Yarborough's management, the establishment quickly became the most fashionable gathering place in Raleigh. The Yarborough was popular with legislators, who considered it the "third house" of the General Assembly, and by 1890 three governors had resided there while in office. There were advances in other areas as well.

In 1856 the Oak City Guards established a reading room on the second floor of the Smith Building at Fayetteville and Hargett, open to subscribers and visitors to the city. Two years later the Gum Spring School was sold to a gas company, which pro-

Sherman and his subordinate generals in the military division of the Mississippi posed for this photograph in 1865. Of the men present in the picture—(from left to right) O.O. Howard, John A. Logan, William B. Hazen, William T. Sherman, Jeff C. Davis, Henry W. Slocum, and J.A. Mower—only Logan, Sherman, and Slocum visited Raleigh that same April. (DAH)

The United States Coast and Geodetic Survey established the Raleigh Astronomic Station—later referred to as the Raleigh Longitudinal Station—consisting of three granite stones on Union Square in 1853. The blocks, slightly northeast of the state's geographic center, were used to help position telegraph lines between Raleigh, Washington, D.C., and Charleston, South Carolina. (DAH)

vided gas lighting to those who could afford it in 1860; a new and better school was built on Nash Square. Dry-goods merchants, florists, printers, photographers, bakers, carriagemakers, music and art teachers, and druggists were all opening new businesses. In 1860 J.H. Kirkham, taking advantage of a current spa craze, sold season tickets for three dollars to partake of the mineral waters issuing from a spring near Smithfield and East streets. Two resident dentists, P. Babcock and L.S. Perry, finally relieved Raleighites of their often painful dependency on traveling dentists.

The General Assembly also passed bills which altered Raleigh politically and geographically. In 1855 the legislature granted the town commissioners the power to tax land, liquor, entertainment, dogs, hogs, horses, and unfenced cattle. The commissioners were authorized to appoint constables, to regulate public streets and bakery products, and to establish standing committees in charge of streets, public pumps, graveyards, and citizen watches. In 1857 the General Assembly changed the title of the "intendant of police" to "mayor." The mayor served in the capacity of a justice of peace; as chairman of the board of commissioners, he cast a vote when needed to break a tie. William Dallas Haywood was the first officially titled mayor, and William H. Harrison served from 1858 to 1867.

The legislature, in 1857, also extended the city limits one-fourth mile in each direction to encompass a total of one square mile—to Oakwood Cemetery to the east, slightly beyond Smithfield Street to the south, to St. Mary's Street to the west, and to North Boundary Street. Not all the new residents were content. Hoping to avoid an increase in taxes and responsibility for the existing city debt, some owners of the annexed property took their case to court, arguing that the affected citizens should decide the issue by vote. The Raleigh commissioners contended that the legislature could "extend the limits of any incorporated town, without the consent and against the wish of the citizens who live on, or own the land comprising the part to be annexed." The commissioners' contention was upheld.

Local politics were overshadowed by the national variety over the next year, however, when President James Buchanan passed through town on his way to attend the June 1858 commencement of the university in Chapel Hill. The Oak City Guards and the Wilmington Light Infantry met the President at Weldon, and D.M. Barringer stood in for absent Mayor Harrison to welcome him officially. Military companies from throughout the state, 10 fife-and-drum corps, and bands from Salisbury, Fayetteville, and the USS *Pennsylvania* marched around Union Square and down Fayetteville Street, escorting the President, Secretary of the Interior Jacob Thompson, and

Governor John W. Ellis to the Yarborough House. The *New York Herald* and the *Richmond Dispatch* sent reporters, and John Spelman covered the events for the *Standard*. In a speech to the assemblage, the President said, "If in the frenzy of political excitement, this great Union should be dissolved, ages yet unborn will curse the day that we had in our trust the liberties of the world." He spoke to an audience that had grown used to being at the center of that political "frenzy."

During the crucial 1850s, William Woods Holden was the man more than any other responsible for guiding—as often by provocation as by advocation—political thought and action in Raleigh and, indeed, throughout the state. The illegitimate son of poor Hillsborough parents, Holden had learned enough law while writing for the *Standard* to pass a lawyer's examination before the North Carolina Supreme Court in January of 1841. That same year he had married Anne Young, the niece of William Peace, one of Raleigh's wealthiest and most respected citizens. He had risen sufficiently in Whig ranks to be a Wake delegate to a state convention in 1842, but he unhesitatingly switched to the Democratic party a year later when he was offered the opportunity first to edit and, soon thereafter, to purchase the *Standard*. Although the newspaper offer was the immediate enticement to change party affiliation, Holden's later political stands were compatible with the philosophy of his adopted party and consistent with his *Standard* motto: "The many instead of the few." His contributions to the emergence of the Democrats as the dominant political force in the state were acknowledged by his appointment as state printer in 1850. But it was as an editor that he exerted his enormous influence on public opinion. In 1854 Thomas Bragg became the Democratic candidate for Senator, tanta-

In 1843 William Holden (1818-1892) became editor of the North Carolina Standard, *transforming it into the most powerful tabloid in the state. Appointed provisional governor of North Carolina by Andrew Johnson in 1865, he defeated Thomas Ashe three years later in the first gubernatorial election to be held under the new (1868) state constitution. Courtesy, North Carolina Collection, UNC Library*

mount to election, almost solely as a result of Holden's editorials in the *Standard*.

But Holden's influence extended far beyond playing the kingmaker and building personal power. He was one of the first state leaders to assert that the right of secession preceded the Union forged by the Constitution. As early as 1851 he wrote that Congress had already dissolved the Union by its failure to protect Southern rights, and he warned that North Carolina would secede if Congress continued in its refusal to enforce the Fugitive Slave Law and in its attempts to regulate slavery. Holden, partly as a boon to Southern independence, encouraged additional internal improvements to develop resources and to open new markets. Historians hold him chief-

William Percival designed the Rufus Tucker mansion, built on the corner of St. Mary's and Hillsborough streets in 1858. The twin turrets housed water storage tanks, which were filled by hand pumps from a pond on the premises. (DAH)

ly responsible for turning public opinion in favor of increased state support of railroads, plank roads, and shipping facilities. Holden was also active in pushing for reform in the penal system and in education, but his first love remained partisan politics.

The Wake County delegation endorsed Holden for governor at the 1858 Democratic state convention in Charlotte, but a majority of the delegates—who still represented the aristocracy—opposed him because of his low birth and his support of the common man. The Whig *Register* observed the donnybrook with sardonic amusement: "The lawyers and upper crust generally are for Ellis, while the unwashed multitude are for Holden. Although not entitled to a seat in a Democratic pew, we have all along been a strong Holden man. We think he is entitled to the nomination, and we are of opinion that it would be a burning shame, if one who has spent his life in making great men out of the very smallest sort of materials, should be refused the reasonable reward which he so urgently seeks." After further infighting, the delegates chose John W. Ellis of Salisbury. The Democrats in the General Assembly later rejected Holden again when he became a candidate for the U.S. Senate, choosing Thomas Bragg instead. Holden remained the faithful Democrat, however, supporting both Ellis and Bragg in the *Standard*.

As a delegate to the Democratic National Convention of June 1860 in Baltimore, Holden saw that Southern extremists were bent on confrontation, and he abandoned his earlier secessionist stance. Holden worked earnestly but futilely to prevent disunion both in his party and in the nation. In the fall campaign, he preferred Stephen A. Douglas but publicly supported John C. Breckinridge, believing him to be the stronger candidate. Even after Lincoln's election and the secession of South Carolina, Holden—like a majority of North Carolinians—opposed any rash action.

Left: *John Willis Ellis (1820-1861), lawyer, legislator, judge, and advocate of states' rights, was elected governor of North Carolina in 1858 and 1860. During his first administration he expanded the state militia, and when hostilities erupted, he quickly seized all federal property in the state. Courtesy, North Carolina Collection, UNC Library*

Hinton Rowan Helper earned widespread opprobrium in Dixie with his book, The Impending Crisis of the South. *Although he was an avowed racist, Helper supported abolition because he felt that slavery contributed to white poverty, much to the economic detriment of the South. Courtesy, North Carolina Collection, UNC Library*

In January 1861 the General Assembly ordered a public election to be held on February 28 to determine if a convention should be called to consider secession. The vote was 47,323 to 46,672 against, but antisecessionist sentiment changed abruptly following the attack on Fort Sumter and Lincoln's request on April 15, 1861, for 75,000 volunteers. Holden's *Standard* and the other 13 unionist newspapers in the state immediately became secessionist. On May 1, 1861, the legislature did not bother with voter approval; it simply ordered the election of 120 delegates to attend a May 20 convention on secession in Raleigh. The assembly voted unanimously to leave the Union. A hundred guns announced the delegates' decision, all the bells in the capital city rang, and Union Square was renamed Capitol Square.

In their eagerness to defend the South and its honor, Raleigh males rushed to form military units even before the convention voted to secede. In late April at the Fair Grounds, Captain S.D. Ramseur organized Company A of the 10th North Carolina Regiment, commanded during the war by Basil C. Manly of Raleigh. Two more companies formed during the early summer. Captain George Furibault headed Company E and Captain William Harrison commanded Company K of the 14th North Carolina Regiment. A year into the war,

Left: *The North Carolina secession flag celebrates two "independence days." On May 20, 1775, the Mecklenburg Committee of Safety allegedly passed a group of resolutions declaring residents of that county free from British rule, and the date below the star commemorates the state's leaving the Union, 86 years later. Raleigh artist William Garl Brown designed the banner. (DAH)*

Above right: *On April 15, 1861, this telegram pushed North Carolina over the brink of secession. Simon Cameron, President Lincoln's secretary of war, ordered Governor Ellis to supply two regiments of state troops to assist Federal forces attempting to relieve Fort Sumter. When the news reached the public, North Carolinians abandoned their predominately pro-Union sentiments. Courtesy, North Carolina Collection, UNC Library*

Right: *Governor Ellis refused U.S. Secretary of War Cameron's request for soldiers, saying, "I regard the levy of troops made by the administration for the purpose of subjugating the states of the South as in violation of the Constitution and a gross usurpation of power. I can be no party to this wicked violation of the laws of the country to this war upon the liberties of a free people. You can get no troops from North Carolina." Courtesy, North Carolina Collection, UNC Library*

Like other Confederate states, North Carolina issued its own currency between 1861 and 1865. These notes are in 5 cent, 75 cent, 10 cent, $10 and $50 denominations, and were printed in Raleigh. (DAH)

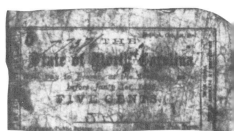

still another company collected in Raleigh—Company C of the 47th North Carolina Regiment with Edward Hill as its captain.

Other segments of Raleigh's population supported the cause with equal fervor and industry. The women of the First Baptist congregation quickly turned the church basement into a factory—producing 1,500 mattresses, 400 shirts, 300 jackets, 200 pairs of pants, and 200 haversacks during the very first month of hostilities. William Jackson Hicks began making gunpowder in his factory north of the city. Captain B.P. Williamson and Colonel J.M. Heck established a firm to turn out belt buckles and spurs, Captain J.W. Garrett, Major W.W. Pierce, and Major H.A. Dowd supervised a Raleigh plant manufacturing uniforms. A cartridge plant sprang into operation at the North Carolina Institute for the Education of the Deaf and Dumb, the Kuester firm began making percussion caps, and other companies converted their facilities to the manufacture of wooden shoes, munitions, and other supplies. Major John Devereaux's skillful management of the Quartermaster Department, headquartered in Raleigh, would keep North Carolina better supplied than any others in Lee's Army of Northern Virginia.

Answering a call from the Confederate government for metal to be cast into cannon, members of the First Baptist Church voted unanimously to send their 1,300-pound bell to a foundry in Fayetteville. The Catholic and First Presbyterian churches followed suit. In a letter to the *Register*, John W. Syme explains the propriety and the practicality of the

sacrifices: "If we do not prevent the Yankees from getting possession of our country, our church edifices will be of little use to us as their pulpits will be occupied by puritanical, Praise-Be-God-Bare-Bones, crop-eared, roundhead Yankee Abolition parsons, who will preach blasphemy through their noses and compel us to pay for it."

The publishing industry in Raleigh continued to thrive during the war, often manifesting the effects of the conflict on Southern cultural life and ideas. Theophilus Hunter Hill of

Ordained in 1840, Braxton Craven (1822-1882) served as pastor of the Edenton Street Methodist Church in 1864 and 1865. He is perhaps better known as president of Trinity College (now Duke University) and as the commandant of the Salisbury Confederate prison camp. (DAH)

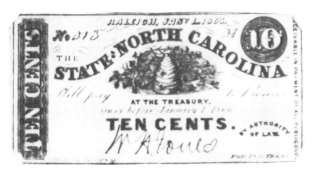

assistants combined to make the city a wartime medical treatment center. At first, the Guion Hotel functioned as a hospital, then Dr. Thomas Hill converted the unfinished Peace Institute building into General Hospital Number Eight in the summer of 1862. But the Fair Grounds Hospital and, later, the Pettigrew Hospital were larger and more active. Raleigh physician Edmund Burke Haywood, who had enlisted as a private in the Raleigh Light Infantry, was put in charge of the Fair Grounds Hospital as well as a training camp capable of handling 16,000 recruits. Dr. Haywood had attended the Raleigh Academy, graduated at the head of his class at the University of North Carolina, and studied medicine at the Jefferson Medical College of Philadelphia. Under his direction, the hospital became the busiest in the state. Between May 20, 1861, and August 1, 1862, when the state transferred it to the Confederacy, the Fair Grounds Hospital admitted 4,731 patients: 4,228 returned to duty, 241 were furloughed, 44 moved to other hospitals, 16 were discharged, 32 deserted, and 170 died. For the entirety of its operation as a state and as a Confederate hospital, the Fair Grounds center lost only 229 out of 6,916 patients admitted, while returning 5,894 to duty.

In June of 1864, Dr. Haywood moved to the Pettigrew Hospital on Rock Quarry Road, also known as General Hospital Number 13. The incomplete and unpainted main building held 394 bedsteads and six cots, but the energetic doctor made Pettigrew safe and efficient despite mounting obstacles. Physicians, medicine, drugs, attendants, cooks — in short, everything except patients — were in increasingly short supply. Like everyone else in Raleigh, Dr. Haywood also had to battle inflation. Between 1862 and 1865 in the local market, the price of chickens rose from 20 cents to $4.50, a dozen eggs from 15 cents to $4.05, a pound of beef from 12.5 cents to $3.33, bacon from 33 cents per pound to $7.50, wheat from $3 per bushel to $50. Despite those formidable problems, a surgeon inspector in December 1864 officially reported to Haywood:

Raleigh published *Hesper and Other Poems* in the fall of 1861, the first book copyrighted by the Confederate States of America. Raleigh printers also published textbooks, some unabashedly biased toward the South. Levi Branson's *First Book in Composition* seems innocuous enough, but Marinda B. Moore's *Geographical Reader for the Dixie Children* leaves no doubt regarding the author's intended audience. Lemuel Johnson's 1864 *An Elementary Arithmetic* was blatantly jingoistic; one problem asked, "If one Confederate soldier kills 90 Yankees, how many Yankees can 10 Confederate soldiers kill?"

The Fair Grounds, Camp Ellis, and Camp Mangum all became major recruiting and training centers, with four North Carolina regiments assembling at Camp Mangum alone during March, April, and May of 1862. When Union General J.G. Foster led some 11,000 troops on raids as far west as Edgecombe County in November of 1863, Governor Zebulon Vance ordered 7,500 state troops into position to defend the capital. He also ordered 10 percent of all capital-area slaves between 18 and 45 to be conscripted to build earthworks, later fortified with 10 batteries of cannon. Foster never attacked Raleigh, but he did prevent Confederate use of the vital Atlantic Coast Railroad east of Goldsboro. Raleigh, however, was considered safe enough for Mrs. Jefferson Davis, three of her children, and Robert E. Lee's daughter Mildred to stay at St. Mary's for a period during the war.

Raleigh's relative safety, its railroad connections to battlefields north and west, and its capacity to provide civilian

Raleigh surgeon Edmund Burke Haywood (1825-1894) established the state's first military hospital. He enlisted in the Raleigh Light Infantry when North Carolina seceded and was appointed surgeon of the North Carolina State Troops. Organizing a hospital on the old Fair Grounds, he eventually became director of General Hospital Number 13 — Pettigrew Hospital — which later became the Confederate Soldiers' Home. (DAH)

Originally a Union sympathizer, Zebulon Baird Vance (1830-1894) volunteered for the Confederate Army when North Carolina seceded. His military career was cut short when he was elected governor in 1862; he defeated W.W. Holden for the same office in 1864. Vance's skill at securing military appropriations from the legislature made the state one of the few that could support troops in the field without outside aid. He also organized a successful blockade-running operation. Courtesy, North Carolina Collection, UNC Library

"The order, discipline and excellent sanitary conditions of your hospital are such as to reflect great credit upon yourself and associate medical officers."

While casualties on the battlefields mounted, the conflict was also incurring political "casualties" in Raleigh and throughout the state. By the summer of 1861, a complete split had been effected between William Holden and the Democrats, who organized under the Confederate party banner. No longer the state printer, Holden organized opponents to the Confederate party and the Richmond government into the new Conservative party, which chose 32-year-old Colonel Zebulon Vance of Buncombe County to oppose Confederate candidate Colonel William Johnston in the 1862 gubernatorial election. Holden and *Fayetteville Observer* editor Edward Hale conducted Vance's campaign, and their charge that nonslaveholders were being called upon to make the greatest sacrifice in a "rich man's war and a poor man's fight" clearly struck a responsive chord. Vance defeated Johnston 54,423 to 20,448, and Holden once again became state printer and an influence in government.

But Holden's alliance with Vance quickly deteriorated. In the summer of 1863, the Heroes of America, also called the Red Strings, formed a peace party that sponsored more than 100 well-attended rallies throughout the state. Holden supported them in the *Standard,* and the similarity between his editorials and many of their resolutions led observers to conclude that he was their guiding inspiration. In response to the widespread agitation for peace, the North Carolina regiments sent representatives to an August convention in Hillsborough that reaffirmed their support of the Confederacy and condemned Holden by name. Virginian authorities forbade the distribution of the *Standard* within their state, and Jefferson Davis wrote Vance asking if Holden's "treasonable action" warranted prosecution. Governor Vance released a proclamation on September 9, 1863, asking the people to curb the

peace movement and "not seek to cure the evils of one revolution by plunging the country into another." Holden responded, "Let the people speak; it is refreshing to hear them."

Two days later Georgia troops, passing through Raleigh under the command of General Henry Benning, vandalized the *Standard* offices. Unionist Mark Williams retaliated by leading a mob that destroyed the presses of the pro-Confederate *State Journal.* Vance restored order, even calling out troops to protect the *Standard* from further violence, but the governor and Holden remained opposed politically.

The *Standard* favored a convention to seek an independent peace for North Carolina. Vance preferred to support Confederate initiatives, and he stepped up his criticism of the Richmond government for excluding North Carolinians from policy-making positions and for acceding to the Union occupation of eastern North Carolina. A peace convention nominated Holden to oppose Vance in 1864, and the governor won reelection by a landslide, 58,065 to 14,471. Holden quickly announced he would support Vance, the state, and the South while still seeking peace. The peace movement was broken, however, by Lincoln's reelection, his adamant refusal to negotiate, and by increasing signs of imminent Northern victory.

On March 11, 1865, General Sherman occupied Fayetteville. On March 19-20 at Bentonville, Sherman defeated General Joseph E. Johnston in the greatest battle ever fought in North Carolina. Johnston resumed his retreat to the north, and General Joseph Wheeler's troops were marching through Raleigh on April 10 when news came of Lee's surrender. Margaret Devereux overheard a conversation in her yard among some cavalrymen, who had dropped in their tracks from exhaustion: "One of the poor fellows, while the column was passing by Christ Church, looked up at the weathercock and remarked to a comrade that it was the first and only instance of Wheeler's boys seeing a chicken which they could not get at."

On April 11, 1865, State Treasurer Jonathan Worth fled west with state records and a large supply train. The next day governor Vance moved to Hillsborough, leaving the elderly former Governor David L. Swain, then president of the University of North Carolina, to surrender the capital. As the last Southern detachments passed through the city, Mayor W.H. Harrison and the board of commissioners decided it was time to take measures to protect the city.

On the rainy morning of April 13, after a delegation headed by Swain had visited Sherman to make preliminary arrangements, Mayor Harrison and a contingent of prominent Raleigh citizens took a carriage out Holleman Road under a flag of truce. They waited just across Walnut Creek until a group of Yankee cavalrymen approached and then escorted them to General H. Judson Kilpatrick, who accepted the surrender. The general agreed to protect the "lives and property of all who yielded obedience to law and order," but promised

The reputation of Union General William Tecumseh Sherman (1820-1891) as a destroyer of private and public property (during his March to the Sea and Carolinas campaigns) preceded him to Raleigh in the spring of 1865, and was one reason why city fathers decided to surrender rather than subject residents to unnecessary hardship. Few people realized that Sherman held a genuine affection for the South, since he had lived there 12 years. (DAH)

Hugh Judson Kilpatrick (1836-1881) was the first Union officer to enter Raleigh after the city surrendered. Nicknamed "Kill Cavalry" because of his exploits in Virginia, he was transferred to the Western theater of operations by General Sherman, who allegedly remarked, "I know Kilpatrick is a hell of a damned fool, but I want just that sort of man to command my cavalry in this expedition." The general was referring to his campaign against Atlanta and the Carolinas. (DAH)

Jonathan Worth served as state treasurer during the Civil War, and acted in the same capacity in William Woods Holden's provisional government. He later defeated Holden in the 1865 gubernatorial race. In 1867 the Charleston, South Carolina Chronicle called him "a quiet little old gentleman sharp as a briar, and with a well of wisdom at the root of every grey hair." (DAH)

to "pursue with relentless fury all traitors in armed opposition to the Union."

As Kilpatrick and his cavalry galloped up Fayetteville Street, an incident occurred to threaten the tenuous peace. A detachment of Wheeler's cavalry, left behind to destroy arms and supplies, had lingered to loot undefended stores and warehouses. One of the men, a Texas lieutenant named Walsh, fired a parting shot at the approaching Yankees and shouted, "Hurrah for the Southern Confederacy." He rode west along Morgan Street, not knowing that a bridge did not span the railroad beyond West Street. When he turned his mount abruptly at that point, his saddle girt snapped and he fell. The Yankees captured him and took him to Kilpatrick at Capitol Square. Walsh claimed he was ignorant of the surrender, but Kilpatrick accused him of being a thief and commanded an orderly to "take this man out where no ladies can see him, and hang him." Walsh proclaimed, "I will die a

brave man." Kilpatrick answered contemptuously, "You die a thief and a villian." Kilpatrick's men hanged Walsh in Lovejoy's Grove just beyond Burke Square. Kemp P. Battle, who witnessed the entire episode, held scant admiration for the foolhardy Texan, who "if his aim had been accurate, might have aroused the invading soldiers to madness. There was no element of heroism in his conduct, only reckless courage. And yet a young lady for many days kept fresh flowers on his grave."

Union forces also captured Commandant Theodore Calhoun James, the last Confederate soldier in the city, who delayed flight too long. He had been wounded at Gettysburg and had lost an arm at the Wilderness. Kilpatrick jailed him for refusing to take a loyalty oath, and the women of Raleigh turned James into a cause celebre, piling flowers outside his cell. After three days, Kilpatrick relented and released James to return to his home in Wilmington.

Approximately 60,000 Union soldiers set up camp in and around Raleigh. A large contingent continued through town in pursuit of Johnston's army, another large body camped at Dix Hill, and a smaller group pitched tents where the Archives and History building is now located. Still others occupied Camp Russell at New Bern and Tarboro streets, Nash Square, and other sites in the city. When Vance left the "Palace," it ceased forever to be the home of North Carolina governors. Sherman used it as his headquarters, and Grant stayed there for three days in late April. The "Palace" would remain a Federal headquarters until 1876.

General Sherman was preparing to leave Raleigh when word arrived via telegraph that President Lincoln had been assassinated. For the next several hours, he and his generals were taxed to their utmost to keep Union troops from taking revenge. General John A. Logan arrived at Rocky Branch just in time to keep his troops at Dix Hill from invading the heart of the city; General John McAllister Schofield restricted all his

Union General John Alexander Logan (1826-1886) kept hostile troops from plundering Raleigh after Lincoln's assassination was announced. The instance seemed to be one of the few times that Logan, usually a quick-tempered man, was able to remain calm. (DAH)

John McAllister Schofield (1831-1906) commanded the 23rd Corps during Sherman's march through the Carolinas, and later commanded the Union army's Department of North Carolina. When news of Lincoln's death reached Raleigh, the general kept his men confined to camp for two days in order to prohibit acts of revenge against city inhabitants. (DAH)

soldiers to camp for two days; and a fire in an abandoned workshop the next morning aroused great concern. Fortunately, tragedy was averted and, all in all, the occupying army treated Raleigh gently. For example, the only damage done to the capitol during the entire period of Federal occupation was a single axe mark (still clearly visible) under the lock of a door leading from the lobby into the governor's office, which had been caused by a soldier forcing entry. Following the establishment of official military rule, General J.N. Stiles was put in command of Raleigh and General Schofield in command of the state. On May 19 the new President, Raleigh native Andrew Johnson, appointed William Holden provisional governor, but he was to hold only briefly the office he had coveted so long.

When Holden became governor on June 8, 1865, North Carolina was bankrupt, there was little local government, racial relations were worsening, and impoverished blacks were rapidly gathering in and around the larger towns. But as devastating as the economic conditions were, the human losses

from the Civil War greatly overshadowed them and were, indeed, incalculable. Raleigh's casualties included many men, both young and old, who might have served it well in the difficult Reconstruction period that lay ahead.

The losses of Jefferson Lovejoy, Lovejoy Academy master, were particularly grievous. Born into a Sharon, Vermont, family, Jefferson, Elijah, and Owen Lovejoy were each victims of the aroused passions that eventually resulted in war. Prior to the war, a mob in Alton, Illinois, had murdered Elijah for editing an abolitionist newspaper. Owen was also an ardent abolitionist and a close friend of Abraham Lincoln. Jefferson became equally enthusiastic for the Confederate cause of his adopted region, an ardor he displayed by drilling his Academy students on the grounds at Burke Square. Two of his sons died in the war. A surviving son, Guy Mannering Lovejoy, described the effect of the war on the relationship between Jefferson and Owen, "Their convictions totally estranged them; the brothers were never reconciled." Aldert Smedes, principal of St. Mary's, lost his son Ives at Chancellorsville and his son Edward at Spotsylvania. The shock of the boys' deaths permanently deranged their mother. U.S. Senator and Raleigh resident William Henry Haywood also lost two sons, Cameron and William Henry, Jr.

Leonidas L. Polk—son of Colonel William and Sarah Hawkins Polk—graduated from West Point, but resigned his commission in 1830 to attend the Virginia Theological Seminary. He advanced in the Episcopalian hierarchy to become the Bishop of Louisiana in 1841, and he was almost solely responsible for founding the University of the South at Sewanee, Tennessee, in 1860. In June 1861 he reverted to his first career and accepted a commission as a major general in command of the Army of the Mississippi. He won the distinction of having defeated U.S. Grant at Belmont, Missouri, on November 7, 1861, but after that he slowly gave way to superior forces in the Mississippi Valley. He died in battle at Pine Mountain, Georgia, on June 14, 1864, during the futile defense of Atlanta. Another Raleigh general died at the Battle of Antietam Creek. Lawrence O'Bryan Branch had come to Raleigh from Enfield in 1844. He served as president of the Raleigh & Gaston Railroad and as a United States Congressman, before volunteering as a private in the Raleigh Rifles in April of 1861. By September he was colonel of the 33rd North Carolina Regiment, and in November Jefferson Davis commissioned him a brigadier general. He served first at New Bern before joining Lee in northern Virginia.

Many Raleigh youths died in battle or from wounds received in battle. Gettysburg took a particularly heavy toll. Captain Campbell T. Iredell, son of former governor James Iredell, died in the field. Wesley Lewis Battle, brother of Kemp P. Battle, fought in several of the battles in northern Virginia. He lost an arm during Pickett's charge at Gettysburg. A surgeon tried to rejoin his arm, but Battle died in a hospital in Philadelphia. Harry King Burgwyn graduated from the Virginia Military Institute in 1861, and at the age of 20 and the rank of major commanded the Camp of Instruction in Raleigh. Promoted to lieutenant colonel, he led the 26th North Carolina Regiment on July 1, 1863, into a battle on Seminary Ridge, during which the regiment suffered 90 percent casualties. Burgwyn's last words, after he fell enfolded in his regimental flag, were, "Tell the General my men never failed me at a single point."

Some returned wounded or with broken health, to resume lives interrupted by the war. Alexander Boyd Andrews, who was wounded at Jack's Shop in Virginia, settled in Raleigh to become a railroad magnate, an aloof personality, and perhaps the most powerful man in the city. Robert E. Hoke fought at Big Bethel, the Seven Days, Second Manassas, Antietam Creek, was wounded at Chancellorsville, and rose to the rank

of major general. After the war he was president of the North Carolina Insurance Company, the Seaboard Air Lines System, and the North Carolina Car Company. Joseph W. Holden—son of William Holden—served a year as a prisoner of war after his capture at Roanoke Island. Paroled, he attended the University of North Carolina and wrote a poem, "Hatteras," included in William Wadsworth Longfellow's anthology *Poems of Places* and the posthumous *Hatteras and Other Poems* in 1925. Joseph Holden served as speaker of the house and, in May of 1874, became Raleigh's youngest mayor. The privations of the prison camp had broken his health, however, and on January 2, 1875, he died in his father's house at Hargett and McDowell.

But many Raleigh soldiers returned from the war healthy of

In 1830, six months after he graduated eighth in his class from West Point, Leonidas L. Polk (1806-1864) left his commission for the Episcopal church. Appointed Bishop of Louisiana in 1841, he became a major general in the Army of the Mississippi after secession in 1861. Victorious over U.S. Grant at the Battle of Belmont, he died defending Atlanta at Pine Mountain, June 14, 1864. (DAH)

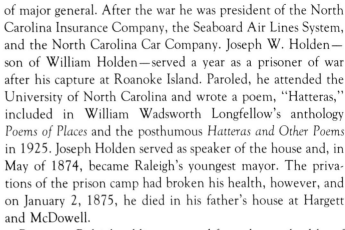

Bennett Smedes (1837-1899) had taught at St. Mary's for 15 years when he became rector in 1877. A Raleigh native, Smedes studied at Lovejoy Academy and Trinity School, graduated from St.

James' College, Maryland, and was ordained an Episcopal minister in 1863. This advertisement for St. Mary's School dates from about 1880. (DAH)

Lawrence O'Bryan Branch (1820-1862), journalist and lawyer, Democratic congressman, and nephew of Governor John Branch, entered the Raleigh Rifles as a private when North Carolina seceded. He rose quickly in rank, was promoted to brigadier general in 1861, served in Virginia under "Stonewall" Jackson, and saw action at Second Manassas and Harper's Ferry. He was killed at Sharpsburg. (DAH)

Graduating from Virginia Military Institute in April 1861 with a letter of recommendation from Thomas Jonathan Jackson, Harry King Burgwyn, Jr., (1841-1863) became lieutenant colonel of the 26th North Carolina Regiment at age 19. Shortly after the state seceded, he was posted to a training camp near Raleigh. Burgwyn saw action at Fort Macon, New Bern, and the Seven Days' Battles before dying on McPherson's Ridge at Gettysburg in 1863. Originally interred in Pennsylvania, his remains were eventually moved to Oakwood. (DAH)

Joseph William Holden (1844-1874) was elected to the state house of representatives in 1868. He served as editorial assistant to his father, William Woods Holden, on the Standard, *was speaker of the (North Carolina) house, and was elected mayor of Raleigh in 1874. (DAH)*

limb and able to lead fully productive lives. Walter McKenzie Clark, for example, had left Tew's Military Academy in 1861 to drill recruits at Raleigh—at the age of only 14. He followed them to join Lee's army, took time off in 1863-1864 to graduate first in his class at Chapel Hill, and became—at 17—the youngest lieutenant colonel in either army. He returned to Raleigh after the war, rose to chief justice of the North Carolina Supreme Court, and compiled without pay 16 volumes of *State Records* and the five-volume *Histories of the Several Regiments and Battalians from North Carolina in the Great War: 1861-1865.* Brigadier General William Ruffin Cox, who had moved to Raleigh from Scotland Neck in 1859, later served in the General Assembly and as secretary to the U.S. Senate. Major General Daniel G. Fowle was captured at Roanoke Island and later paroled. After the war he won election to the General Assembly, was chosen superior court justice, and became the third governor of North Carolina from Wake County.

But Raleigh's most poignant experience with the Civil War, perhaps, involved the burial of the dead. During the war, soldiers who died in the hospitals and bodies brought in from battle—both Rebel and Yankee—were interred in the Rock Quarry Cemetery near the Pettigrew Hospital. In late 1866 an agent from the U.S. Registration of Graves Service arrived to select a cemetery for Union dead who had been temporarily buried at the Bentonville battlefield. Union forces were using the hospital facilities as barracks, and the agent ordered Mayor Harrison to remove the Confederate bodies or see them "thrown into the public road."

Mrs. L. O'Brien Branch, Miss Sophia Partridge, and others had formed in May 1866 the Ladies Memorial Association of Wake County and they now volunteered to organize the removal of the bodies to a tract of land donated by Henry Mordecai. In February and March of 1867, the transfer was made to the Confederate Cemetery. Other bodies continued to arrive, and in 1871 the Ladies Memorial Association once again organized a mass burial. Caretakers at Arlington National Cemetery had threatened to plough up the area containing North Carolinians who had died at Gettysburg. The Association prepared graves at the Confederate Cemetery, businesses closed, and the city observed a day of mourning on August 25, 1871, when the bodies arrived by train. The Reverend R.L. Mason conducted funeral services. The graves were strewn with flowers by Raleigh's women and children. The August 28 *Sentinel* describes the solemn event: "One hundred and three graves with open, hungry mouths to receive a like number of human bodies was a scene rarely witnessed by human sight." One of the dead was Raleigh native Lieutenant R.M. Harvey of the 14th North Carolina Regiment who died in battle the day after he had captured the flag of the 150th Pennsylvanian Regiment. Lieutenant Harvey's dying request was that the flag be sent to President Davis. Later the General Assembly voted $250 per year for upkeep of the cemetery, and the United Daughters of the Confederacy joined the Association in caring for the grounds.

A controversy of an entirely different nature arose when President Andrew Johnson visited the city of his birth in June 1867. Clerks in state offices had raised money to erect a suitable monument to his father, Jacob Johnson, and Governor Worth and Mayor Haywood had invited the President to attend the dedication. He arrived on June 3 accompanied by Secretary of State William H. Seward, other dignitaries, and reporters from the Associated Press, the New York *Herald,* and the New York *Times.* An infantry company, a squadron of cavalry, a black band, and city officers escorted him to the Yarborough House. When called upon to speak, Johnson refused to address politics, but in the course of his remarks he apparently said something that provided sufficient interest. One observer reported that he referred to Jacob as a man "said to be my father." Thirty years later, another eyewitness remembered the words to be, "I come today to take part in the ceremonies connected with the erection of a monument

Walter McKenzie Clark, pictured here circa 1895, spent 35 years on the state supreme court, serving as chief justice from 1902 until his death in 1924. The Halifax County native moved to Raleigh in 1873, and was an author, historian, and advocate of women's suffrage. He also spearheaded the drive to have the dates May 20, 1775, and April 12, 1776, included on the state flag and "esse quam videri" chosen as North Carolina's official motto. (DAH)

over the remains of a man whom I claim to be my father.'' Others present denied that he said anything of the sort. Johnson left for Chapel Hill the next day, but his postwar brief visit provided abundant fuel—perhaps specious—to feed controversy.

The wounds from the long and bloody war would be exceedingly slow in healing, and the controversies that had resulted in the "Lost Cause" would continue to disrupt the region politically, economically, and socially for years to come. William Holden, as provisional governor, would once again find himself at the center of those controversies. Some former leaders, opposed to Holden in spirit, still felt he could rule effectively if given half a chance. But veterans immediately damned Holden for taking the amnesty oath, and he further alienated the Confederate faithful by appointing only loyal Unionists to state and local positions, inevitably making many poor choices in the rush to establish order. Among his Wake County appointees were Richard Badger as a private secretary, Sion Hart Rogers as attorney general, Daniel G. Fowle as superior court judge, S.M. Parrish and J.D. Pullen as clerks, and Jonathan Worth as state treasurer.

Governor Holden convinced the federal government to suspend the crippling 25 percent cotton tax and to pay for the property—including cotton—sold in the state after the armistice. Those measures allowed him to finance a constitutional convention, which convened in Raleigh on October 2, 1865. The convention repealed the Ordinances of Secession, abolished slavery, and repudiated the war debts—which distressed bankers, politicians, educators, and private citizens. Jonathan Worth opposed repudiation, ran against Holden as a Conservative in the November election, and defeated him 31,643 to 25,704 in a light turnout resulting from the disenfranchisement of large portions of the electorate.

President Johnson and Radical Republicans interpreted the vote to be an expression of defiance by Confederate diehards. Further Southern "obstreperousness" resulted in the Reconstruction Act of March 2, 1867, which reestablished military rule and demanded a new constitution prior to readmittance into the Union. A second Constitutional Convention met in Raleigh between January 14 and March 17 of 1868. Republicans outnumbered Conservatives (i.e., Democrats) 107 to 13, including 18 "carpetbaggers" and 15 black delegates. Little was expected of the convention, but surprisingly it produced a document which, with very few modifications, remains in effect. The new constitution abolished slavery, guaranteed universal manhood suffrage, established a public school system, reformed government, and moderated the penal code. Voters approved the constitution by a vote of 93,084 to 74,015.

The first election under the 1868 constitution restored Holden to the governorship, although he would be impeached for his own and his party's excesses. The Republican-controlled legislature voted its members $8 per diem and 20 cents per mile travel reimbursement. It also issued over $42

Andrew Johnson (1808-1875), 17th President of the United States, was a man surrounded by controversy. Less than a year had passed between his visit to Raleigh—where he raised the curiosity of city residents with remarks about his father—and February 24, 1868, when Congress failed by a single vote to pass a resolution of impeachment against him. Courtesy, North Carolina Collection, UNC Library

million in state bonds at a time when the state's total tax base was only $120 million. The legislators opened a bar upstairs in the capitol, and the careless transportation of whiskey barrels up and down the steps left still-visible scars on the stairs. A majority of the bonds were issued to repair and to build new railroad tracks, and the bonds became a bonanza for corrupt lobbyists and legislators.

Milton S. Littlefield, a carpetbagger who had moved to Raleigh, directed the railroad lobby, and he alone spent hundreds of thousands of dollars lavishing cash and favors on legislators. The bonds rapidly decreased in value, approximately $13 million was wasted, the state debt topped $28 million, and taxes rose radically. Littlefield and some of his cohorts fled when the bubble burst, leaving Holden to take the blame, although he had been uninvolved in the corrupt manipulation. The episode further damaged Holden politically, but many of the most pressing and complicated problems facing him simply resulted from the transition North Carolina now had to make from a slave state to a free one.

At the end of the Civil War, large numbers of legally free but impoverished blacks began congregating in Raleigh, as they did in other Southern cities. In 1860 Raleigh's 2,087 blacks made up 44 percent of the population; by 1870 the number had grown to 4,094 comprising 53 percent of the population. The black influx helped make Raleigh second in size only to Wilmington by 1880. The influx was inspired, in part, by the numerous relief agencies that set up headquarters in Raleigh, attracting many blacks seeking assistance in embarking on newly independent lives. Local charity organizations helping blacks included the New York Southern Relief Association, the Presbyterian Board of Missions for Freedmen, the Peabody Fund, the Avery Estate, and the American Missionary Society. Of these groups, the American Missionary Society was the most influential. Among other endeavors, it bought property in the south of town around the "Palace" and sold inexpensive lots to black families. This led, in the 1870s,

Now known as Peace College, Peace Institute opened in 1872. It was named for William Peace, bachelor businessman and Raleigh Presbyterian elder who was a strong advocate of higher education for women. In 1879 the institute operated the first kindergarten in the South. (DAH)

to the creation of the first black neighborhood in Raleigh.

But by far the most influential—for good or ill—of the black-oriented assistance organizations in Raleigh was the government-approved Freedmen's Bureau, which established offices in the Peace Institute and was directed by Dexter E. Clapp. The Freedmen's Bureau did much with food, shelter, regimental doctors, and legal assistance. But it also was responsible for creating personal hardship and racial disharmony. It organized the Freedman's Saving and Trust Company to provide banking services for former slaves in 1865, but inept management and outright corruption caused the bank to fail in 1874, with black depositors suffering most of the losses. The Freedmen's Bureau also encouraged people to join the Union League, an organization ostensibly designed solely to benefit blacks but actually used as well to recruit voters into the Republican party. As elsewhere, Union League members, which included almost all of the adult blacks in Raleigh, formed armed militia-like companies and some extremists in the organization burned barns and killed livestock in Wake County.

The success of the Union League in stimulating the newly enfranchised blacks to vote can be measured by breaking poll taxes down by color: in 1867 whites paid $1,581 in poll taxes and blacks paid $1,297. The ratio remained roughly consistent until the late 1870s, when black disenchantment caused many to leave the state or to drop out of the political process. But both the excesses of the Union League and its effectiveness in increasing the black Republican vote spurred many discontented whites to join in Ku Klux Klan activities, further exacerbating already strained race relations and eventually leading to Governor Holden's downfall. The Conservatives, the major opposition party during this period, began utilizing the KKK, initiating some 260 incidents between 1867 and 1869, 174 of which were directed against blacks. To combat the Klan, Governor Holden called on Colonel George Kirk, who had commanded North Carolina volunteers in the Union Army

during the Civil War. During the "Kirk-Holden War," Kirk jailed suspected Klan members and Holden kept them in jail by refusing them the right of habeas corpus. When Chief Justice Richmond Pearson chose not to challenge Holden, *Raleigh Sentinel* publisher Josiah Turner lashed out with a vengence.

A native of Hillsborough, Turner had represented Orange County in both houses of the General Assembly between 1852 and 1862. An opponent of secession, he had nonetheless volunteered for active duty and served at New Bern. He later entered the Confederate House as a peace representative and had vocally opposed Jefferson Davis. After the war Turner returned to Hillsborough, where he was elected to the U.S. Congress but not seated because of his Civil War activity. From Hillsborough he published the stridently anti-Holden *Sentinel*. When Holden accused him in 1870 of being an Orange County Klan leader, Turner replied in the *Sentinel* under the banner "LIES LIKE A THIEF": "The governor has been lying on us for twelve months . . . and . . . lies on us to-

Although initially a Union supporter, Josiah Turner, Jr. (1821-1901), raised a cavalry company in North Carolina and served in the Confederate congress after North Carolina seceded. He purchased the Sentinel *in 1868 and used it as a means of attacking William Woods Holden and his government of "scallawaggers and carpetbaggers." (DAH)*

day by calling us a Ku Klux. If we are, why don't the pumpkin-faced rascal arrest us?" Turner's next editorial was even more defiant: "Gov. Holden:—You say you will handle me in due time. You white-livered recreant, do it now. You dared me to resist you; I dare you to arrest me. . . . Your ignorant jacobins are incited . . . by your lying charges against me that I am King of the Ku Klux. You villain, come and arrest a man. . . . Yours with contempt and defiance—*habeas corpus* or no *habeas corpus.*"

Holden ignored his advisors, who counseled restraint, and had Kirk arrest Turner. Turner soon gained release and triumphantly journeyed to Raleigh to taunt Holden further. After President Grant had instructed the governor to recognize duly issued writs of habeas corpus, and after the Conservatives had regained control of the legislature in the 1870 elections, Holden discharged Kirk and declared the problem solved, but the Conservatives had one more card they insisted on playing.

Frederick N. Strudwick of Orange County introduced a motion to impeach Holden on December 9, 1870, and his formal trial began February 2, 1871. Former governors William Graham and Thomas Bragg were on the team of prosecutors who sought to convict Holden on eight charges, ranging from illegally declaring an insurrection to making illegal arrests to denying the right of habeas corpus. After the trial ended on March 23 the Senate convicted Holden on six charges and immediately removed him from office. Zebulon Vance said the whole episode was "the longest hunt after the poorest hide I ever saw." Later in the year, a Wake County jury found *Sentinel* editor Randolph Shotwell guilty of having been a leader during the period of Klan activity.

Holden retained the respect of the black community, as evidenced by a letter from a black resident of Raleigh, Charles N. Hunter, in March of 1876: "A considerable portion of them here, are under the impression that you are still their Governor, while not a few anxiously inquire if, and hope that, you will be a candidate on the Republican ticket for Governor in the next election."

Despite all the political turmoil, some aspects of black life in Raleigh were decidedly improved during this period. Black secondary education was an immediate concern for all the governmental and charitable groups working to help newly freed blacks. The North Carolina Freedmen's Convention, meeting in Raleigh in October of 1866, sought to improve black education and the Freedmen's Educational Association began constructing black schools. The Freedmen's Bureau helped to establish the Johnson School, in which five teachers were instructing 292 students by 1869. The American Missionary Society founded and ran the Lincoln School at East Cabarrus and South and set up the Washington School, with Fisk P. Brewer as the first principal. These schools were not adequately equipped or supplied, however, and most of the teachers were poorly educated if well-intentioned white women from the North. But the most important black educa-

This artist's conception of Shaw Collegiate Institute appeared in Branson's North Carolina Business Directory *for 1872. Shaw was the first black coeducational collegiate institution in the country. Courtesy, North Carolina Collection, UNC Library*

Washington Graded School for Negroes was located at 137 West South Street. The T-shaped frame building, pictured here circa 1916, was originally designed to accommodate 480 students. (DAH)

tional institution in Raleigh, Shaw University, did emerge from this period to become a lasting influence.

In 1865 former Union Army chaplain, H.M. Tupper—with the help of Massachusetts industrialist Elijah Shaw, General Andrew Porter, and the Freedmen's Bureau—had begun conducting theology classes for young blacks in a cabin outside Raleigh and in the basement of the old Guion Hotel. The Baptist Home Mission Society assisted the black educator, and in 1868 Tupper and the Shaw students began building the $8,000, four-story Shaw Hall. Tupper purchased more property, and by 1874 he had completed Estey Hall, named after Vermont supporter Jacob Estey and believed to be the first building in America built especially for the education of black women. Shaw University was incorporated in 1875; a women's college and the Leonard Medical School became operative in 1880. In that year, 267 students were enrolled, most of them seeking to become teachers or ministers.

Ministers and teachers could also receive training at St. Augustine's Normal and Collegiate Institute, which the Protestant Episcopal Church established in cooperation with the Freedmen's Bureau in 1867, on land once owned by Raleigh founder Willie Jones. The Reverend Jacob Brinton Smith taught the first students a curriculum of Latin, algebra, geography, grammar, natural science, and theology in an abandoned Confederate Army barracks. The Freedmen's Bureau provided $6,248 in 1867, the Avery Fund added $25,000 in 1869, and the Barry Fund contributed $26,716 in 1870. Those gifts allowed the Reverend Smith and his successor, the Reverend John Esten Cook Smedes, to build the necessary facilities, and the abundance of applicants allowed the directors the luxury of setting high entrance requirements.

In 1881 black educators formed the North Carolina State Educational Teachers' Association expressly to encourage the formation of county teachers' organizations, the use of uniform textbooks, and the improvement of teaching methods. The group published the *Progressive Educators,* hoping to advance "progressive education in North Carolina to the elevation and culture of the colored race." The Association ultimately proved ineffectual as a statewide organization, largely because it was too Raleigh-oriented.

In 1881, too, North Carolina blacks would call a Colored State Convention in Raleigh to protest that the Republicans had failed to appoint blacks to positions of genuine authority. But many black men did gain elective and appointive offices. James Young became the Wake County register of deeds, a post office official, and a worker for the Internal Revenue Service. A former slave from Washington, North Carolina, Stewart Ellison had worked on the insane asylum and other buildings under construction in Raleigh in the 1850s. After the war, he moved to Raleigh, opened a store, and went into the construction business—building offices for the Freedmen's Bureau, houses, schools, and other public buildings. He was a city commissioner from 1868 to 1876, director of Central Prison for four years, and a representative to the General As-

sembly. Other black representatives included James Harris (1868-1870) and Willis Morgan (1870-1872). In Reconstruction-era city government, Norfleet Dunstan served as assistant police chief in charge of 11 black policemen, and several blacks were elected commissioners.

Blacks in Raleigh made strides in the private sector as well. In 1875-1876, more than 700 had steady jobs, although most were in unskilled positions. Some 150 were servants; more than 350 were laborers, barbers, laundresses, nurses, waiters, and the like; about 200 worked in industry and manufacturing; and 13 (27 by 1880) were professionals, including eight preachers, four teachers, and one physician. In 1875-1876, there were 31 black-owned businesses. Blacks operated all six capital barbershops; the five black-run restaurants were the most popular in town; and there were six grocers, four blacksmiths, four dealers at the city market, three shoemakers, and one cabinetmaker-undertaker, a harnessmaker, and a boardinghouse manager.

In 1879 Raleigh blacks founded the North Carolina Industrial Association "to encourage and promote the development of the industrial and educational resources of the colored people of North Carolina." The organization predated the Raleigh Chamber of Commerce by almost a decade. It established, also in 1879, the *Journal of Industry,* the first stable black-oriented paper in the capital. That November the directors held the first of several annual fairs, which over the years attracted national figures, such as Booker T. Washington, and gained widespread support, such as reduced railroad fares for visitors. The first fair had 13 categories of exhibits, including such finds as agriculture, manufacturing, fine arts, mechanical arts, and penmanship. The largest of the fairs occurred in 1886, but the percentage of blacks in servile positions persistently increased during the 1870s and the 1880s, and the fairs ceased after it became apparent that their mission had failed.

During the 1870s and the 1880s, black clubs proliferated in all areas of social life. There were seven lodges of the Independent Order of Good Samaritans, two lodges of Masons, two national guard units, the Oak City Brass Band and the Citizens

GENERAL VIEW OF THE FAIR-GROUNDS, SHOWING THE WALKING-MATCH BETWEEN NEGRO PEDESTRIANS.

Coronet Band, four literary and debating societies, several temperance and religious orders, and the reverently titled Grand Limited Order of Brothers and Sisters of Love and Charity. The clubs turned out en masse for the annual Emancipation Day celebrations, forming an orderly procession that ended with a lively rally at the Metropolitan Hall. Even though postbellum religious and social groups tended to attract either totally white or totally black memberships, neighborhoods remained remarkably integrated for a decade or more following the war. The 1870 census listed 1,901 black and 1,361 white residents in the east ward, 611 black and 510 white in the middle ward, and 1,582 black and 1,818 white in the west ward. It was the formation of the Oberlin and Brooklyn sections in the 1870s and the concentration of blacks in the south section of the city that turned Raleigh into an overtly segregated city.

Oddly enough, many Raleigh residents—black and white—felt some sense of loss when Federal troops finally ended their occupation of the city. Many of the Northern soldiers at Camp Russell had married Raleigh women. The soldiers fielded baseball teams to compete with local clubs, and they joined their North Carolina militia counterparts to march in patriotic celebrations. Downtown merchants would also miss their business. Fred A. Olds later wrote that he and many of his fellow

THE PROCESSION PASSING DOWN FAYETTEVILLE STREET, ON THE WAY TO THE GROUNDS.

Left: The North Carolina Industrial Association, an organization formed to encourage economic and educational development among blacks, held its first Grand Fair November 17-20, 1879, in Raleigh. The event was captured in Frank Leslie's Illustrated Newspaper *on December 6. Fair participants and one of the city's black marching bands are depicted here, parading down Fayetteville Street toward the fair grounds. Courtesy, North Carolina Collection, UNC Library*

EXHIBITORS MAKING ENTRIES AT THE OFFICE OF THE SECRETARY.

One of the Grand Fair's athletic events (far left), "the walking-match between Negro pedestrians," was illustrated. Also, exhibitors were sketched registering their fair entries at the office of the secretary. Courtesy, North Carolina Collection, UNC Library

This lithographic montage from Frank Leslie's Illustrated Newspaper *gives a final overview of some of the exhibits and exhibitors present at the North Carolina Industrial Association's Grand Fair. Courtesy, North Carolina Collection, UNC Library*

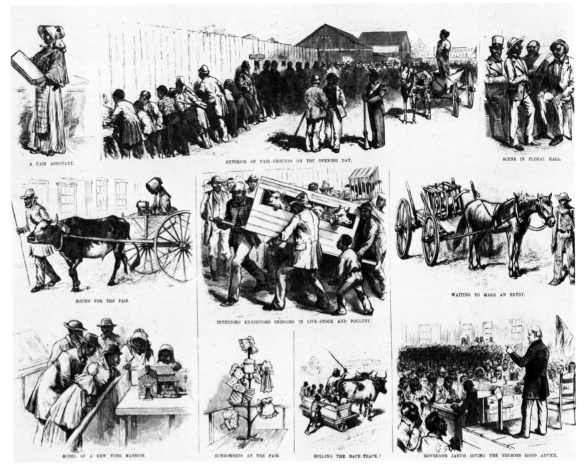

A FAIR ASSISTANT.

EXTERIOR OF FAIR-GROUNDS ON THE OPENING DAY.

SCENE IN FLORAL HALL.

BOUND FOR THE FAIR.

INTENDING EXHIBITORS BRINGING IN LIVE-STOCK AND POULTRY.

WAITING TO MAKE AN ENTRY.

MODEL OF A NEW YORK MANSION.

SUNBONNETS AT THE FAIR.

ROLLING THE RACE-TRACK.

GOVERNOR JARVIS GIVING THE NEGROES GOOD ADVICE.

citizens felt genuine sorrow at seeing the garrison leave in 1876. The state militia occupied the old Pettigrew Hospital buildings for a time, and the facilities were used for a variety of state and municipal activities.

When the occupying forces left the "Palace" (which they had taken great pains to preserve), the city of Raleigh purchased it to house the Centennial Graded School, which was the first graded school in the city and opened August 1, 1876. Captain John E. Dugger, the principal, ran the school on funds provided by school taxes, the Peabody Fund, and contributions from parents. On the first day, 240 students attended classes in four grades—primary, intermediate, grammar, and high school. Dugger was soon able to accommodate an additional 125 male students in a new building next to the "Palace" and in rooms rented on Fayetteville Street.

Raleigh's oldest school, the former Raleigh Academy, which had become the Lovejoy Academy, continued under new owners and a new name after "Old Jeff" Lovejoy became incapacitated in 1876. Captain John Frey and Mr. Hugh Morson of Virginia had taken over the private Atkinson-Scott school for boys on New Bern Avenue, and they moved it to the Lovejoy campus on Burke Square in 1878. The school, which fielded a championship baseball team in the 1880s called the Swiftfeet, moved to North Bloodworth Street in 1884 after the state had razed the old structure to make way for a new governor's mansion. When John Frey died in 1884, Captain Claude Denson and J.D. Hodges became partners

with Morson, and the school became known as Morson and Denson's Academy (with 150 students paying $25 tuition for 20 weeks of instruction in 1887). The school's name was later simplified to the Morson Academy and, finally, to the Male Academy.

For businessmen in general, the immediate postbellum years were certainly not the best of times, but neither were

A native of Fredericksburg, Virginia, Hugh Morson (1850-1925) came to North Carolina in 1874. Teaching first in Hillsborough, Morson, a specialist in Latin and mathematics, settled in Raleigh three years later. After teaching at the Raleigh Male Academy, he became the first principal of Raleigh High School in 1905, a post he filled for 16 years. (DAH)

Wood samples, leather goods, and cotton plants were among the items displayed in the Wake County exhibit of the 1884 North Carolina Industrial Exposition (above). The Exposition's dining hall advertised ice cream (right). The railroad tracks, visible on the lower right, were part of a line installed especially to facilitate tourist attendance of the fair. (DAH)

Left: *Sewing machine sales-men await customers in the 1884 North Carolina Industrial Exposition's main building. (DAH)*

Right: *Nineteenth-century Americans loved European fashions. E. Besson's French Tailoring Establishment, pictured along with its 1865 advertisement, helped keep Raleigh's citizens in step with the latest Parisian styles. (DAH)*

they the worst of times. Less than four months after the armistice, Thomas H. Briggs started a hardware business that is today the oldest continuing business in the capital. An unknown Yankee soldier opened a candy store on Fayetteville Street in 1865, but returned to Philadelphia after six months. Before he left, the soldier sold his business to his assistant A.D. Royster who (with his brother V.C. Royster) manufactured candy on the premises and ran the store for 65 years. In the same year, William H. Dodd and W.G. Upchurch established a retail business on Hargett Street. They prospered, built the Dodd Building at Wilmington and Martin in 1867, and after Dodd retired (to become mayor in 1884) his partner built the Upchurch Building at Market Square in 1886.

L. Rosenthal & Company on Fayetteville Street specialized in quality men's clothing, and M.A. Parker opened another Fayetteville dry-goods store with a total stock worth only $100. Parker's business burned two times, but he persevered, expanded into dealing in cotton and selling groceries, and by 1878 had built a large brick building at Martin and Wilmington. Also on Fayetteville Street, beginning in 1867, Alfred Williams published school catalogues and other materials, furnished supplies to schools and colleges in every county of North Carolina and out of state by mail order, edited and published *The North Carolina Teacher* from 1883, and, according to the *State Chronicle*, had become "the widest known business house in North Carolina" by 1884. The

Stronach brothers, George T., W.C., and A.B., built a retail grocery in 1866 at 6 Exchange Place; the Stronachs soon developed into one of Raleigh's leading families.

In 1867, W.H. and R.S. Tucker built the 1,200-seat Tucker Hall on the third floor of their Fayetteville Street mercantile firm. The auditorium—at 43 by 120 feet and with its parlor, saloon, dressing and anterooms for performers, and a 40-foot by 27-foot gaslit stage—served for decades as a cultural center. The Tucker offered acts as dissimilar as tenor Pasquale Brignoli, actor Joe Jefferson, Colonel W.F. "Buffalo Bill" Cody, the D'Oyly Carte Company performing *Pirates of Penzance,* and Governor Vance's 1877 inaugural address.

Raleigh's largest publishing firm, Edwards and Broughton, started in 1871 when Needham Bryant Broughton and Cornelius Bryant Edwards bought $500 worth of old *Standard* printing equipment from Major W.A. "Billy" Smith of Johnston County. Smith sold the partners the equipment and loaned them $100 for supplies, with the understanding that he would not foreclose "so long as I find you with your coats off and hard at work." Their business received a boost in 1873 when they formed a partnership with the publishers of The *Biblical Recorder,* and another boon in 1887 when they began publishing specialized materials for schools and hospitals.

Most of these enterprises, however, were relatively small and nonindustrial. Following an exhaustive study of business and personal records, J. Carlyle Sitterson has concluded that

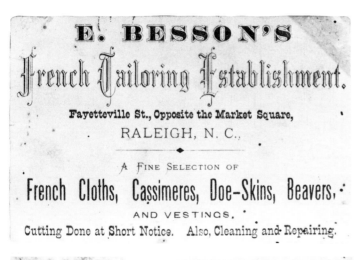

E. BESSON'S
French Tailoring Establishment.

Fayetteville St., Opposite the Market Square,
RALEIGH, N. C.,

A FINE SELECTION OF

French Cloths, Cassimeres, Doe-Skins, Beavers,
AND VESTINGS.

Cutting Done at Short Notice. Also, Cleaning and Repairing.

nonagricultural manufacturing in eastern North Carolina was virtually nonexistent on the eve of the Civil War, being essentially limited to blacksmithing, fishing, tanning, harnessmaking, lumbering, carriagemaking, and the production of naval stores. By 1870 manufacturing establishments in Raleigh still represented a capital investment of only $225,000 in total, producing a scant $425,000 in goods and employing a mere 305 workers. Ten years later Wake County led the state in total manufacturing operations, but it ranked only sixth in the value of goods produced. By 1885 capital investment in Raleigh factories would climb to $791,500, and their output would amount to $1.16 million. But the figures for Raleigh would continue to lag behind those for the state as a whole,

and by the mid-1880s city newspapers, led by the *State Chronicle,* would become increasingly critical of local investors for being too cautious.

Manufacturing may not have been doing well on the large scale, but trade and industry began to boom for smaller proprietors when the economy stabilized in the late 1870s. Downtown merchants could rely on a steady trade from state government officials and the visitors attracted to the capital, as well as from the officers and men at Camp Russell until 1876. The mercantile establishment of the Tucker brothers, who had made enough money from their store to build the lavish Tucker Hall, was still the city's largest. But other dry-goods merchants challenged the Tucker firm, among them the Norris and Carter at 203 Fayetteville, Joseph P. Gulley at Fayetteville and Exchange Place, A. Creech & Company at Fayetteville and Hargett Streets, and W.T. Woodard at North Market Square and Wilmington.

None was more industrious, however, than P.S. Waitt. Waitt came to Raleigh as a youngster in 1862 and went to work making envelopes for W.L. Pomeroy in his bookstore. Waitt rapidly became so proficient that he used up all of Pomeroy's stock and worked himself out of a job. Not despairing, Waitt made currycombs for the military, clerked for Pomeroy, sold papers, attended Lovejoy Academy after the war, and set type for the *Standard.* In 1872 he opened a clothing store at 215 Fayetteville, and by 1876 he had done well enough to move to larger quarters next door.

J.S. Pescud, A.S. Lee, and Dr. Eugene Grissom bought the P.E. Pescud & Sons drugstore at 118 Fayetteville in 1869. They opened an additional store at Martin and Fayetteville in 1879, which immediately became the "in" place with the youth of Raleigh. The fastest-moving items were cigars, sodas, mineral water, toilet articles, and medicines. The January 12, 1884, *State Chronicle* was justly impressed with the owners' unstinting determination to provide their faithful clientele with a multiplicity of refreshments: "They have made an order for a new opera soda fountain, which will dispense 22 syrups and 10 mineral waters. It is to cost $2,500, and will be one of the handsomest and most complete soda fountains in the Southern States."

Captain B.P. Williamson was certainly one of the most successful, if not the most successful, of Raleigh's postbellum businessmen. A Wake County farmer, he purchased a $75 license to engage in general commission business in 1865. A few years later W.G. Upchurch joined him to form Williams & Upchurch, and in 1881 their mercantile business grossed an incredible $465,428.77.

Some small industries were succeeding, although they catered primarily to local clients. G.M. Allen and William Cram owned shops on Hargett Street at the junction of the railroads. They operated a foundry that included a 15-horsepower steam engine, and they specialized in repairing sawmills, gristmills, cotton gins, and engines. They also made bearings, did customized iron and steel work, and made plows

There was more to Tucker
Hall than just the North
Carolina Land Company.
The building also housed a
1200-seat theater where
Raleighites could enjoy shows
by nationally acclaimed per-
formers and local talent.
(DAH)

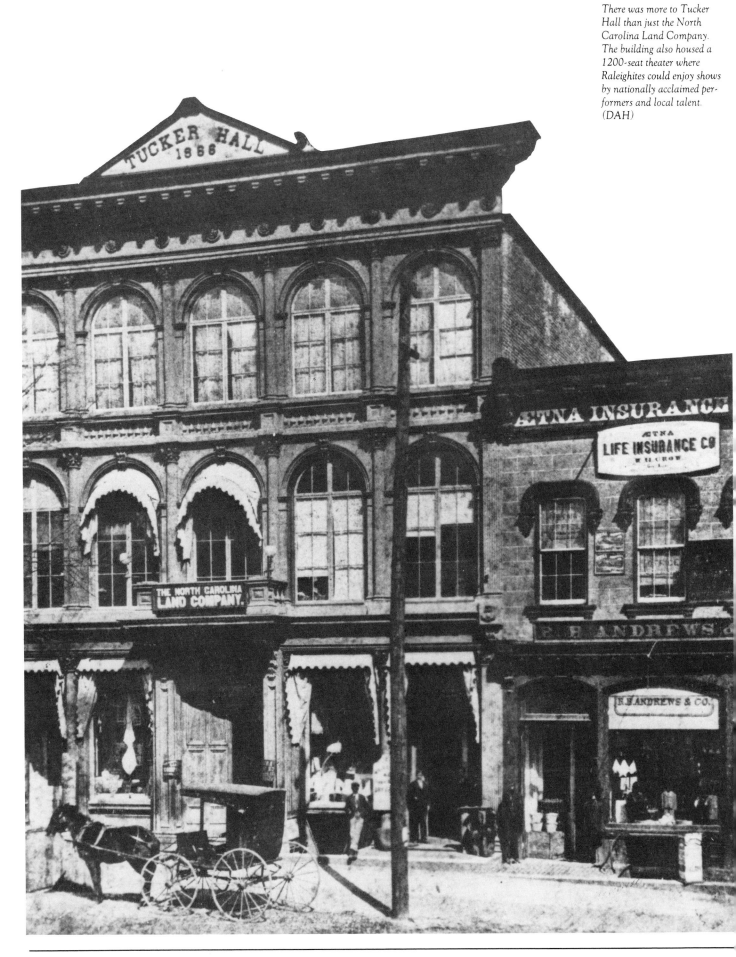

and other castings. Colin H. Hawkins and J.C. Kearney ran the Pioneer Manufacturing Company at West Davie and West streets near the North Carolina Depot. They purchased hardwood and scrap iron, and they made plows, fertilizer, cotton planters, stalk choppers, plow points, andirons, grates, and other castings. They also distributed machinery, such as the Diamond Stalk Chopper and Philpot's Manure Distributor. In June 1873 Kemp P. Battle, W.R. Cox, W.C. Stronach, W.H. Dodd, R.T. Fulghum, and others put up $100,000 to incorporate the North Carolina Fertilizer Company, which manufactured and sold "Manipulated Guano."

The hotel business was thriving as always. The old Guion Hotel had been a conscription headquarters and a hospital during the war and a temporary haven for homeless blacks briefly after the war. Remodeled as the National Hotel in 1865, it became the headquarters for the State Agriculture Department in 1879. The Buttermilk Tavern on Morgan Street between Blount and Wilmington, which had quartered troops embarking for the Mexican War, remained open after the war. The Lawrence Hotel on the site of the old Indian Queen burned in the 1860s. The William Bain Hotel across the street from the capitol occupied the space later used for the Olivia Raney Library. The Planters Hotel at Wilmington and Martin probably accommodated few genuine planters, flanked as it was by some of the sleaziest grog shops in the city, a competitive congregation that kept the price of liquor to 10 cents per quart in the area.

For a longer period than Casso's Inn, the Indian Queen, or the Guion Hotel before it, the Yarborough House had constituted a congenial "third house" for legislators desirous of attending to business of state before and after formal sessions. A veteran barkeeper describes a typical day in the Yarborough House to a *Sentinel* reporter in November 1876: "There is a rush to the barroom from 7 to 9 a.m., for the morning drams. Then there is a lull in the clink of glasses until 11 a.m. But the grand rally is from 10 o'clock at night until 1 in the morning. Then it is that the legislators and their friends surge in like the waves when navies are stranded and business is livelier than ever."

The construction industry lagged behind the hotel business in recovering. The next major addition to Raleigh's forming "skyline," following the building of Tucker Hall, was undertaken by Thomas Briggs. In 1874 he built the four-story Briggs Building on Fayetteville Street, then the tallest building in eastern North Carolina and still the home of Briggs Hardware. Surely no other space in Raleigh has been put to more uses than its upper floors. It has housed the YMCA, a Catholic church, professional offices, the State Hall of History, and the State Museum. In World War I the national guard used the Briggs Building for instruction, leaving bullet holes as evidence of the thoroughness of their training; and it was the first home of the Raleigh Little Theatre. "Hurricane Hazel" claimed the roof in 1954, but downstairs business continued unabated.

The cornerstone was laid for a new federal courthouse and

The North Carolina Department of Agriculture moved into the old Eagle (which became the Guion, and then the National) Hotel building in 1887. This picture, taken from Union Square, shows the iron fence and gaslights that once surrounded the capitol grounds. (DAH)

The Raleigh National Bank—known as the "Round Steps Bank" because of its most prominent architectural feature—was built about 1868 at the corner of Fayetteville and West Hargett streets. This picture, taken between 1885 and 1890, shows the city's early electric street-lighting system. (DAH)

Post Office building at the corner of Fayetteville and Martin the same year the Briggs Building went up. By the time the building was completed in 1878, its cost had risen to about $400,000. The granite for the building came from Goldsboro,

Left: *The Briggs building (which has always housed the Briggs family hardware business) contained at various times on its upper floors a church, YMCA, theater, museum and rifle range. (DAH)*

The Century Post Office was the first postal facility constructed in the South after the Civil War. Pictured here in 1900, the building's cornerstone was laid in 1894. (DAH)

The "house" that Edwin Marshall Yarborough built survived until 1928. For more than 75 years the hotel served as the city's premier social center. Frequented by state lawmakers when the General Assembly was in session, Yarborough House earned the sobriquet, "third house of the legislature." It was also the unofficial residence of North Carolina governors between 1871 and 1891. (DAH)

The fortress-like Central Prison was built with convict labor, the stone for its walls quarried on the construction site. (DAH)

and the structure had one striking architectural peculiarity — the front and the rear were identical. At the cornerstone-laying ceremonies, participants preserved a road map, coins, stamps and a cancelled envelope, a copy of Post Office regulations, and photographs of President Grant, other federal dignitaries, and building architect Alfred B. Mullett. (After the new Federal Building was completed in 1970, the old one became the Century Station.)

During the postbellum period, the state government also expanded its physical facilities, adding one major new institution and rebuilding the governor's mansion. Since the beginning of the 19th century, political leaders, newspaper editors, and other reformers had agitated for the construction of a humane state prison, but it was not until the constitutional convention of 1868 that the movement bore tangible fruit. The constitution included a provision calling for the construction of a prison and the 1868 legislature appropriated $200,000 for the project. After a long debate, the General Assembly voted to locate the facility in Raleigh and agents purchased a section of the Boylan estate from Kate Boylan, where the Central Prison would be built. Workers began erecting a temporary prison to house the convicts who would be used to build the state prison, which was to be designed by William Jackson Hicks, who had manufactured gunpowder during the war.

Some laborers other than convicts were used in building the prison, including a young native of Pennsylvania who had learned to carve stone in Baltimore before arriving in Raleigh. William Oliver Wolf married Hattie Watson of Raleigh, divorced her, and then married Cynthia Hill. He earned his living by working as a stonecutter on the Central Prison job,

Above: *William Oliver Wolfe, pictured with his wife circa 1900, wanted to be an actor when he was young, but he was apprenticed to a stonecutter. (DAH)*

and while in Raleigh he added an "e" to his surname. When Cynthia died, he moved to Asheville where he married Eliza Pentland who, on October 3, 1900, gave birth to Thomas Wolfe—North Carolina's most famous author.

Designer William Hicks also supervised work at the prison, and by 1875 sixty-five cells were ready for occupation. When the project was completed in 1884, the state had a penal facility that would serve its needs into modern times, requiring alterations primarily to accommodate modern conveniences. (Hicks later designed the Labor Building, the Park Hotel, and supervised the convicts—several of whom left their initials in the bricks—who built the new governor's mansion. Samuel Sloan and A. Gustavus Bauer of Philadelphia designed the mansion, and Governor Daniel G. Fowle was the first governor to move in on January 5, 1891. Fowle died there three

months and two days later.)

Between 1860 and 1880 the population of Raleigh was increasing rapidly. By 1890 it would reach 12,678, three times the 1860 population of 4,780. Naturally such increases dictated alterations in city government, and the General Assembly repeatedly moved to solve evolving problems. In 1875, for the first time, the mayor became subordinate to the board of commissioners, 17 of whom represented five wards and chose a nonmember as mayor. Officials at the same time were struggling to pay off the city debt, which stood at $126,000 in bonds and $40,000 in scrip in January of 1874. Income for the preceding year had been $50,000, expenditures had totaled $36,000, leaving $14,000 to pay interest and to redeem scrip. In 1881 the General Assembly made several more changes. The city limits were extended one-half mile in each direction

The Raleigh Light Infantry parades at the capitol around 1875. City and county militias like this one were forerunners of National Guard units. (DAH)

from Capitol Square. A board of aldermen chose the mayor, hired civil servants, and also chose commissioners to oversee streets, police and fire departments, the waterworks, public education, sanitation, street lighting, the upkeep of the city cemetery and parks, the city market, and hospitals.

In an 1881 pamphlet entitled *The Streets of Raleigh: Their Condition and Remedy*, City Engineer T.D. Hogg claimed that perpetual dust or mud "impede the necessary traffic upon our streets, give strangers an unfavorable impression of the city, and in manifold ways hinder our growth and development. Unless the progress of the city is to be severely retarded, it is evident that something must be done, and that without delay." Among many other suggestions, Hogg proposed that 20-foot-wide median strips should divide Fayetteville, Halifax, Hillsborough, and New Bern; that trees should line all the

main streets; and that a "steel rail cart-way" should be constructed on busy streets to attract heavy vehicles. Kemp P. Battle objected to the plan to level sidewalks and to cut all trees within five feet of the streets to assure straight curbs. He asked, "Are the people willing to ruin the fine row of elms from the Park Hotel to the Holden corner for the sake of a scientific curb?" Street Committee chairman John C. Drewry defended the plan with another rhetorical question, "Must we then destroy the uniformity of that curbing by running out a foot here and several feet yonder, in order to preserve a few craggy old elms?"

Kemp lost his battle, and the men poised to push Raleigh into the "age of industry" had aligned their forces solely to look forward, devil take the hindmost and a few craggy old elms.

I n the winter of 1880, 19-year-old Herbert Hutchinson Brimley of Willington, Dedfordshire, England, saw Raleigh for the first time. He was not favorably impressed and later recalled, "It was the damndest place I had ever seen." What he saw were uncomfortable hotels, dilapidated sidewalks—where any existed—and a main street distinguished chiefly by the varying depth of its mud. But beneath the surface details of a depressed city recovering from war and occupation, Brimley detected a spirit exuding hope and promising progress: "Raleigh conveyed the impression of being comparatively raw, the cows and hogs roaming the streets giving it something of a rural atmosphere. However, there was a restless, pushing air about the place and its people that impressed me."

Brimley decided to establish roots in Raleigh, and his personal fortunes in the years ahead would bear more than a passing resemblance to those of his newly adopted city.

CAPITAL IMPROVEMENTS:

V

1880 - 1905

Raleigh was slow to lose its image as a lazy, defeated Southern "town," and Brimley failed at his initial attempts to make a living at farming and teaching. Soon, however, Brimley and a brother set up a successful taxidermy shop and biological supply house. Brimley went on to become curator and director of the respected North Carolina State Museum, an internationally honored naturalist, the author of important scientific papers, and the coauthor of two classic books, *Fishes of North Carolina* (1907) and *Birds of North Carolina* (1919). Raleigh, like Brimley, vigorously adopted the new technological advancements of the 1880s and the 1890s. Within 30 years, Raleigh would come of age as a center of education, a "metropolis" welcoming hundreds of thousands of visitors per year, and the home of numerous (if modest) industries—while remaining the center for ever-increasing governmental activities.

The first of the modern marvels to come to Raleigh was the telephone. On September 20, 1879, B.W. Starke began using a line he had run between his home and his Western Union office at Fayetteville and Martin. He then installed an Edison Telephone exchange in all his offices and it operated for about a year before becoming obsolete. J.F. Reynolds of Southern Bell Telephone canvassed businessmen in 1881 regarding the prospects of establishing an exchange in the capital and the response was positive. The first Southern Bell exchange, headquartered over the Pescud, Lee, & Company drugstore at 118 Fayetteville Street, went into 24-hour service on April 1, 1882, with 29 subscribers, who paid 80 cents a year in city taxes per phone. Southern Bell gradually built up a commercial and residential system in the heart of the city. One hundred and thirty-five phones were in use by 1893, 365 by 1899, and 790 by 1908.

Raleigh businessmen saw the financial promise of the new device and soon provided Southern Bell with local competition. In 1898 Will A. Wynne opened the Interstate Telephone and Telegraph exchange over the Wake Drug Store at 301 Fayetteville. Under William Boylan, who succeeded Wynne as manager, the Interstate would merge with Southern Bell in 1907 to form the Capital City Telephone Company and be completely taken over by Southern Bell in 1912. But other local competition would fare better, under the able leadership of Will Wynne.

Will Wynne learned the telephone business by building North Carolina's first long-distance line between Raleigh and Goldsboro in 1896 and by managing the Interstate. In 1900 he installed his own Raleigh Telephone Company exchange at

Minnie Moring, Pattie Moring, Lilly Ferrel, Emmie Drewry, Pearl Myatt, and Margaret Myatt (left to right) were playing along Blount Street in the vicinity of the Executive Mansion when this photograph was taken around 1900. The driver of the ox cart was related to local personality Aunt Betsy, who piloted a similar horseless carriage around Raleigh. (DAH)

In 1903 Will A. Wynne (who opened a city telephone exchange in 1898) and his business associate Mr. Brewer constructed what could have been the nation's first vehicle built specifically to transport telephone poles. It was also Raleigh's first truck. (DAH)

130-1/2 Fayetteville. A consistent innovator, Wynne in 1903 purchased an engine, parts, and materials from which he built a truck to haul telephone poles—reportedly the first truck made in the United States. Wynne retired from the telephone business in 1922, although he retained an active interest in seeing that the region's communications interests were well-served. During the 1930s, he led a protest that succeeded in forcing Southern Bell to reduce rates and to refund $538,000 to North Carolina customers, including $26,000 to Raleigh users. So great was the respect afforded Wynne, however, that when Southern Bell later converted from a manual system to an automatic exchange in Raleigh, its executives invited Wynne to throw the ceremonial switch.

Long after the telephone had ceased to be a novelty, Raleigh's streets remained dusty in dry weather and often impassable in wet. When Raleigh voters defeated a $50,000 bond issue for street improvement in 1883, the General Assembly facetiously chartered a ferryboat company to supply service on Fayetteville Street. The ridicule was lost on Mayor William H. Dodd, who used surplus taxes not to improve city streets but to pay debts—in order to reassure industrial managers of the financial soundness of Raleigh. Public pressure and general dissatisfaction had a cumulative effect, however, and in 1886 city officials voted to "macadamize" Fayetteville Street. It was a slow process and only about one block per year was paved for several years. But residents were willing to meet the expense and a $100,000 bond issue in 1889 reserved $25,000 for street work. Street Commissioner W.Z. Blake credited the revenue from the bond issue with making possible a record of 10,793 square yards of Belgium block paving and 3,796 feet of curbing the next year.

Raleigh's old street lamps were also inadequate for an age of nightly downtown activity. In 1882 the city contracted with the Raleigh Gas Light Company to light the streets. The company put up scores of lights, but technology was already making gas lighting obsolete. In 1885 the Thompson Huston Electric Light Company agreed to supplement the existing gas lights with electric bulbs for $3,000 per year. On December 3, 1885, a large crowd gathered in the late afternoon at a site listed variously as the Raleigh Street Railway Company or the North Carolina Car Company to witness Frederick C. Olds (son of Colonel Fred A. Olds) and Robert L. Gray (later editor of the *Times*) throw the switches to light the street lamps for the first time. The rejoicing was soon replaced by complaints, however, because the lights were dim and bulb replacement slow. City officers were so upset over the service that in 1890 they refused full payment of their bill.

The locally owned Raleigh Electric Company next took on the job, but then progress was slow. Responding to a seemingly hopeless situation, the Light Committee in 1902 suggested that the city provide its own service, but a lasting solution was soon in the offing—in the form of a hydroelectric plant on the Cape Fear River.

During construction of what was then the largest hydroelectric plant in the region at Buckhorn Falls, 11 men died, part of a dam broke in a flood, and the developers went bankrupt before completing the project. The Electric Bond & Shore Company finished the job and installed General Electric generators. Then Electric Bond & Shore was joined by the Raleigh Electric Company, the Consumers Light & Power Company of Sanford and Jonesboro, and the Central Power Company of Fayetteville to form the Carolina Power & Light Company. When CP&L began service in 1908, enough electricity was finally available for Raleigh's primitive street-lighting system.

In spite of the poor condition of city streets, a growing

Southern Bell hired its first female operator in 1895, a trend which had obviously caught on by the time this photograph was taken. This is how the main switchboard appeared during the first decade of the 20th century. (DAH)

Despite his failure as a farmer and teacher, Herbert Hutchinson Brimley (1861-1946) became one of Raleigh's best-known citizens and one of the world's foremost naturalists. He also served as curator of the state museum from 1895 to 1928, and as director from 1929 to 1937. (DAH)

Above: *City residents relied on wells to meet their water needs until 1881, when the Raleigh Water Works Company was formed. This photo-* *graph of the original pumping station and filtration plant was taken around 1900. (DAH)*

The water tower at 115 West Morgan Street stood abandoned for 14 years until 1938, when architect William H. Deitrick purchased it, converting the structure into an office building. It became the headquarters of the state chapter of the American Institute of Architects in 1963. (DAH)

tators. The *State Chronicle* reports: "Col. Scott, letting exuberance get the upper hand and embuing his charger with the same commodity, his horse fell and both rolled over in the mud from which both were extracted totally unharmed, and aside from its serious appearance, the episode added to the mirth of the day." No mirthless fellow himself, Colonel Scott announced that his thrilling feat was a trick he reserved exclusively for railway inaugurations.

Dr. V.E. Turner, R.T. Gray, and F.H. Busbee later purchased the company from Snodgrass, and converted from mule to horsepower. They, in turn, sold to Dr. E.H. Jacobs of South Dakota, who contracted with the General Electric Company in 1890 to construct 10 miles of electric lines parallel to the tracks. Soon Jacobs was providing electric-car service at seven-minute intervals over seven miles of track, but passengers and nearby residents complained of discourteous operators, noisy bells, and poor tracks. Jacobs' income was not enough to meet expenses and he defaulted in 1892. General Electric took down the lines, repossessed and repainted the cars, and moved them to Charlotte, where for years the street-car system operated as the "Raleigh Street Railway Company."

The expanding population also complicated efforts to maintain Raleigh's water supply. In 1880 city aldermen ordered wells deepened to meet increasing water needs, and the next year health inspectors began the routine inspection of residential and business sanitation facilities. In 1881, too, private investors formed the Raleigh Waterworks Company and began preparing a watershed north of town, laying a network of one-inch pipe and building a water tower. No historical structure in Raleigh remains in better condition than the original water tower at 115 West Morgan Street. Finished in 1887, the tower has a 30-foot octagonal lower section, built from three-foot slabs of granite, which still soundly supports the additional 55 feet of brick that, until 1924, held a 100,000-gallon tank. In 1913 the city—which had had to build its own waterworks to reduce rates and to improve service—came into possession of the tower. (The structure stood vacant from 1924 until 1938, when architect William H. Deitrick bought it to use as offices. Since 1963 it has been used as offices by the North Carolina chapter of the American Institute of Architects.)

An adequate water supply was also essential to proper fire protection. The decade of the 1880s was fortunately a time of relatively low fire damage, but the fear of fire remained a disturbing constant. As early as 1890, Fire Chief E.B. Englehard suggested the city employ full-time firemen, but until 1913 only Raleigh's well-equipped volunteers kept diligent watch. A robust rivalry developed with volunteer units in other cities, and Raleigh's volunteer firemen eagerly awaited annual statewide competitions testing their skills. The Raleigh Capital Hose Company won gold medals in the state competition of 1889 and successfully defended its championship in Charlotte in 1890. The fire chief began installing electrical alarm boxes

population and an expanding city enhanced the prospects for the lucrative operation of a streetcar system. A small operation began in 1886 when Texan George M. Snodgrass imported three railroad carloads of mules from his native state and formed the Raleigh Street Railway Company. By Christmas Day of 1886, he had completed three routes, including the main line running from the Centennial School to St. Mary's. Inaugural ceremonies brought hundreds of spectators, business leaders, and all city officials. At four p.m., Miss Maggie Moring rang a bell starting the first scheduled run. Snodgrass drove the first car, carrying dignitaries from the Hotel Florence at Fayetteville and Davie toward St. Mary's.

One of Snodgrass' Texas friends provided sufficient excitement to mark the event permanently in the minds of the spec-

Will Wynne photographed Raleigh's championship volunteer fire company in front of its Fayetteville Street headquarters in 1890. (DAH)

This mule-drawn streetcar was resurrected for the Centennial Parade of Transportation held in Raleigh on May 21, 1940. Such vehicles plied the city's streets during the last decades of the 19th century. (DAH)

Above: *The third Rex Hospital opened in May 1937. A fourth facility, at 4420 Lake Boone Trail, replaced it in 1980. (DAH)*

Above: *Mary Lewis Wyche (1858-1936) had an unparalleled impact upon North Carolina nursing. Graduated from Philadelphia General Hospital in 1894 at age 36, she became head nurse, matron, and bookkeeper at Rex Hospital, established the Rex Hospital Training School for Nurses (the first such school in the state), revitalized the moribund Raleigh Nurses' Association, and organized the North Carolina State Nurses' Association. (DAH)*

Right: *The North Carolina legislature had passed a bill establishing the state's first insane asylum in 1848. Dorothea Dix Hospital did not admit patients, however, for another eight years. In 1896 the staff of the hospital included (left to right) Dr. Kirby, Mrs. Whitaker, W.R. Crawford, Dr. Faison, and Dr. McGeachey. (DAH)*

throughout the city in the late 1880s; by 1890 the business district was saturated and 18 boxes had been placed in residential areas.

Financial instability was another disturbing constant. By the mid-1890s, city expenditures were exceeding income. In 1895, for example, the city took in $66,000 from taxes, market rents, and other fees; but it spent $74,000. Voters approved an additional $50,000 bond issue in 1897, providing revenue for additional services but sinking the city deeper into debt. Raleigh was also burdened by the expenses incurred by the Health Department's operation of a charity hospital. Some residents accused attendants at the hospital of abusing patients in the mid-1880s, and officials strictly regulated prescriptions written there in 1894. But few were critical when the hospital staff vaccinated over 80 percent of the population against smallpox during an epidemic in 1899, while at the same time operating a Pest House on Old Garner Road to quarantine those already infected.

By the early 1890s, St. John's Guild of the Good Shepherd Church was struggling to keep the St. John's Hospital open in the old Manly house at South and Salisbury, where the Guild had formed the first public hospital in Raleigh in 1877. The Rex Fund had once again grown to more than $30,000, and the aldermen decided to use the money to buy and enlarge the St. John's facilities. The city and the Rex Fund then shared

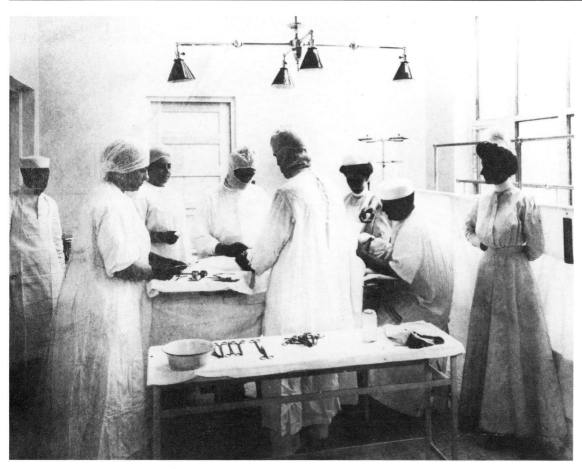

Dr. H.H. Royster (fourth from the left) is shown performing surgery at Rex Hospital in 1909. Also appearing in the picture with the hospital's chief (and only) surgeon, are Alex, an orderly (far left), Dr. Abernethy, anesthesiologist (second from the right), and Nurse Orchard (far right). (DAH)

the purchase price of $4,500 in August 1893. When Rex opened in May 1894, it was the first hospital in the state to implement a nurses-training program, headed by Mary Wyche of Philadelphia, and the first to require its staff nurses to be registered by the State Executive Board of Health. Additions to the old Manly house were not long in coming: trustees added an eight-room annex; the Ladies Hospital Aid Society contributed an operating room; and the Ministering Circle of King's Daughters donated an annex to the children's ward. The staff treated 345 patients in 1904, and services expanded considerably with the completion of a new building in 1909.

Mrs. Aaron Burtis Hunter, wife of the principal of St. Augustine's, deserves credit for taking the initiative to rectify the chronic shortage of health care available for the majority of blacks in the Raleigh area. She collected more than $1,100 to start another hospital in 1895, which she named St. Agnes in honor of the late wife of chief contributor I.L. Collins of California. St. Agnes Hospital opened in 1896 in the former residence of the Reverend Robert B. Sutton, past principal of St. Augustine's. It was modernized in 1903 with a new operating room, tile floors, a new sterilization room, and other improvements. When the executive committee of the Board of Trustees approved a new building in 1904, Mrs. Hunter went to work again, this time raising an impressive $15,000. With great joy, staff and patients moved into the new hospital in June 1909. But St. Agnes was destined to be plagued with problems, mostly caused by insufficient financial support, far into the future.

Newspapers continued to be important factors in the charged political atmosphere of Raleigh, and their editors continued to become men of influence in the community and state. Foremost among the newspapermen of this era was Josephus Daniels. Daniels was given his start in the newspaper business by Durham tobacco manufacturer General Julian S. Carr, who had been willed the majority of the *State Chronicle* stock by former owner Randolph A. Shotwell. Josephus Daniels, a recent arrival from Wilson, called on Carr in August 1885 to propose continuing the paper under his editorship. Carr had previously been unaware that he owned the stock, but he was impressed with the youthful Daniels and gave him the stock with the provision that Daniels would pay for it only if the paper succeeded. In his first editorial on October 16, 1885, Daniels announced his unabashed intention of publishing a Democratic newspaper that would adhere to the principles of Thomas Jefferson, "The greatest of Americans." In the same month he received his law degree from Chapel Hill, but he never practiced for pay.

Josephus Daniels came from a decidedly middle-class background. When Josephus was only three, his shipbuilder father was accidently killed by Southern cannon fire at Washington, North Carolina, and his mother had then moved to Wilson, where she became postmistress. As an up-and-coming young man about Raleigh, he became friends with Adelaide Worth Bagley, the grandaughter of former Governor Worth. Emboldened by the lack of success more socially elevated young men were having with "Addie," he embarked on a

Randolph Abbott Shotwell (1844-1885) established the New Bern Journal of Commerce *and the Rutherfordton* Vindicator *before coming to Raleigh, in 1878, as editor of the* Farmer and Mechanic. *He also served in the state house of representatives during the 1876 session, and wrote* Three Years in Battle *and* Three Years in Federal Prisons *about his Civil War*

experiences. Shotwell's shrewd abilities as an editor and writer eventually led to a merger of the Farmer and Mechanic *and the* State Chronicle *in 1885. (DAH)*

Samuel A'Court Ashe (1840-1938) led a varied life as a soldier, conductor on the Wilmington and Weldon Railroad, lawyer, politician, and historian. He edited the Biographical History of North Carolina, *was a founder of the* News and Observer, *and served as clerk of the federal district court in Raleigh from 1918 to 1936. (DAH)*

long courtship that resulted in their marriage on May 2, 1888. The *News and Observer* noted that "the crème de la crème of Raleigh society" attended the wedding, but Daniels knew they did not come to see him. More than 50 years later he would write his son Jonathan, "You and I may get in on our wives' tickets, but in conviction and in radicalism we belong to the proletariat."

Daniels failed to make a profit from the *Chronicle,* but he succeeded in attracting attention and in establishing a reputation for incorruptibility. To supplement his income, he sought and won the office of Printer-to-the-State in 1887, beating out his fellow Democrat Samuel Ashe of the *News and Observer.* Ashe seethed over losing to a relative upstart, and one night in 1891 his anger boiled over. He attacked Daniels in an alley outside the *News and Observer* offices, although a state senator separated the two before any harm occurred. When he learned that the *News and Observer* staff had released a report to the Associated Press stating that Ashe had "cowhided" him, Daniels sent his own telegram to the AP: "I understand that a telegram has been sent that Captain Ashe struck me with a cowhide. This is a lie. He did not touch me with anything and will not dare to do so."

The following day the men met in the lobby of the capitol and wrestled each other to the floor, but the Mecklenburg legislator, Captain W.E. Ardrey, broke up the struggle by cuffing each of the ineffectual combatants indiscriminately and chiding them, "I am ashamed of you both. It is a disgrace to North Carolina that you two editors should be turning into thugs." As a matter of principle, Daniels won the printing contract again in 1893, but he gave the work to other publishers.

After Daniels' attempts to keep the *Chronicle* afloat through merger and to start a Democratic weekly, *The North Carolinian,* had both failed, General Carr once again came to the young editor's assistance. In the summer of 1894, Carr bought the foundering *News and Observer* and turned it over to Daniels. From Washington, where he had accepted a post in President Cleveland's administration, Daniels wrote a now-famous letter to 100 leading North Carolina Democrats asking each to purchase $100 in *News and Observer* stock. Seventy responded and the paper was temporarily solvent. Daniels returned in 1895, finally able to turn a serious-minded newspaper into a profit-making enterprise. Later he bought back all the outstanding stock, even though some of the holders made him pay dearly.

As editor of the *News and Observer,* Daniels consistently opposed the railroads as they were then managed, unregulated trusts, and liquor. Just as consistently, he supported white supremacy, a graduated income tax, the direct election of U.S. Senators, free public education, and women's rights. Over the years, his paper became known as "the old Reliable" to his allies, the "Nuisance and Disturber" and the "Nauseous Lie Server" to his enemies, who became legion. Judged by the prevailing concepts of today, Daniels was an intolerant reactionary. Judged by the prevailing concepts of turn-of-the-century

The campus of St. Augustine's School boasted four major buildings in 1899. They were (from left to right), Taylor Library, the Chapel, Lyman building, and Smith building. (DAH)

North Carolina, he was in the mainstream of popular opinion. Without doubt his most controversial campaign took place during the 1898 elections.

Republican Daniel L. Russell had won the governor's race in 1896 with the help of the black vote, and the return to "white supremacy" became the key political issue in the state. Black editor Alex L. Manly published an editorial in his August 18, 1878, *Wilmington Daily Record* suggesting that white women, especially the poor, were guilty of luring black men into trysts, for which the males were held responsible and too often lynched. The editorial created a storm of anger and Daniels launched an unstinted pro-white anti-black campaign during which he predicted that white voters were becoming an "irresistible unit in their determination not to longer submit to the humiliation and indignations which have followed in the wake of negro rule."

The attack on Governor Russell was as cruel as it was exaggerated, perhaps reaching its nadir on September 30, when the *News and Observer* carried a front-page cartoon by Norman Jennett depicting Russell dressed in a checkered suit (with the head of a black man in each square) and listening to Wake County black political leader James Young whispering "do this, do that" into his ear. Daniels never apologized for his methods, claiming that "no quiet voice could have been heard in those times" of poverty and bitterness. But he did confess to excesses: "I can look back and truly say that no personal ambition or enmity of individuals guided my action, and when the contests ended I bore no resentment toward any with whom I had differed. But I look back, also, amazed at my own editorial violence at times, even when I understand the circumstances which surround it."

(In his future career, Daniels became Secretary of the Navy, mentor to Franklin D. Roosevelt, and longtime ambassador to Mexico, but he always happily returned to Raleigh and the *News and Observer* whenever time allowed. When he died in 1948, Josephus Daniels had been North Carolina's most famous citizen for over a generation.)

While politics occupied considerable time during the turn of the century, Raleigh citizens remained as committed as ever to their churches. In 1887, out of a total church membership of 3,590, the Baptists led with 2,005, the African Methodist Episcopal Church was next with 1,305, the Congregationalists had 130, the Episcopalians 75, and the Presbyterians 25. The black churches showed the greatest rate of growth. African Methodist Episcopal members built St. Paul's on Edenton Street in the mid-1880s; there were nine black churches in Raleigh by 1891 and 20 by 1901. St. Paul's burned on July 4, 1909, but the congregation responded quickly by rebuilding the church still in use.

Yankee preacher R.G. Pearson conducted a well-attended revival in May 1888, and secular activity continued on a large scale. The Women's Baptist Home Mission Convention, formed in Raleigh in 1884, supported the Oxford Orphan Asylum for Negroes, financed African missionary work, encouraged Bible reading, spurred Sunday school attendance, and assisted the poor. Another orphanage was begun by the Reverend Thomas Frederick Price. The Wilmington man, thankful for having survived a violent storm at sea, pledged to pay his debt to providence by building an orphanage in the capital. He financed the beginning of work on the Catholic Orphanage in 1898; Holy Name Chapel was completed in 1902 and the dormitory finished in 1903.

Raleigh's long-suffering temperance advocates recognized a golden opportunity to promote their cause in the 1890s, and they unified into a dedicated, cohesive band to take advantage of it. Down Fayetteville Street, within easy walking distance of the capitol and across the street from the Wake County Courthouse, Jim Miller ran a bar and gambling hall in Raleigh that was most popular among legislators and well-heeled residents and visitors. His was the brightest-lit establishment downtown and the most lavishly decorated public house in the city. Occasionally, complaints forced authorities to investigate, but Miller was able to prevent grand jury action largely because of the influence of his clientele. All that changed in January of 1886, when newly appointed Superior Court Justice Walter Clark resolved to prosecute Miller for running an illegal gambling hall.

When Clark chose Swift Galloway as prosecutor, most observers believed the prosecution would be half-hearted because Galloway was a frequent customer of Miller's establishment. Miller and his lawyers were, therefore, taken by surprise when Galloway attacked with all the forces at his command. A jury convicted Miller, Judge Clark sentenced him to work on the roads and fined him $2,000, and the North Carolina Supreme Court upheld the verdict. The fine and lawyers' fees broke Miller, who never returned to Raleigh, but that was only the beginning for prohibitionists.

Josephus Daniels, a teetotaler who would change some drinking customs on a national scale when he became Secretary of the Navy, applauded the outcome of the trial, and other abstemious-minded capitalites took heart. Although Raleigh voters had defeated prohibition 1,248 to 480 in 1877, the vote against had been only 1,185 to 780 in 1881. The 1886 prohibition fight was led by printer and Baptist State Convention Secretary Needham B. Broughton, by the unsuccessful 1884 gubernatorial candidate Captain Octavius Coke, by the Reverend W.H.R. Leak, and by the faculty and clergy at Shaw. Daniels supported the cause with frequent editorials in the *State Chronicle.* Outside temperance leaders lent their support, too, and the combined effort paid off with a 1,237 to 1,177 victory at the polls.

Broughton, Daniels, Leak, and others celebrated in the Metropolitan Hall the night of the election, but their victory was less than complete. Saloonkeepers simply moved their establishments immediately across the town borders, erected signs inscribed "Last Chance" on the side facing those entering town and "First Chance" on the side facing those leaving town, and resumed business as usual.

Cockfighting, horse racing, and other forms of gambling also survived outside the town limits in the barrooms and grog shops, but new, more acceptable sports were growing in favor. After years of attending amateur events, Raleigh spectators in 1885 got their own professional team in the North Carolina Baseball Association, a league that also included Goldsboro, Durham, Oxford, and Wilmington. Professional baseball would grow to dominate local sports pages before the end of the century, but another new sport of the period also aroused popular interest. On October 18, 1888, a team made up of University of North Carolina sophomores played Wake Forest College in the first football game held in Raleigh.

Sports were not the only diversion, however. No event of the year excited youngsters of all ages so much as the annual

The Source of the Governor's Inspiration.

Top: *Daniel Lindsay Russell, Jr. (1846-1908), headed a Fusion government of Republicans and Populists from 1897 to 1901. As governor, he opposed the state's white supremacy movement, and was castigated in the Bourbon Democrat-controlled press for doing so. This Norman Jennett cartoon, showing Russell taking advice from black Wake County political leader James Young, appeared on the front page of the* News and Observer, *September 30, 1899. Russell was the last Republican governor of North Carolina until James E. Holshouser, Jr., was elected in 1972. (DAH)*

Above: *As secretary of the navy during both of President Woodrow Wilson's terms in office, Josephus Daniels (right, 1862-1948) made decisions which pleased some and perturbed others. One of the latter was his directive banning liquor from officers' messes. He used his position as editor of the* News and Observer *to champion causes like prohibition, anti-Ku Klux Klan measures, the League of Nations and World Court, and child labor laws. Daniels also served as ambassador to Mexico from 1932 to 1941. (DAH)*

arrival of the circus. Spectators crowded the curb for a closer look at the parade of animals and performers down Main Street, and the smells and dust associated with the Big Top contributed an ambience never to be forgotten. Those desirous of more refinement were undoubtedly pleased in 1885, when Major E.J. Hardin, Dr. A.W. Knox, and Professor J. Kurssteiner of St. Mary's organized the Raleigh Philharmonic Society. On December 22 of that year, an orchestra, mixed chorus, and soloists gave the Society's first public performance in the Chapel of the Institute for the Education of the Deaf, Dumb, and Blind. Dr. Kurssteiner was the guiding spirit of the organization, and when he left Raleigh the Society folded.

In the hall of the Olivia Raney Library on October 12, 1905, the Johnsonian Club performed an evening of music inspired by Shakespeare. The Johnsonians had originally been organized in 1895 by Miss Mattie H. Bailey and Miss Jane Ward as a book club, and similar groups followed from time to time, including the Fortnightly in 1899, Olla Podrida in 1899, and Tuesday Afternoon around 1903.

Beginning in the 1890s, Sherman Upchurch also began booking top-flight attractions into the Academy of Music at Martin and Salisbury. Upchurch had himself toured with "Buffalo Bill" Cody's Wild West Show, and he presented Raleigh audiences with such Broadway stars as Maxine Elliot, William Faversham, Nat Goodwin, Maude Adams, and De Wolf Hooper. The Academy's wide spectrum of dramatic productions included *The Taming of the Shrew, The Village Bride, The Bohemian Girl, The Circus Girl,* and *The Grand Duchess.* Upchurch reserved the most popular acts for fair week, at which time he raised his top price to as high as $2.50 per seat.

Around 1900 Upchurch had competition from an entirely new medium, and no phenomenon ever attracted attention — both positive and negative — from a wider range of Raleigh's population. The "movies" came to town with traveling "projectionist" Lyman Howe, who would set up his projector, a screen, and a gramophone in the second floor of the old City Market at Fayetteville and Exchange and show one-reelers to capacity audiences. Mr. Foster and Mr. Mansfield foresaw future trends and converted the market hall into the Gem Theatre in 1905, charging 10 cents admission. When they opened the tentlike Airdome on Fayetteville Street to provide eager customers with an option of bills, they incurred the wrath of local ministers for presenting "sinful amusement."

Jim Weaver and Ben Tongue opened the Gaiety, complete with a mechanical piano, and Foster and Mansfield built the Revelry to replace the Gem in 1908. Barney Aronson and O.B. Browne, lately of Henderson, bought the Revelry and renamed it the Almo in 1909. John C. Drewry literally rushed to accommodate anxious patrons by having carpenters work all day one Sunday in 1909 to complete the Grand in time to open on Monday and thus not lose any of the week's business. Drewry interspersed vaudeville acts and movie showings, but

the next competitor, Herbert and Jerome Rosenthal's Lyric, adhered strictly to film fare.

Competition was keen. The standard bill consisted of a one-reel comedy, a drama, and a western. When the market finally became saturated, proprietors resorted to various types of advertisement to attract audiences — newspaper ads, billboards, traveling displays. Once when the Third Regiment band had contracted to play in front of a movie theater to attract a crowd, Sherman Upchurch sent one of his performers to the scene. The actor, using a megaphone and "neat oratory which would make a seasoned politician green with envy," erroneously informed the crowd that Upchurch had hired the band out of a sense of civic duty to entertain his beloved fellow citizens. Despite such tactics, the movie business continued to grow in Raleigh, although by necessity at a more moderate pace. The more traditional institutions of culture also grew at a moderate pace.

The sustained interest in cultural activities, even of a relatively low order, was one reflection, perhaps, of increased educational opportunities during this period. Raleigh residents became relatively generous in their support of public education, although they did not always approve requests for new primary schools or expansions of the curriculum. In 1877 voters had approved a school fund levy of 10 cents per $100 in property value, which allowed the purchase of the Washington and Garfield schools for black students and the construction of a new black school in Oberlin. But 1885 was the watershed year for Raleigh schools. In that year state taxes provided $6,730.35 to the school fund, district taxes $6,249.80, private subscriptions and donations $800, and a bond issue $25,000. Administrators were thereby able to purchase the old "Palace" property for the Centennial School; but, far more important to long-term advancement, they convinced Edward P. Moses to move from Goldsboro to become superintendent of the Raleigh school system.

The indefatigable Moses was precisely the man for the times, and he earned the enduring respect of citizens from all stations by instituting new programs and by making Raleigh schools effective and efficient. He fought prejudices against remedial education, and he struggled to change the idea that education should be restricted to the upper classes and that public schools were a form of charity. Moses was also responsible for founding the Archibald De Bow Murphy School on Person Street in 1887 — the last school built in Raleigh in the 19th century.

But Moses ran into overwhelming opposition when he called for the establishment of a high school. Opposed were businessmen, who would pay a large share of the taxes; Peace and St. Mary's which would lose students to a competing institution; and the majority of voters, who were not yet willing to keep children in school after the traditional apprenticeship age. Moses' plan was defeated. In 1889, he became the center of another storm of protest from business interests when a shortage of money forced him to close the schools after

Although construction of the main building at Peace Institute began in 1858, the nearly finished structure was used as a hospital during the Civil War, and as the Freedman's Bureau for a few years afterward, before classes were *able to commence in 1872. The Presbyterian church bought the school in 1907, and in 1943 it was renamed Peace College. (DAH)*

Leonidas Lafayette Polk (1837-1892) served in the state legislature in 1860 and 1864-1865, edited the Raleigh News from 1880-1881, and published the Progressive Farmer in 1886. However, his lasting contribution to the people of North Carolina was his successful fight for a state department of agriculture, of which he became the first commissioner. (DAH)

sent to the General Assembly a counterpetition containing 164 signatures supposedly representing the owners of $4 million of Raleigh's $5.38 million of taxable property. When supporters of the bond issue compared the claims of the counterpetition with tax rolls, they found that the 164 had listed only $2 million for taxes. Josephus Daniels claimed the list constituted "a roster of the biggest liars in Raleigh" and threatened to publish it. After more gloves-off political wrangling, the General Assembly passed the bill by a landslide vote in both houses, and voters approved the measure 2,688 to 1,718. Nevertheless, Moses had to drop the eighth grade, which he had initiated in 1888.

School terms varied widely from year to year, depending upon available funds and the weather. Students attended a record high of 200 days in 1884, the number dropped to a meager 74 in 1886, rose to 162 in 1888, and dropped again to 91 in 1890. To accommodate the maximum number of students, the schools operated two sessions per day: one from nine a.m. until noon, and the other from noon until 2:30 p.m. There were statistical differences between the white and the black schools, but they were not great. In 1885-1886, 13 teachers averaging $33.75 per month taught 784 white students; 15 teachers averaging $30.50 per month taught 1,133 black students. All schools operated for six and a half months that year; average daily attendance for white students was 76 percent, for blacks 65 percent. Students could advance a maximum of three grades per year.

The task of all who labored to improve primary education in Raleigh was truly Herculean. The 1900 census revealed that North Carolina had the unenviable distinction of being the most illiterate state in the Union. But, ironically, higher education had never fared so well, and Raleigh gained two new schools to add to its four existing institutions of higher learning.

Beginning in 1875 the General Assembly used the $7,500 per year in interest accruing from the Morrill Act land-grant fund to run an Experimental Agriculture Station at the University of North Carolina. The state's first commissioner of agriculture, Leonidas L. Polk, the second influential figure in Raleigh history to bear that name, campaigned to have the Station moved to Raleigh. To widen his support he suggested that it become an agricultural and an industrial college. Chapel Hill advocates naturally objected, but in 1881 the General Assembly voted to move the Station to Raleigh and bought the National Hotel to house it after remodeling.

After Polk stepped down as Commissioner of Agriculture, he continued his efforts to benefit farmers and to set up an agricultural college in Raleigh. In 1883 he gained some invaluable allies. *State Chronicle* founder and editor Walter Hines Page, attorney W.J. Peele, and several other young Raleigh men formed the Watauga Club for the expressed purpose of starting a school in Raleigh patterned after the Massachusetts Institute of Technology. Page stressed the chief advantage to Raleigh: "Our people need it and have sought it

five months. The next year he could count on only enough money to keep the schools open for three months. His dilemma was complicated further by constitutional restrictions, which required the schools to operate a minimum of four months but which also limited taxation for schools to 10 cents per $100 property value. Moses proposed that the city seek General Assembly permission for a $100,000 bond issue. Mayor Alfred A. Thompson strongly approved of longer sessions and upgrading the schools, and Dr. Richard H. Lewis, Needham Broughton, and Raleigh & Gaston chief mechanic Peter Fleming organized and led the campaign.

Strong opposition to the bond issue was voiced by leaders in the newly formed Chamber of Commerce. They drafted and

because they wish to see Raleigh a place of manufacture and this she must be if anything more than a seat of government.''

When Page realized he could not make the *Chronicle* pay, he left Raleigh "without a dollar or a job" and moved to New York, where he worked on several papers. But Josephus Daniels ably took his place, and the Wataugans had certainly prodded their legislators into alertness. In 1885 the General Assembly voted to establish an agricultural and industrial college in a city that would donate land and contribute to construction costs.

Many cities wanted the school, and Raleigh had to win it. Business leaders offered to contribute $8,000, city officials offered the use of the Exposition Building and 20 acres at the Fair Grounds, William Stronach added another acre, R. Stanhope Pullen promised another 8.5 acres, and city officials guaranteed the Board of Agriculture complete control over the school. Leonidas Polk called farmers to Raleigh in January 1887 to pressure the legislature, and the Watauga Club drew up a bill. On March 3 the General Assembly approved the bill and appropriated money to purchase a farm adjoining the Fair Grounds.

Classes at the North Carolina College of Agriculture and Mechanical Arts began October 3, 1889, and later in the month the cornerstone was laid for the Main Building, designed by Baltimore architect C.L. Carson and renamed Holladay Hall in 1915 in honor of the first president, Alexander Quarles Holladay. Six professors taught 45 students the first year, 84 the second, and 110 the third. Students paid $30 per year tuition, and they could attend in relative comfort for only $130 per year in total expenses.

Raleigh gained its sixth and last major institution of higher

Alexander Quarles Holladay (1839-1909), first president of North Carolina College of Agriculture and Mechanic Arts, was also one of the six original faculty members and the school's first bookkeeper. The school was to become North Carolina State University. (DAH)

education in 1889, when Baptist leaders decided to establish a Baptist Female Seminary and invited bids from cities desirous of being home to the new school. Businessmen and Baptist officials in Durham submitted the highest bid, and they were resentful when Raleigh was chosen over them. The *State Chronicle,* ever eager to boost the capital, explained the logic behind the decision: "The college will always have most desirable surroundings; it will enjoy the greatest convenience to all our churches, public buildings and halls; it is protected every hour of the day and night by police and sanitary regulations; it is on the main streetcar line, surrounded by water and sewer mains." The first students attended classes in a large, four-story brick building at Blount and Edenton. The curriculum was extensive: psychology, pedagogy, ethics, logic,

Holladay Hall, the first academic building erected at North Carolina College of Agriculture and Mechanical Arts, was named for Alexander Quarles Holladay. Courtesy, North Carolina State University Archives, Raleigh

Latin, Greek, French, German, Spanish, English, math, science, history, business, art, elocution, music, and "domestic accomplishments." The Baptist Seminary became the Baptist University for Women in 1905, and in 1909 trustees renamed it Meredith College to honor Baptist leader Thomas Meredith. Meredith had urged the Baptist State Convention of 1838 to locate in or near the capital "a female seminary of high order that should be modeled and conducted on strictly religious principles, but that should be, so far as possible, free from sectarian influences."

Gaining the Female Seminary may have pleased Baptists and boosters, but it would have significant repercussions. Encouraged by their success, civic leaders hoped to attract Trinity College in 1891, when its trustees announced that they were interested in moving from Randolph County to the city offering the greatest incentive. Negotiators for Raleigh signed an agreement promising a contribution of $20,500 to bring Trinity to the city, but all efforts came to naught when Durham entered the competition. Not wanting their town to again lose out to rival Raleigh, Washington Duke offered $85,000 and General Julian Carr promised 65 prime acres if the trustees chose Durham. Raleigh generously released the trustees, Trinity moved to Durham, and in 1924 it became Duke University, now one of the most prestigious and well-endowed universities in the world.

Although Raleigh lost out to Durham on acquiring Trinity College, the very fact that it was in the bidding indicated some degree of economic recovery. Boosters began to clamor for immediate and massive industrial development in the 1880s. They eagerly assisted efforts to conduct an industrial fair in North Carolina following the success of the North Carolina display at the 1883 Boston Exposition. A Walter Hines Page editorial of 1884 is typical of contemporary thinking: "Raleigh must put up or shut up. If we are to have the Great State Exposition, we must subscribe the cash and subscribe it now and a good deal of it." Raleigh put up, hosting an exposition in conjunction with the 1884 State Fair to show off North Carolina products to buyers from other states, to educate farmers, to promote investment in manufacturing, and to speed up railroad expansion. The fair was a success, and Northern investment, especially in cotton mills, picked up markedly as did the shipment of machinery into the state. But little of either came to Raleigh.

As much as anyone then living in the city, R.S. Tucker was aware of the fluctuations of Raleigh's economy through the years. Born into the city's leading mercantile family, Tucker had been quartermaster and commissary in Raleigh during the Civil War, a captain of the cavalry, clerk of the House of Commons, director of the North Carolina Railroad, an official of the Raleigh & Gaston Railroad, and for 18 years, the director of the Institute for the Education of the Deaf, Dumb, and Blind. At his store he sold expensive "bond" taffeta in large quantities, French velvet at $5 per yard, and French brocade at prices reaching $10 per yard. He knew money for investment was present in the capital.

On May 27, 1888, Tucker scheduled a meeting in the

Facing page: *Gustavus Adolphus Bauer, designer of the Executive Mansion, also drew the plans for the Baptist Female University building. The five-story structure was completed in 1899 at the corner of Edenton and Blount streets. In 1909 the institution received its present name, Meredith College, in honor of Thomas Meredith, founder and editor of the* Biblical Recorder. *When the school moved to its new campus in 1926, the old turreted building was transformed into the Mansion Park Hotel. It was razed in 1967. (DAH)*

Left: *Fannie Wilson and a classmate, photographed on campus at Baptist University for Women, wear clothing typical of the first decade of the 20th century. (DAH)*

mayor's office for persons interested in forming a Raleigh Chamber of Commerce and Industry. When more than 300 businessmen arrived, the meeting was moved to Metropolitan Hall. The Chamber of Commerce was organized and Tucker elected president. The Chamber's immediate goals were to establish a cotton mill, to increase tobacco sales, to keep taxes low as an incentive to outside investors, and to improve streets and roads. Within a year, the Chamber's efforts were rewarded by the location in Raleigh of the North Carolina Wagon Company, the Greystone Granite & Construction Company, the Wetmore Shoe & Leather Company, the Cider & Vinegar Manufactory, the Suspender Company, and a charter for the Raleigh Cotton Factory. In his annual report for 1890, Mayor Thompson accented the shift in emphasis: "The territory tributary to Raleigh is so restricted that, however enterprising our merchants may be, it can never become a great commercial center. With cheap water and cheap gas we can make it—what would appear to be better for our whole people—a great manufacturing town." He urged unrestricted efforts to attract additional industry.

The drive to establish a cotton mill was an old one, but now it took on a new vigor. Advocates pointed to the increase in estate values, the hundreds of jobs, and the increased capital a mill would bring Raleigh. The Chamber of Commerce began selling stock, and by the summer of 1889 it had raised $62,000, selected company directors, and purchased six acres of land, even though all pledges had not been honored. By March 1890 the building was ready for machinery. Expecta-

tions knew no bounds, as evidenced by an anonymous letter to the May 10, 1890, *State Constitution:* "Now, listen to me: A Raleigh cotton mill can pay just as great a per cent as any mill anywhere, and I want to record a prophecy right here, right now, that the Raleigh mill will make as good a report after the first year as any mill operated in this whole country. You will see it too."

The Raleigh Cotton Mill, on what is now Downtown Boulevard, went into production in the summer of 1890, turning out 1,500 pounds of spun yarn during an 11-hour day, and much of the output was going to Northern markets. The Caraleigh Cotton Mill went into operation in 1892 and the Pilot Mill in 1893. Raleigh ironically had become a fledgling "cotton-mill town" just as the price of cotton was dropping; it plummeted to four cents a pound at the Raleigh exchange in 1894. Area farmers rapidly shifted to other crops, ending Raleigh's brief reign as the cotton-trading capital of North Carolina.

Even with the increased activity, Raleigh remained less industrialized than most other North Carolina cities. But retail business grew steadily, and the creation of the Insurance Department in 1899 spurred companies to set up headquarters in or near Raleigh. Still, new industrial concerns continued to locate in the capital. The American Transportation Company began building refrigerated railroad cars in 1889, thereby opening up distant markets for local producers of fruit and vegetables. A Coca Cola Bottling plant opened on Halifax Street in 1903. Julius Lewis & Company began manufacturing

windmills and pumps in 1905. The General Assembly also remained an inspiration for investment, both in session and out.

So many legislators pleaded with druggist Henry T. Hicks to "fix me something for a headache" that he concocted "Hicks' Capudine Liquid Headache Reliever" in 1894. The substance worked so well to relieve legislative discomforts brought on by long sessions in chamber and in the Yarborough House afterwards that Hicks was hard pressed to keep up with demand. He formed the Capudine Chemical Company in 1904 and began selling his mixture nationwide. The company stayed in the family until 1960 when descendants sold it to Pearson Pharmacal Company of Miami, Florida.

Not all residents were upset by the relatively low level of manufacturing growth in the area. In a Centennial Celebration speech in October 1892, Charles M. Busbee evaluated Raleigh's condition positively: "Fortunate it is for us that we have never had a boom. The growth of the city, although slow, has been sure and steadfast. What we have gained we hold. We are a conservative people and go safely if slowly. We have builded upon a rock. No commercial disorder has ever wrecked us. No financial storm has overwhelmed us."

A passage from a Chamber of Commerce pamphlet of 1894 demonstrates some of the negative aspects of overly enthusiastic boosterism. It is clearly aimed at Northern industrialists weary of dealing with organized labor: "The colored people constitute the best labor on earth, and large numbers are taking places as skilled workmen in certain lines with a capacity which cannot be surpassed. Under fair conditions they are loyal and faithful and watchful of the interests of the employer. They will ever prove a bar to the incoming of hordes of the foreign scum which is held accountable for the serious labor disturbances, the disastrous strikes and the interruption of business so frequently experienced in those sections where the scum locates itself. Such events are yet to come to a section where the greater part of the manual labor of business enterprise is performed by the colored people."

The Chamber of Commerce pamphlet guaranteeing labor peace did not exaggerate. Following the lead of the typesetters a generation past, printer John R. Ray organized a Raleigh chapter of the Knights of Labor in 1884, and the Knights elected John Nichols of Raleigh State Master Workman. Ray was a dedicated booster of Raleigh, and his primary goal was to assist local workingmen by abolishing the use of convict labor in the city. The Raleigh Knights of Labor denounced the participants in the Hay Market Riots of 1886, and they emphatically disassociated themselves from agitator J.A.

James N. and W.H. Williamson, father and son, founded the Pilot Cotton Mill in 1892. The mill building (below) was photographed around 1900. The spinning equipment (opposite page, left) and looms (left) were photographed in the early 1930s. At the turn of the century the plant boasted 11,000 spindles and 425 looms. (DAH)

Strickland of Durham who was suspected of implication in the Chicago bombing. The only strike to occur in Raleigh in the 19th century involved the black workers for the Raleigh Waterworks in April 1887. They demanded higher pay, but their strike failed. Ray won his only victory, and that a very dubious one, in 1889. The Raleigh Board of Aldermen agreed to prohibit the use of convict labor on city jobs, but they simply ignored their own edict and continued old practices. By the mid-1890s, the North Carolina labor movement was again dormant.

The rise in commercial investment and in trade created conditions conducive to banking once again. J. Stanhope Wynne founded the Raleigh Savings Bank in 1885, the first savings bank in North Carolina. Herbert Jackson, business manager of the Wetmore Shoe Factory (which used convict labor to make shoes inside Central Prison), joined with Sid Johnson, teller of Citizens National Bank, and with A.F. Page, a lumber and railroad investor, to start the Commercial National Bank of Raleigh. The Raleigh Building and Loan Association opened in 1905 when the construction industry began recovering from a severe recession.

But the building industry, in the 1880s and early 1890s, was by no means depressed. By 1892 railroad lines connected Raleigh to western North Carolina and the Raleigh & Augusta Airline had extended tracks as far as Hamlet. Consequently, Raleigh's importance as a rail center was enhanced. Boosters were proud to point out that 60 buildings were going up during centennial week itself, and in 1893 A.F. Page built the Academy of Music, adding a magnificent new auditorium for cultural, social, and political events. The artist who designed the curtain for the Academy stage used artistic license with the abandon of the true romantic: he depicted Sir Walter Raleigh

landing on Roanoke Island, a spot some points west of the nobleman's actual travels. After a slowdown during the late 1890s, construction once again increased. In the summer of 1903, no less that 65 buildings (representing an investment of more than $300,000) were being erected. In 1907 the Masons introduced a new form of construction to Raleigh when they built the $120,000 Masonic Temple, designed by Charles McMillian, at Fayetteville and Hargett. It was the first building using reinforced concrete in North Carolina.

In 1911 the city received a much more impressive structure employing reinforced concrete. Discontented legislators had pressured the Board of Aldermen to build a larger municipal auditorium by threatening to move the capital to Greensboro unless the Board erected a hall large enough to accommodate the State Democratic Convention. City officials quickly introduced a $125,000 bond issue, voters approved it, and a

Alexander Boyd Andrews (1841-1915) constructed five railroads in the state, served as president of five more lines, and completed the Western North Carolina Railroad. He was general agent of the receivers of the Richmond & Danville Railroad when the company went bankrupt in 1892. Andrews stayed with the firm after its reorganization as the Southern Railway Company. A Raleigh native, he refused the presidency of the Southern because the job required moving to Washington, D.C. Courtesy, North Carolina Collection, UNC Library

committee of Raleigh's leading citizens selected P. Thornton Marye of Atlanta to design the Municipal Auditorium. J.B. Carr & Company of Atlanta won the bid, dignitaries broke ground in March 1910, and Carr completed the building in October 1911. The auditorium was built from reinforced concrete and brick trimmed with limestone and terra cotta. In addition to a 5,000-seat main hall, it housed municipal offices, a jail, police headquarters, and a courtroom. A goodly portion of the Raleigh population turned out to attend the dedication ceremonies on the evening of October 17, 1911. The governor delivered an address, and city officials paid tribute to the committee that guided the project to completion and spoke glowingly of Raleigh's future. Edwin S. Folte christened the auditorium as a cultural center by conducting the Third Regimental Band in renditions of Offenbach's ''Overture,'' Manzia's ''Dance Caprice,'' and Emmett's ''National Airs.'' Wade R. Brown led the Raleigh Choral Society in the ''Hallelujah Chorus'' and Gaston's ''Carolina! Carolina!''

While the Raleigh population at large continued to make economic and cultural strides during the last decades of the 19th century, the black community suffered devastating reversals. More than 3,000 blacks left North Carolina in 1879 alone, and a decade later black leaders gathered in Raleigh in a futile attempt to slow another upsurge in black emigration. The extent of the black exodus is plainly revealed in school statistics. Black enrollment accounted for 63 percent of Raleigh public-school students in 1890, but only 43 percent in 1899 and 39 percent in 1901. Daily attendance also fell, from 60 percent in 1890 to 50 percent in 1899, as blacks came to realize the magnitude of the economic and social barriers they faced. Occupational statistics show that in 1896, 25

percent of working blacks were laborers and a staggering 63 percent held servile positions; by contrast, only 7 percent practiced trades and a sparse 2 percent were professionals. Of those professionals, two were editors, two doctors, four lawyers, 37 preachers, and 40 teachers. There was a corresponding falloff in black-owned businesses during the 1890s. Administrators at Shaw tried to alleviate the problem by placing a greater emphasis on teaching the trades.

The political power of blacks had also declined since Reconstruction days, although there were four black Representatives to Congress between 1875 and 1900 and 10 state legislators as late as the period 1895-1899. On the local level, at least one black alderman served in Raleigh throughout the 1880s; there were three in 1887 and five in 1888. But black political influence reached its post-Reconstruction peak in 1896 when a ''Fusion'' between the Populist party of the Farmers' Alliance and the Republicans gave blacks the swing vote that elected Republican Daniel L. Russell governor by a narrow plurality in a three-way race.

In Raleigh the black community was divided during the 1896 election. Wake legislator James H. Young supported Russell, but Dr. L.A. Scruggs, Dr. James E. Shepard, and lawyer Edward A. Johnson objected to Russell on the grounds that he had made racist statements. They organized the State Convention of Colored Republicans, which met in Raleigh on July 2, 1896, with the Reverend W.H.R. Leak as chairman and Shaw Professor L.B. Capehart as a platform committee member. The Convention endorsed Populist William A. Guthrie of Durham, an action that helped the Democrats carry Wake County but which had little effect on the statewide

In 1887 Colonel Fred A. Olds (1853-1935), with no financial backing whatsoever, founded the State Hall of History by donating his entire collection of historical relics and documents to the people of North Carolina. Raleigh's self-appointed tour guide, Olds was an inveterate walker; at age 75 he could still cover 12 miles a day, claiming that he could ''out-hike'' any Boy Scout in the city. ''Walking is nothing but putting one foot before the other,'' he told a reporter. (DAH)

outcome. When the Democrats recaptured the government, they drew up a suffrage amendment containing a "grandfather clause," which allowed the disenfranchisement of illiterate blacks while protecting the right to vote for illiterate whites. When voters approved the amendment 182,217 to 128,285 in the 1900 election, black political influence essentially vanished.

While changes were taking place in the participation of blacks in local government, the structure of city government itself was altered between 1891 and 1913. The legislature revised the charter in 1891, districting the city into five wards represented by 17 aldermen, extending their terms to two years, and allowing the mayor to vote only when the aldermen deadlocked. By 1905 the list of city officials had grown to include a full-time attorney, a chief of police, a treasurer, a street commissioner, a sanitation inspector, a chairman of the sinking fund commission, a board of equalization, and a board of audit and finance. In 1911 election officials introduced the direct primary, and in 1913 the General Assembly once again reordered city government by introducing a new commission system.

The look of the town was also undergoing dramatic changes, not all of them welcome. Since Burke and Caswell squares had long been lost as open areas, the citizens of Raleigh jealously guarded against losing Nash and Moore squares. When legislators moved to sell the plots in 1888, the Raleigh Street Committee firmly objected. A spokesman proclaimed: "The day is not far distant when they will be highly prized by our people, and they will not be willing to part with them for love or money," foreshadowing modern-day struggles between preservationists and developers, especially regarding Moore Square. Henry Steinmetz was contracted by the city to improve Nash Square and continue the work begun by horticulturalist A.B. Fairchild, but the park was used for recreation and leisure as much by livestock as by people. In 1887 R. Stanhope Pullen donated 60 acres for a public park with the provision that the land be returned if any investor offered to build a cotton factory valued at $50,000 on any portion. Fortunately for generations of Raleighites, no investor appeared. A streetcar line made it more accessible in the 1890s and Pullen Park remains today the splendid attraction it has been for decades.

In 1885 Fayetteville Street still remained an exclusive residential neighborhood as well as being the commercial center of town. Judge Daniel Fowle, later governor, lived in a fine, two-story house where the Sir Walter Hotel was later built. For years the house was remembered for the life-sized iron dogs that flanked the front steps. The family of widower Alfred Williams, whose wife was the widow of David Stone, occupied a house built in 1818 by Stone. Judge William H. Battle's English red-brick, Doric-columned mansion, with a large conservatory, occupied a lot covering an entire oak-lined block. Charlie Upchurch built a modern house, with a fountain in front and large stables in the rear, on property that extended all the way to Salisbury Street. There were scores of other fine houses in the older sections, but Raleigh was literally on the move.

In 1880 its population was second only to Wilmington's in North Carolina, and Raleigh was experiencing the problems of growing from a town to a city. The 1884 legislature enacted a

Automobiles had not yet dominated the traffic on the 200 block of South Wilmington Street when this photograph was taken in about 1903. (DAH)

stock law requiring owners to fence cattle and hogs, but opposition to the law was so strong that, in 1886, the unimaginable happened—the Republican ticket carried the county. Prices were increasing at such a rate that the white Institute for the Education of the Deaf, Dumb, and Blind moved to Morganton in 1891, after lengthy efforts by civic leaders and the principal to keep it in Raleigh. A riot at Central Prison in the mid-1880s also disturbed the peace of mind of Raleigh citizens, many of whom were severely critical of the prison director, the Reverend Frank Reid, who preferred prayer to force as a means of quelling the rioters.

In order to increase the tax base, the legislature in 1907 again extended the city limits one mile in each direction from Capitol Square—to Central Prison in the west, Bragg Street to the South, Tarboro Street to the east, and the Glenwood development to the north. The well-to-do were turning Glenwood into an area of elegant homes, and east of Glenwood the working class were building in Smokey Hollow, an area now devoted to industry and commerce.

By 1910 Raleigh had 19,218 residents, a streetcar system, 11 roads entering and leaving town, 20 miles of paved roads,

45 miles of unpaved streets, 55 miles of water mains, and 1,900 telephones. The lack of industrial development, however, had caused the city to drop to fifth statewide in population. Nevertheless, by 1907 the city had six cotton mills and 33 other manufacturing concerns. It was the state leader in printing and newspaper publishing, and the arrival of the headquarters of the Jefferson Standard Insurance Company in 1907 further entrenched it as a regional center of this relatively new industry.

A visitor spending the night in Raleigh around 1900 might have thought, from the early-morning sounds, that he was in a great metropolis. The Catholic Orphanage bell rang at five a.m.; the State Asylum laundry whistle sounded at six; the State Blind School whistle blew at six; the Central Prison bell tolled at 6:15, 6:30, and 6:45; the State College whistle blasted once at 7:55 and twice at eight, accompanied then by the bell of the Institute for the Education of the Deaf, Dumb, and Blind. Once up and around, the traveler would have realized his mistake, but he would have heard the bells and whistles periodically all day, sounding in unison at noon. He, no doubt, would have confessed relief when they ceased at six p.m., but he would still have had to endure the incessant train whistles.

The influence of Raleigh citizens on the rest of the state was moderate but significant. Colonel Fred A. Olds of Raleigh was almost solely responsible for establishing the State Hall of History in 1887, in which Olds himself soon became an "institution" by conducting thousands of tours for schoolchildren and by establishing himself as Raleigh's best-informed historian. Herbert Brimley's work in the State Museum continued to draw favorable attention to the city. In 1900 the Vance statue on Capitol Square was unveiled, and the Raleigh Post Office was the first in the state to receive a first-class rating.

During the 1890s Raleigh was also the scene of several widely attended events, some local in interest but others of larger significance. The Centennial Celebration was the most stupendous local event of 1892. Every whistle and bell in town sounded at seven a.m. on November 18 to begin the festivities. Colonel Jonathan M. Heck was the grand marshal of the biggest parade in the long history of grand parades in Raleigh. One hundred and eighty-seven marshals representing every occupation in the capital were distributed among the 13 major divisions in the mile-and-a-half string of floats, marching bands, and dignitaries. A float with Lafayette viewing Canova's statue of Washington won first prize. Miss Susie Tucker rode on another float dressed as the "Goddess of Peace," and the Raleigh Bicycle Club entertained with precision riding. During the evening ceremonies at Stronach's auditorium, Miss Minnie May Curtis won $25 for submitting the best poem on Raleigh, Captain C.B. Denson read the poem, and Dr. Kemp P. Battle delivered—for one hour and 40 minutes—a lecture on the history of early Raleigh. The next day a "Wild West" show and horse racing highlighted events at the Fair Grounds; and in the evening, celebrants attended dances throughout the city, including a Grand Centennial Ball in costume and wigs. A fireworks display at Moore Square entertained those with less elegant tastes.

The following May Raleigh was the scene of a solemn ceremony that aroused all the emotions attendant upon the "Glorious Lost Cause." At 1:10 p.m. on May 30, 1893, a train arrived transporting the body of Jefferson Davis, who had died in 1889, to a permanent burial site in Richmond. Mayor Thomas Badger and representatives for Governor Thomas M. Holt led a mounted honor guard to meet the train. Two of Davis' daughters declined an invitation to refresh themselves in the governor's mansion, preferring to visit the Yarborough House instead. The guard passed the casket through a window of the train and transported it ceremoniously to the capitol, which had been draped in black for the occasion. The body lay in state in the lobby on a catafalque banked with flowers and ornate wreaths. Old soldiers by the hundreds weepingly paid their respects; Confederate flags contributed a false sem-

Left: *Raleigh celebrated its centennial during the autumn of 1892. One of the events commemorating the city's 100th anniversary was a one-and-one-half-mile-long parade on October 18, part of which is shown here. (DAH)*

Right: *The remains of Jefferson Davis toured the South in 1893, enroute to final burial in Richmond. Raleighites turned out in scores to catch a glimpse of the coffin as it was drawn up Fayetteville Street on May 10. (DAH)*

Right: Nearly 20,000 people witnessed the unveiling of the Confederate monument on May 20, 1895. Granite for the statue was quarried in Mount Airy; the figures on the statue were modeled after Raleigh resident and Confederate veteran William R. Dicks. (DAH)

blance of jubilation; and over 5,000 people viewed the casket during its brief stay. The Davis daughters and the mayor of Richmond held a reception on the platform of their private car as preparations were being made to resume their northern journey. An estimated 1,000 people shook their hands, and many thousands witnessed their 3:40 p.m. departure.

In the early 1890s women of North Carolina formed the North Carolina Monument Association to push for the erection of a Confederate memorial on Capitol Square. Mrs. Armistead Jones headed the fund-raising drive, and chapters organized in every county of the state. In 1893 the legislature contributed $10,000, and the Association contracted with the Mulloon Monument Company of Louisville, Kentucky, to build a 72.5-foot monument for $25,000. The Association raised another $5,000 and laid the cornerstone facing Hillsborough Street on May 20, 1894. The General Assembly appropriated an additional $10,000 in 1895 to make final payments for the work.

Left: *Concerned that North Carolina should commemorate its Civil War dead, citizens formed the North Carolina Monument Association to secure funding to erect an appropriate statue on Union Square. Mrs. Armistead Jones, seated second from the left in this photograph of the organization's leaders, directed money-raising efforts for the project. (DAH)*

Right: *William Jennings Bryan (seated right and facing left), the Democratic party's nominee for President, was photographed on Fayetteville Street during his 1896 campaign visit to Raleigh. Over 15,000 people crowded Nash Square on September 17 to hear him speak on such topics as federal corruption and the coinage of gold and silver. (DAH)*

Left: *Ensign Worth Bagley, serving aboard the USS Winslow, was the first American naval officer to die in the Spanish-American War. A younger brother of Mrs. Josephus Daniels, he was buried in Oakwood Cemetery. The statue was erected on Union Square in 1908. (DAH)*

The Memorial Association held a grand reception on Sunday, May 19, 1895, preparatory to the Monday dedication of the monument, and some 20,000 visitors filled the railroad coaches arriving in Raleigh. Churches held special services in honor of the occasion, and Confederate veterans proudly prepared their uniforms and flags.

The Monday ceremonies began with the obligatory military parade, led by grand marshal O.J. Carroll. Mrs. "Stonewall" Jackson, the widow of General D.H. Hill, and General W.R. Cox were honorary guests. At the dedication, the Reverend Bennett Smedes opened with a prayer. Captain Samuel Ashe welcomed visitors and told them, "This monument we unveil bears witness that North Carolina, a generation after the Southern Confederacy faded away into the realms of the irrevocable past, cherishes a mother's pride in the valor of her Confederate sons and regards them as noble examples for the patriots of future ages." Colonel A.M. Waddell delivered an address to 150 dignitaries and veterans on the grandstand,

2,000 seated on the grounds, and 15,000 standing outside the iron fence that then surrounded Capitol Square. Eight-year-old Julia Jackson, granddaughter of "Stonewall" Jackson, unveiled the monument amid a sea of Confederate and Union flags. The next day the *News and Observer* carried an ode by a Professor Meares dedicated to Mrs. Armistead Jones in appreciation of her work on the project, noting that "Prof. Meares is as good a Rebel as ever lived, having lost three brothers in the Confederate war."

A few years later, a new war would distract the attention of Raleigh from the lost cause three decades old. After Congress declared war on Spain on April 25, 1898, the First North Carolina Regiment formed at Camp Bryan Grimes near Raleigh on May 2—this time to defend national rather than regional honor. Only nine days later, Ensign Worth Bagley, younger brother of Adelaide Worth Bagley Daniels, was killed aboard the USS *Winslow* at Cardenas Bay, Cuba. A statue on Capitol Square paid for by popular subscription now honors

Left: *President Theodore Roosevelt reviews the troops marching in a parade held in his honor during his visit to Raleigh in October 1905. (DAH)*

Right: *Richard B. and Olivia Cowper Raney were only married a year and a half when Mrs. Raney died in 1896. Mr. Raney constructed the Olivia Raney Library in her memory. It was completed in 1900 at the corner of Hillsborough and Salisbury streets. (DAH)*

Ensign Bagley—the first naval officer to die in the Spanish-American War. A less ennobling event occurred in Raleigh on October 20, 1898, more than two months after hostilities had ceased. Following payday, soldiers from Camp Bryan Grimes rioted on Fayetteville Street, shooting out streetlights and frightening civilians in general.

The most famous "alumnus" of the brief war paid a public visit to Raleigh on October 10, 1905. Theodore Roosevelt arrived via special railway coach, then made a trip up Fayetteville Street, escorted by a parade of Mexican War and Confederate veterans and a dozen National Guard companies. Colonel D.Y. Cooper gave every student at St. Mary's a flag to wave as the procession passed. The first President to visit Raleigh under Secret Service guard, Roosevelt delivered a prepared speech at the Fair Grounds in which he praised North Carolina, asked for support for his Appalachian preservation program, and called for further regulation of the railroads. While in Raleigh, he presented the Patterson Cup for the best literary work of the year by a North Carolinian to John

Charles McNeill, who had composed poems later published as *Songs Merry and Sad.*

Five years earlier the capital had finally received a library housing works of literature not only by its native sons but by authors from around the world, thanks in large part to Richard Raney. Richard B. Raney had moved from Granville County as a youth of 18 and taken a job as clerk at the Yarborough House. An industrious young man, he became manager in 1883. After prohibition, he started selling insurance, quickly becoming one of the leading agents in the state, accumulating wealth which he later added to by investments in a wagon factory, a cotton mill, a fertilizer factory, and banks. The insurance business brought him into contact with Pulaski Cowper, who had his own business and later became president of the North Carolina Fire Insurance Company, and Raney fell in love with and married Cowper's daughter Olivia. Olivia was greatly respected and active in the social and cultural life of Raleigh, and after her premature death, her husband decided to memorialize Olivia in a way that would most benefit the city that had treated him so well.

At the corner of Hillsborough and Salisbury, Raney built what the *Farmer and Mechanic* described at its completion in October 1900 as "the handsomest library building in the State, and the most complete and modern one in the South." The three-story Olivia Raney Library included a residence for the librarian, a reception room, and store areas to generate income on the first floor; stacks for 5,000 books, a reading room, a "smoking room for gentlemen, a reception room for ladies," and offices on the second floor; and a music hall on the third floor, also intended to generate money. Miss Jane Albott came from Lincoln, Nebraska, to set up the library. In view of the use Raleigh citizens have made of the Richard

Raney's gift through the years, the January 1901 report in the *News and Observer* is hardly an overstatement: "The opening of the Olivia Raney Library last night was the most notable event in the history of North Carolina in the early days of the Twentieth Century."

In the 30 years or so from the end of Reconstruction to the first decade of the 20th century, Raleigh had tried hard to assume a role in the industrial South. All things considered, it had failed, but not so completely that it would give up the effort in the prosperous years that lay ahead. As had been true so many times in the past, however, Raleigh had survived and continued to be important largely because of governmental activities, even when the General Assembly lacked the prescience to adequately provide for those activities.

In 1903 Governor Charles B. Aycock headed a commission including Wake Senator H.E. Norris and Wake Representative John C. Drewry to investigate the feasibility of modifying the capitol to accommodate the expanding state government. The plan they submitted to the legislature would have altered the capitol beyond recognition. It proposed constructing a new north wing, a new south wing, a new east wing, and raising the dome to conform with the new dimensions. The General Assembly refused to approve the $500,000 measure, a move that would come back to haunt the state and the capital many decades later when government had unquestionably outgrown the meager facilities of the aging capitol.

The Yarborough House continued to be the scene of many social events into the 20th century. A banquet held there in about 1900 attracted such notables as Wesley N. Jones (left, with napkin on knee) and S.W. Brewer (holding newspaper). (DAH)

Between 1910 and 1940 Raleigh learned that it could greatly benefit from and contribute to a rapidly expanding national economy; but it also discovered for the first time it could be unabridgedly fettered to that same economy when it contracted drastically. In the severe depression following 1837, the massive outlay of funds to build a new statehouse and the arrival of the first railroad had helped to maintain stability, even to bring moderate prosperity. The effects of the Panic of 1873 had been largely diluted by the many problems that abounded following military defeat. The city had bounced back quickly from the depression of 1893. But 1929 would be a different matter. Not even the presence of state government would be able to shore up the battlements against the ravages of the Great Depression.

VI

FROM PROSPERITY TO DEPRESSION:

1905 - 1940

In 1913 the state initiated a period of building expansion with the new State Administration Building, designed by Atlanta architect P. Thornton Marye, who had planned the Municipal Auditorium. In June of the same year, the city bought a lot on East Martin Street "to be used for the erection thereon by the City of Raleigh of a market." State University graduate James M. Kennedy designed the complex, which included an up-to-date refrigeration plant. The *News and Observer* expressed its redundant approval on September 9, 1914, upon the completion of a sanitary market in which "Dainty slippered lassies may trip into the new sanctum of the stockyard and the farm without hesitation and without reluctance." Wake County contributed to the building upsurge in a tried and true manner. Commissioners arranged for the reliable P. Thornton Marye, by now Raleigh's "staple" architect, to design a new courthouse, the fourth to occupy the same site. Assisted by Frank B. Simpson of Raleigh, Marye completed the building in 1915. (It stood until 1967, when it was razed to clear space for the fifth and latest Wake County Courthouse.)

In education, the old dream of Edward Moses materialized in 1905 when the school board approved implementation of a Raleigh High School. Hugh Morson accepted the principalship, thereby ending one tradition while beginning another. He closed the Male Academy, which had trained generations of Raleigh youth since 1802 when it had opened as the Raleigh Academy. When a second high school was built in the 1920s to relieve overcrowding, it was named the Hugh Morson School in recognition of Morson's achievements.

Another Raleighite recognized by the naming of an educational institution was Dr. Jane S. McKimmon. As a director of the Home Demonstration Office, Dr. McKimmon occupied offices in the old National Hotel in the prewar years. She eventually headed more than 75,000 North Carolina women members of Home Demonstration and 4-H clubs. She experimented with preserving vegetables in tin cans, and during the 1918 influenza epidemic, she supervised successful Demonstration Club efforts to care for the sick and to feed the hungry. Dr. McKimmon earned undying recognition as a humanitarian and as a scientist, a recognition recently demonstrated anew when the continuing-education complex at State University was named in her honor.

The private sector was still more active. Carolina Power & Light Company had taken over the streetcars in 1908 and gradually expanded the system to include 14 cars clamoring along 14 miles of track. They extended service into the growing number of Raleigh residential areas. The publishers of the *Biblical Recorder* erected new

Officials of Commercial National Bank must have watched the construction of Citizens' National Bank with some dismay. When it was completed in 1914, Citizens' took Commercial National's place as the tallest structure in the city. (DAH)

By *the second decade of the 20th century, Raleighites had come to embrace the automobile as a viable form of personal transportation. Salesmen and new cars await customers at Carolina Cadillac, circa 1916. (DAH)*

Below: *Lynne's Popcorn Wagon traveled the streets of Raleigh early in the 20th century, soothing the hunger pangs of city residents with fresh-roasted peanuts and hot, buttered popcorn. (DAH)*

Right: *The originator of home demonstration work in North Carolina, Dr. Jane Simpson McKimmon (1867-1957) was also the state's first home demonstration agent. She, in conjunction with Dr. I.O. Schaub of the North Carolina Agricultural Extension Service, developed a nationally acclaimed and widely copied program of instruction for rural homemakers. Courtesy, North Carolina State University Archives, Raleigh*

headquarters at 119-121 West Hargett Street in 1911. That same year, the ubiquitous Marye finished plans for the Commercial National Bank Building at South Wilmington and East Martin. When completed in 1913, the 10-story edifice was the tallest in Raleigh, but the Citizens National Bank on Fayetteville Street topped it by a story within a year. B.F. Montague, believing the business district was about to move southeast, built the three-story Montague Building at South Blount and East Hargett in 1912. But Fayetteville's reign as "downtown North Carolina" still had a period to run.

In 1907 the General Assembly extended Raleigh's borders once more, bringing the Mordecai house within the city limits. The multifarious neighborhoods that so distinguish the landscape of modern Raleigh began to proliferate in the early decades of the 20th century. The old Boylan plantation became Boylan Heights, and in 1910 the Parker-Hunter Realty Company earnestly began to develop Cameron Park. Opponents to unrestricted development organized and spoke out, but they had little effect. Mrs. Charles Mulford Robinson and fellow Women's Club members in 1913 fought to restrict outdoor advertising and to have power lines buried, believing "the electrical and advertising interests" were profiting by making "Raleigh streets ugly and unsafe." The automobile, as much as anything, would be responsible in the 1920s for the development of Hayes-Barton, Mordecai Place, Wilmont, Fairmont, Hillcrest, Anderson Heights, Whitaker Park, Country Club, and many more outlying residential areas.

But in the early years of the 20th century, automobiles were

The old Raleigh Market House, between Market Place and Exchange Street, housed Metropolitan Hall and city hall in its upper floors, while farm produce vendors hawked their wares on the first. The basement held the jail and the police headquarters. (DAH)

tions—and prices—attended special films. Sherman Upchurch booked *The Birth of a Nation* complete with live orchestral accompaniment into the Academy of Music at $2 per seat, selling all seats for the three days the film played. (A cotton corporation purchased the Academy in 1922 and turned it into offices, leaving the Municipal Auditorium with a near monopoly on concerts and other popularly attended events.) Most movie houses kept the admission price down to five cents, although proprietors raised it to 10 cents for special programs, such as *The Passion Play* at the Almo (the old Revelry) just prior to World War I.

Moviegoers in Raleigh, however, were soon to feel the

Above: American soldiers put a 30-ton British tank and two French Renaults through their armored paces at Camp Polk, near Hillsborough Street, in 1918. (DAH)

still something of a novelty. City officials enacted the first speed limit in 1907—six miles per hour. Drivers operating vehicles within the city were required to be licensed in 1913—a full 20 years before state licensing became mandatory. Mrs. Ashby Baker, daughter of R.S. Tucker, shocked many with her extravagance in 1912, when she paid $3,500 for a 42-unit, battery-driven automobile, capable of going 60 miles per recharge. (Mrs. Baker used the car until 1928, by which time it had become a familiar roving "landmark.") In 1919 the first drive-in service station catering to automobiles of the gasoline-consuming variety was opened at Fayetteville and Cabarrus by R.M. Allen.

Leisure time could be spent taking a ride in an automobile, either for its own sake or to reach sites of recreation. In the years leading up to World War I, more refined forms of entertainment began to compete with vaudeville and the movies in popularity. On February 13, 1914, Mme. Nellie Melba, billed as "The Greatest Singer of All Times," headed an operatic program at the Municipal Auditorium. Tickets were scaled from $1 to $3. On April 14, 1915, Walter Damrosch conducted the New York Symphony Society Orchestra in a performance in conjunction with the Festival Chorus, the Meredith College Choir, and the Wake Forest Glee Club. Enthusiasm ran so high that both afternoon and evening performances were offered.

But Raleigh continued to be a good investment market for movie-theater owners. The Hines brothers came from Roanoke, Virginia, to build a theater on West Martin Street, although the structure burned in 1914 when still relatively new. Also lost in the fire were the *News and Observer's* offices, composing rooms, and presses. Until about 1920 film programs usually changed daily, although favorites such as Sarah Bernhardt in *Queen Elizabeth* and the Civil War action drama *Blue and Grey* ran for extended engagements. Special prepara-

Below: Workers at Gill Iron Foundry pause for the camera before returning to the production of army shell casings. Before World War I, English civil engineer F.H. Gill established the foundry (at the corner of Davie and McDowell streets) to cast agricultural implements, machine parts, and building materials. (DAH)

This truckload of captured German helmets was parked in front of the post office to encourage the sale of "Victory Loan Bonds" to city residents. (DAH)

Soldiers of the 317th Ambulance Company find respite from war in a chapel at Vaux, France, in 1918. Attached to the 80th Division, the unit was formed and recruited mainly in Raleigh. (DAH)

effects of the accumulation of soldiers in training at Camp Polk. Admission prices would rise dramatically from five cents in the early months of 1917 to 40 cents by the end of 1918. When the United States declared war on the Central Powers on April 6, 1917, 60 of the residents of the Confederate Soldiers Home rushed to volunteer for active service. Their patriotic gesture was declined, but within two months 2,558 other Raleigh men had been accepted for duty. Raleigh citizens purchased more than their quota of Liberty Bonds, and several Raleigh women joined the medical corps as nurses. By May of 1918, 775 Raleigh and Wake County volunteers were on duty in France, and on May 30, 1918, Lieutenant T.

Harry Watson became the first Raleigh soldier with the American Expeditionary Forces to die overseas.

On the local scene, Camp Polk off the Hillsborough Road was used as a training ground for tank corps. Raleigh residents opened their homes to accommodate the thousands of soldiers who had layovers in town or who were in the vicinity for temporary training. Governor and Mrs. Thomas W. Bickett converted the second-floor ballroom of the governor's mansion into a makeshift barracks when traffic was at its heaviest in 1917. Raleigh ladies of the Red Cross met every single troop train with refreshments. They operated a bathhouse for weary soldiers in transit, and made hospital supplies whenever time

Raleigh's Red Cross members distributed food and reading material to soldiers passing through the city on their way to Europe's battlefields. Volunteers are pictured meeting a train at the railroad siding west of Nash Square. (DAH)

During the First World War thousands of soldiers passed through Raleigh on their way to unfamiliar European battlefields and uncertain fates. Many of them found a friendly face, a kind word, and other comforts of home at the lcoal Red Cross headquarters. (DAH)

allowed.

Before the end of the war, 1,657 Wake County men served in the Army, 352 in the Navy, and nine in the Marines; 12 women joined the Nurses Corps. Out of the more than 2,000 Wake citizens to serve in World War I, 893 were black.

Two months after the Armistice, Camp Polk was deactivated, but Raleighites reserved their greatest celebration for March 23, 1919. On that day more than 50,000 people came to the city, arriving by automobile, bus, carriage, wagon, or on foot, and filling every incoming train to capacity. For several blocks around Capitol Square, traffic was hopelessly stalled. The crowds became impatient, the excitement built, and

then, at seven in the evening, the multitude erupted into one prolonged shout as a train's whistle signaled the approach of what they had all been waiting for—the train pulling into the old Cabarrus Street depot carrying Raleigh native Colonel Albert L. Cox and the 113th Field Artillery. Cox's father, General William R. Cox, had ordered the last Southern volley fired at Appomatox in a losing cause. Colonel Cox and his regiment had led the break in the Hindenburg Line (enduring 85 percent casualities), which in September of 1918 had helped to turn an Allied stalemate into victory. The greeting for Cox and the 113th was the greatest celebration Raleigh had ever witnessed. All businesses were closed and all houses

On March 23, 1919, Colonel Albert Cox led the men of the 113th Field Artillery, American Expeditionary Force (AEF) down Fayetteville Street to the cheers of a crowd 75,000 strong. The unit was raised in the state and served with distinction in the St. Mihiel and Meuse-Argonne offensives during the war. (DAH)

Born in Raleigh, Albert L. Cox (1883-1965) was a hometown attorney until active duty took him to the Mexican border as captain of the Third North Carolina Infantry. As state National Guard colonel he organized the First North Carolina Field Artillery, retaining command when the unit became the 113th Field Artillery, AEF. Recipient of the Distinguished Service medal, he moved to Washington, D.C., in the 1930s, served as provost marshal of the capital during World War II, and retired from the Army National Guard as a major-general in 1949. He died in Goldsboro. (DAH)

been built in the city since 1920. Capital spent on construction had risen from $862,332 in 1920 to $4,653,124 in 1924. The city had six state banks and two national banks, three major hotels and three hospitals; it was host to 4,000 college students and 50 conventions in 1924; and it had 55 wholesale and jobbing firms.

The 1920s were marked by numerous large-scale projects—including the $750,000 Sir Walter Hotel in 1922; the $264,000 State Theatre, the $200,000 School for the Blind, the $336,000 Odd Fellows Building, and about one million dollars of additions at Meredith College, all in 1923; the $335,000 Agriculture Building in 1923; the $335,000 Professional Building in 1925; and the $614,000 Carolina Hotel, the $265,000 Raleigh Branch Banking and Trust Company offices, and the $280,000 Capital Club in the years 1928-1930. Income and spending also peaked in the late 1920s. In 1929 retail sales for Wake County were over $30 million; per-capita spending was $318.22.

Most of the expansion in Raleigh's labor force between 1910 and 1930 was in government. In 1909 only 1,249 of the 19,218 residents of Raleigh worked in manufacturing. Five years later, the number of workers had remained remarkably consistent at 1,255, but total wages had risen from $384,000 to $515,000, a 34 percent increase. In 1928 the Chamber of Commerce counted 1,397 Raleigh employees in manufacturing who were earning $1,638,892 during a year in which they turned out $6,215,229 worth of products.

The nonmanufacturing positions were, for the most part, in service areas or in construction. There were 33 law firms (not surprising in a political mecca), 19 automobile sales and/or service companies, eight banks, eight general building contractors, five accounting firms, 11 physicians, 10 department stores, and four advertising agencies.

were open; over 75,000 people lined Fayetteville Street; and a parade more than three miles long welcomed the returning heroes.

The end of the war ushered in a period of unparalleled prosperity for Raleighites. Raleigh's "grandson" Thomas Wolfe wrote the classic account of 1920s speculation and boom in a Southern city in *You Can't Go Home Again*, describing what he had observed in Asheville. The same fever hit Raleigh. City building inspector John Mangum later estimated that over $26 million had been spent between 1920 and 1931 on building businesses, hotels, churches, schools, homes, and offices. A 1925 Chamber of Commerce pamphlet, *Facts and Figures about Raleigh*, claimed that 2,645 new buildings had

Agriculture still thrived in Wake County and, during the 1920s, the Chamber of Commerce worked to establish a mutually profitable cooperation between Raleigh and the surrounding farming district. Gains in farming efficiency would increase sales and purchases in Raleigh and, consequently, income for all concerned. In 1930, 6,475 farms on 158,562 acres of cropland produced 20,000 bales of cotton, 20 million pounds of tobacco, a million bushels of corn, and approximately 200,000 bushels of grain, 400,000 bushels of potatoes, and 7,000 tons of hay. Large quantities of fruits and vegetables contributed further to the value of total farm production, as did 150,000 laying hens, 7,000 milk cows, and 10,000 hogs. Total farm income from the sale of produce for 1930 was estimated to be $6,883,622.

The prosperity of the 1920s also brought increased social activity to the capital. Downtown merchants had begun holding an annual Fall Festival around 1915. In the beginning it was little more than a back-to-school sales campaign during which businessmen sponsored social gatherings attended by guests invited from Raleigh and other North Carolina cities and towns. However, as the Fall Festival became more and more formal, its organizers began to be more selective in sending out invitations and more particular in planning the events. In 1920 Mrs. Adelaide Boylston was chosen chairman of the committee that arranged for the presentation of young girls from cities throughout the state. On the evening of September 27, Governor Cameron Morrison escorted the Queen of the Coronation Ball (Miss Mary Louise Everette, daughter of the secretary of state) to the dance floor and another Raleigh institution, the Debutantes Ball, was born.

The merchants and the Chamber of Commerce sponsored the Debutantes Ball for several more years; then they turned its management over to the young men of the Terpsichorean Club, formed especially for the occasions by socially acceptable young men of Raleigh, most of whom were undergraduates at State University. Sherwood "Possum" Jones was the first president of the Terpsichoreans, and Emily Storr and Annette Tucker, both of Raleigh, led the first ball held under the club's sponsorship. (After the Municipal Auditorium burned in 1930, the Ball moved to the Frank Thompson Gymnasium on the State University campus until the Memorial Auditorium offered more dignified accommodations.)

Although the Terpsichoreans intentionally limited the number of debutantes invited, the event grew over the years—from 30 debs in 1921 to about a hundred in 1928. (Elaborate private parties now accompany Ball Week, and all aspects of the Ball stretch over a period of months.) The Terpsichorean Club had been preceded by the Capital Club for social-minded men of the area. Other clubs of social prominence included the Circle and the Nine O'Clock Cotillion. These clubs, and the genteel set of Raleigh in general, had as their central location the 300 to 500 blocks of Blount Street. Since 1900 Raleigh had revolved around this area of the city, because it was home to Colonel A.B. Andrews of the Southern Railroad, several state leaders, successful businessmen, and some of the well-established families of the city. (Blount Street would retain its social distinction until the World

Lassiter's Mill, named for 1908 owner Cornelius Jesse Lassiter, occupied a site favored by mill operators since the 1760s. N.C. State's civil engineering class of 1921 was photographed near the building during a field trip to Crabtree Creek. Fire destroyed the mill in 1958. (DAH)

War II years.)

A new social center of "official" Raleigh also emerged during this period when, in 1923, General Albert Cox and Josephus Daniels formed the Capital Construction Company and began work on the Sir Walter Hotel. When it was near completion, the owner of the Yarborough House, B.H. Griffin, bought in as a partner for $100,000. Griffin and Alton Bland, Sr., comanaged the new hotel and it was an immediate success. In 1925 more than three-fourths of the legislators stayed there while in Raleigh. The Yarborough House, which the Sir Walter replaced as the most important hotel and gathering place, was unfortunately lost in a fire on July 3, 1928. It had been the home of three active governors and a large contingent of legislators, having served as the General Assembly's "third house" for over 70 years.

Only two years earlier, fire had also destroyed part of a Raleigh landmark dating back to the 1850s. On April 10, 1926, Raleigh and Durham fire fighters rushed to Dix Hill to control flames in the west wing of the State Hospital for the Insane. Captain Sprague Silver supervised National Guard troops and State University ROTC students, who guarded more than a thousand patients—some of whom were criminally insane—who had vacated the building without injury. The "fire" of progress claimed the old National Hotel, when state authorities decided to tear it down to make way for new Agriculture Department offices. Concerned citizens organized to protect the former Confederate headquarters and hospital, but they failed to deter the General Assembly, which appropriated $425,000 for the project. C. Murry Nelson and Thomas Wright Cooper of Raleigh designed the Agriculture Building, completed in 1923. A new Department of Revenue building followed in 1927 at Salisbury and Morgan. Architect Philip Schwartz directed a $102,000 renovation and restoration of the capitol in 1923-1925. He built new bathrooms and new steps, repaired internal decorations, and replaced deteriorated materials. In 1928 the federal government donated $16,000 and the state added $15,000 to beautify the grounds. Workmen landscaped the area, added grass plots and walkways, and built Memorial Mall—now flanked by the statues of Charles Brantley Aycock and Governor Vance, and inhabited by a flock of pigeons whose welfare is attended to daily, in all seasons, by purveyors of peanuts and popcorn.

The 1920s also brought changes in local government. The General Assembly extended the city limits in 1920 and again

Above: *The Municipal Building and City Auditorium on Davie Street was constructed in 1910 after the North Carolina legislature threatened to move the state capital to Greensboro because Raleigh had no convention facilities. (DAH)*

Right: *The Yarborough House, a Raleigh landmark since 1852, burned on July 3, 1928. Ben Dixon MacNeill captured the conflagration in this photograph he took from the sixth floor of the Hotel Sir Walter. Courtesy, North Carolina Collection, UNC Library*

A cotton broker inspects a client's crop in front of the Commercial National Bank building, 14 East Martin Street, about 1913. Wagons like this were a common sight in the city at harvest time. (DAH)

Below: *Loomis MacGoodwin of Raleigh invented the mechanical, self-propelled cotton picker, built by Dillon Supply Company around 1919. (DAH)*

in 1923, each time infuriating at least some of the new residents, as in earlier annexations. The 1923 bill expanding the city limits also set annual salaries for city officials: $4,500 for the mayor; $4,200 for commissioners; $3,300 for the city court judge; and $1,800 for the prosecuting attorney.

Durham, Greensboro, High Point, Charlotte, and other cities in the Piedmont Crescent tended to grow sporadically, as investment in industry and commerce surged and waned. The state government's influence on the local economy was sufficient to keep Raleigh's growth slow but steady. Population in 1920 stood at 24,416—a 27 percent increase over the last census. On paper the 53 percent increase to 37,379 in 1930 looks dramatic, but, in fact, the two extensions of the city limits were largely responsible, and real growth was due chiefly to increases in state and federal government administrative offices. Another boon to slow but steady growth came in 1921, when the General Assembly granted zoning power to Asheville, Wilmington, and Raleigh. Mayor T.B. Eldridge was pleased with the new authority because he believed the city had started to expand in "crazy-quilt patches that have been stuck on the sides and hung on the corners of the original city plan, without thought of the effect on the future city." Mayor Eldridge wanted, above all, to protect established residential sections. (The Depression would do what ordinances failed to do, and post-World War II prosperity would bring the return of rapid development.)

Education, too, made gains during the decade, although it would also be beset by controversies. Administrators had been plagued by chronic underfunding until the early 1920s. Mayor T.B. Eldridge dramatically brought the issue to public attention on March 12, 1920, when he came out against a $200,000 school bond issue. He declared that a minimum of $1.5 million was urgently needed to overhaul a deplorably overcrowded and dilapidated system, and he argued that $200,000 would only allow for the maintenance of an unacceptable status quo. The next day E.L. Harris of the Raleigh Township School Board answered the mayor, arguing that the university records of former Raleigh students validated the past performance of Raleigh schools, that the work done was more important than the building in which it occurred, that the people and not the mayor or the board should decide the issue, and that the mayor's proposal was impractical, negative, and impossible under the present tax ordinances.

Harris' argument carried the day and major action was delayed, although not for long. On April 4, 1922, voters approved a one-million-dollar bond issue that allowed the superintendent to build four new elementary schools, to begin the Hugh Morson High School, and to renovate other schools. In 1926 another $1.3 million issue provided funds to complete projects in progress, to build one elementary school for black students and three for whites, and to build the Needham

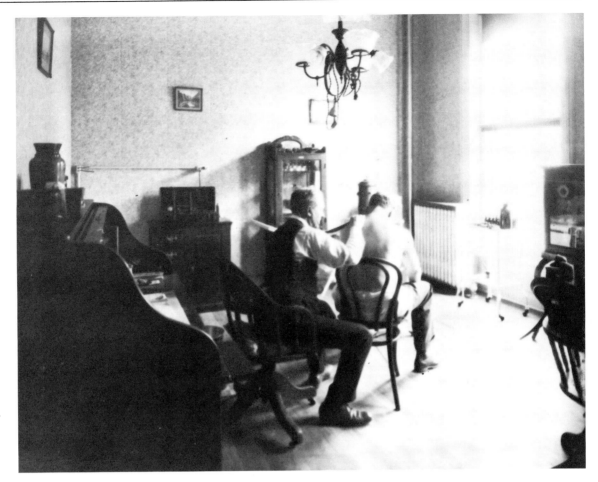

Dr. William C. Horton examines an unidentified patient in his office at 307 Fayetteville Street circa 1925. (DAH)

Below: In 1926 Meredith College classes were moved from the original building at the corner of Blount and Edenton streets to a new campus at 3800 Hillsborough. Johnson Hall, the administration building, is shown here. (DAH)

Broughton High School. Physically and fiscally, Raleigh public schools were finally on a sound foundation.

In the private sector, Hardbarger's Business College entered competition in 1924 with King's Business College, which had been founded in 1901; and, in 1936, the Sacred Heart Cathedral School opened for students in grades one through eight. The Reverend M.L. Lotta enjoyed less success. Born on Duncan Cameron's old plantation on the Neuse River, Lotta had experienced harsh treatment as a youth under white overseers and harsher treatment yet under black overseers. He earned a teacher's degree from Shaw University, and in the years before World War I he had attempted to found Lotta University "to solve the race problem." Lotta did not begin on a shoestring budget: he obtained 276 acres and built several wooden buildings. But he never attracted more than 30 students at one time—boys paid $6.50 per month tuition and girls $5. In the end, all Lotta's land and property had to be sold in the 1920s when banks foreclosed.

But funding problems took a back seat between 1920 and 1927, when a great battle raged in North Carolina over the teaching of evolution in public schools and state-supported colleges and universities. *News and Observer* columnist Nell Battle Lewis became one of the foremost defenders of Darwinism, and the Raleigh journalist played a leading role in the eventual acceptance of texts that explained evolutionary theory. Except for Lewis' column, the *News and Observer* supported the fundamentalist point of view, even carrying vehement attacks on Darwin in regular columns written by William Jennings Bryan. Lewis accused evangelists such as Mordecai Ham and Billy Sunday of distorting "the Gospel of Jesus" to the extent that they actually uttered blasphemies in their determined attempts to persuade audiences.

As the fundamentalists intensified their emotion and language, Lewis turned to equally bitter diction. She described the leading evangelists as "barnstormers" and their tactics as "thoroughly contemptible." When Governor Cameron Morrison rejected two biology textbooks in 1924 for presenting the theory of evolution, she called his act an "executive decree extraordinaire by which science has been put in its place in North Carolina." When David Scott Pode, a Raeford legislator, introduced a "Monkey Bill" in January 1925 banning the teaching of evolution, Lewis called the bill "utterly uncivilized." Her consistent rallying of support among citizens,

One of the heaviest snowstorms recorded in North Carolina occurred in March 1927. Although the vicinity of Union Square looked charming in its blanket of white, elsewhere the city was littered with felled trees, poles, and power lines. (DAH)

educators, and public officials made her a key factor in leading her side to ultimate victory.

Other social issues facing Raleigh and attracting Lewis' attention were equally complex. *News and Observer* publisher Josephus Daniels frequently admitted to being guided by a pronounced disposition toward puritanical, even prudish, concepts. But he was also a good newspaperman, and his instinctive recognition of an excellent journalist caused him to give Nell Battle Lewis complete freedom to write what she pleased,

A graduate of St. Mary's School and Smith College (where she was Phi Beta Kappa), Nell Battle Lewis volunteered for the YMCA Canteen Service at age 19, serving on French battlefields with the AEF during World War I. Returning to Raleigh, she championed social causes, was licensed to practice law in 1929, wrote the column "Incidentally" in the News and Observer for 26 years, and in 1948 became associate editor of The Raleigh Times. She died in 1956. (DAH)

even when (as in the case of evolutionary teaching) her views diametrically opposed *News and Observer* policy. In her column "Incidently," Lewis urged citizens of Raleigh and North Carolina to apply and to accept serious criticism of themselves and their area. However, when she accused North Carolinians of "bloated self-glorification," "artistic barrenness," and "intellectual inertia," she did not always reap universally favorable response from an appreciative audience.

As ascerbic as her remarks sometimes were, Lewis realized that Raleigh's provincialism was not entirely negative. She once observed that: "In spite of census figures and papers of incorporation, the difference between a town and a city is largely a matter of atmosphere. With a city one usually associates an air of sophistication, a complex social life, relationships superficial and formal, busyness and bustle. Raleigh, North Carolina is a town."

Noting that Raleigh had never had a grand opera and that it did not currently have a concert series, being content with road shows and women's literary clubs, Lewis stated, "Indeed, the arts do not trouble Raleigh unduly." But she also noted approvingly that "Raleigh flatly refuses to be peppy" in an unrelenting search for industry. She realized that Sinclair Lewis might have found Babbitts and booster clubs aplenty in Raleigh, but she also believed he would miss much if he confined his search to those elements of society alone. "For good or ill," she wrote, "Raleigh insists on being herself." The same, in retrospect, could be said about Nell Battle Lewis.

Right: WPTF's first truck with a remote radio transmitter was photographed around 1930 at the north entrance of the capitol. The radio station's call letters stand for "We Protect The Family"—appropriate because its parent firm was and is an insurance company. Courtesy, North Carolina Collection, UNC Library

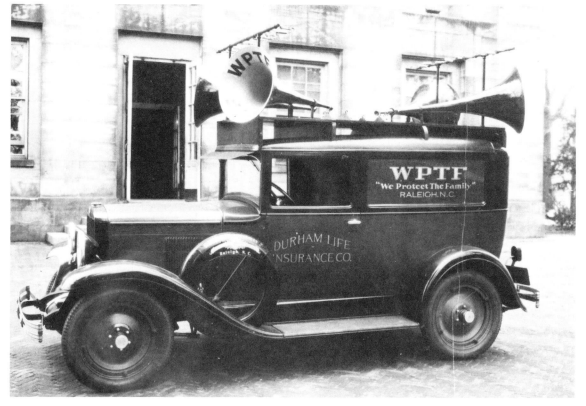

Below: Three WPTF employees—(from left to right) Andrew Massey, Willard Dean, and Henry Hulick—were photographed on October 7, 1932, carrying the radio station's homemade portable VHF transmitter. Courtesy, North Carolina Collection, UNC Library

William Avera Wynne (left, 1896-1951) operated the city's first telephone exchange and its first radio station, built and owned Raleigh's first truck, was the first North Carolinian to play on a major league baseball team, and opened, in 1922, the oldest exclusive radio dealership in the state. Wynne was also a champion trick rider (on bicycle); he tried to ride down the steps inside the Washington Monument in Washington, D.C., but guards stopped him and his friends before they finished assembling the dismantled bicycle that they had smuggled inside. (DAH)

During a period when science, in the form of evolution, was encountering determined resistance, other innovations were received with enthusiasm. Raleigh enjoyed a significant first in 1922 when Captain Chandler Cox, assistant professor of electrical engineering, supervised the installation of a broadcast transmitter at State University. He and his students were thrilled when their first test broadcast was picked up as far away as Wilmington by a State alumnus. Local Baptist ministers were preparing to conduct a revival, and they asked Captain Cox to inaugurate his system by broadcasting the sermons of Dr. George W. Truett, who had come from Dallas, Texas, to lead the services. Will A. Wynne provided a telephone-line linkup between the church and State University, and the first radio program broadcast in North Carolina went on the air in the first week of March.

Cox and his students hoped to make the operation permanent during the fall semester, and they licensed their experimental station WLAC. On October 16, 1922, they invited several distinguished speakers to initiate regular service: Governor Cameron Morrison, Josephus Daniels, Highway

Commissioner Frank Page, Mayor T.B. Eldridge, State Superintendent of Public Instruction Eugene Clyde Brooks, and Edith S. Vanderbilt, president of the North Carolina State Agriculture Society and director of the State Fair.

WLAC stayed on the air until it was forced to shut down in 1925 due to a shortage of funds. But one year later Will Wynne had formed the Wynne Radio Company of Raleigh and begun broadcasting on 50-watt WFBQ. Later in the year, Wynne changed his call letters to WRCO (standing for the Wynne Radio Company). He moved from the C.R. Boone Building to improved facilities in the Sir Walter Hotel and raised his power to 100 watts in 1926. The next year he boosted his power again and gained a license to broadcast beyond sunset. In 1927 Durham Life purchased the station and changed the call letters to WPTF. (WPTF moved to the now-familiar 680 in 1929, and in 1933 incorporated as the WPTF Radio Corporation, grew to 5,000 watts, and moved to Cary.)

The airplane also enjoyed widespread acceptance in the post-World War I era. Raleigh had been introduced to the "flying machine" on November 16, 1910, when I.A.D. McCurdy flew an airplane into the capital, setting it down on the old downtown Fair Grounds. Local enthusiasm for the airplane grew and, in 1920, Captain D.H. Robertson (who had flown for the British Royal Air Service) opened a flight-training school. However, area pilots remained restricted to pastures and ballfields until 1929, when Truman and Marie

Miller opened the Raleigh Municipal Airport south of town. The Millers ran it for the Curtiss Wright Flying Service until 1933. In 1931 Raleigh became an airmail stop on the New York-Miami run, and in 1933 the city took over the field. (The Millers purchased the property in 1944 and maintained the airport until they sold the 256-acre facility to developer Donald K. Appleton in 1972.)

The number of movie houses steadily increased during the "Golden Age of Cinema." The new State was in operation when the Almo burned in 1925; the Palace in 1926 preceded the destruction by fire of the Grand in 1928; and in 1933 the Capitol and the Wake intensified downtown competition. The Carolina Coach Company set up headquarters in Raleigh during the 1920s, as buses began to break the railroad's

Top: *The Ambassador Theater opened around 1936 at 115 Fayetteville Street. It closed after more than 30 years of entertaining Raleigh-area residents. (DAH)*

Left: *The facilities at Raleigh Municipal Airport were dedicated October 5, 1934. Fifty-three planes and 100 government and aviation officials and pilots—including Captain Eddie Rickenbacker and Pan American Airways Vice President R.G. Thach—turned out for the occasion. (DAH)*

Right: Sherwood Battle Brockwell (1885-1953) became the chief of Raleigh's fire department in 1911, and a year later organized the city's first full-time fire fighting unit. In 1913 he became North Carolina's first fire marshall, and he established the first statewide firemen's training program in the country. (DAH)

Top: Raleigh relied on volunteer fire fighters until 1912, when the city hired full-time companies. This is the crew of Station Number One, perched on the roof above a horse-drawn hook and ladder. Some of them are wearing scaling equipment around their waists. (DAH)

Right: The crew of Station Number Three pose at the corner of Hargett and Blount streets, with hook and ladder, circa 1913. Firemen present for the picture are (left to right) C.F. Gaston, Luther Thomason, Earnest Holland, Eugene Jones (standing), Henry Parrish, and Mathews Baker (driver). (DAH)

Berry O'Kelly (1860-1931), businessman and educator, founded the Berry O'Kelly Training School. He was a realtor, an insurance executive, and a board chairman and vice-president of the city branch of the Mechanics and Farmers Bank. O'Kelly was also a founding member of the National Negro Business League. (DAH)

monopoly on long-distance travel. As elsewhere in the nation, the bus increasingly became the accepted form of intercity transportation at least until the post-World War II automobile boom.

The Stock Market Crash of 1929 and the Great Depression that plagued America during the 1930s brought a halt to Raleigh's prosperity. Building slowed abruptly when the Great Depression hit. The $3,864,573 spent in 1928 fell to $1,938,516 in 1929 and to $969,307 in 1930. After the Capital Club, no major commercial structure rose in the city until the Durham Life Building in 1942.

No industry suffered more in the short term during the 1930s in Raleigh than banking. In 1920 there were eight locally owned and operated banks in the city. By September of 1927 only two of the people working in those banks were still active in banking in the capital, and all the banks had either closed or been absorbed. Wachovia purchased Merchants National in 1923. North Carolina Bank and Trust Company absorbed the Citizens National Bank of Raleigh in 1929 and the Raleigh Savings Bank and Trust Company in 1932, but the new Raleigh branch lasted only until 1937. First Citizens took over the Wake County Savings Bank on December 29, 1934, and moved into the old Commercial Bank Building, retaining W.W. Vass as a vice-president and William P. Little as a cashier. The others, including the old National Bank (which had become the Raleigh Bank and Trust Company) and some newer entries in the field, simply failed. At the end of 1937, five banks were operating in Raleigh, including the Mechanics and Farmers Bank. Founded in 1923 by Calvin Lightner and Berry O'Kelly, Mechanics and Farmers was the only black-owned bank in town and the only local bank to survive the Great Depression.

By 1933 retail sales had fallen to less than $17.5 million and per-capita spending to $184. In the very depths of the Depression, Louis M. Wade and others formed the Raleigh Junior Chamber of Commerce to fight back. The struggle was

long, but by 1939 recovery was complete. In Raleigh alone, per-capita spending in 619 retail outlets reached $547, well above the peak 1929 figure.

Although manufacturing, too, would decline, industrial ventures did not cease entirely during the 1930s. The Aeroglide Corporation, now at 7100 Hillsborough Road, began in 1928, weathered the lean years, and currently makes grain driers, process machinery, charcoal-briquet production equipment, fruit-and-vegetable handling equipment, and other products. The National School and Industry Corporation on Glenwood Avenue went into production in 1936, a particularly chancy year. (It now concentrates on manufacturing bank alarms, burglar and fire alarms, audiovisual equipment, and institutional drapes.)

As if to symbolize the onslaught of the Depression, Raleigh lost a cherished institution in 1930. Although it had stood for less than two decades, the Municipal Auditorium had long been the center of entertainment and political activity. The leading attractions of the period were routine fare: Will Rogers, Paderewski, John Philip Sousa, Galli-Curci. The political giants of the age, including Theodore Roosevelt, William Howard Taft, and William Jennings Bryan, had also appeared there before capacity crowds. In 1928 Al Smith attended a rally at the Auditorium, but not exactly by choice. After bands from Carolina, Duke, and State universities had welcomed Smith when he arrived on a campaign tour, enthusiastic supporters escorted him to the Auditorium stage and introduced him to an expectant audience before he could protest that he had not prepared a speech. Smith compensated for any disappointment by donning a State freshman's cap, signing autographs, and exhibiting thorough pleasure over his rambunctious reception.

On the evening of October 24, 1930, however, the Municipal Auditorium ceased forever to be a stage or a forum. During the Negro State Fair Marshal's Ball, flames raced through the hall. Prisoners were removed from the jail in the adjoining municipal portion of the structure, which fire fighters managed to save, but the Municipal Auditorium was damaged beyond repair. Without hesitation, city officials moved to replace the lost facility, and within two years the York Construction Company had built Memorial Auditorium on the grounds previously occupied by the "Palace" and Centennial School. Dedicated to the war dead of Raleigh, Memorial Auditorium contained facilities capable of providing meals for 1,800 diners and seating for 3,067 spectators, with room for a thousand more temporary seats. Memorial Auditorium ably replaced the Municipal Auditorium and, for decades, it has been the scene of the governor's inauguration, the annual Debutantes Ball, concerts, theatrical performances, and a host of other functions.

About the only other significant construction activity during the years of the Great Depression involved federally assisted Works Progress Administration projects. In 1938 alone, WPA funds provided 45 percent and state revenues 55 percent of the $5,271,416 alloted for contruction and renovation in the vicinity, with $1.4 million going to State University for five new dormitories, a new chemistry and textile building, new dairy barns, and other building and repair work. The city water department received $700,000, and the Wake County School System got $250,000. But the largest single outlay was for the new Justice Building.

To prepare a site for the Justice Building, the state bought the property at Fayetteville and Morgan containing a brick structure built on the site of the old Casso's Inn. George W. Mordecai and Gavin Hogg had purchased the property in the 1830s. Hogg's deed had passed down through his family and the Mordecai family had also retained ownership of its portion. The state paid $175,000 for the property and spent an

Top: *The Superba Theater, 222 Fayetteville Street, was in the City Bank building. Motion picture advertisements were placed in the corridors on either side of the bank entrance.* (DAH)

Above: *The Justice building, at Morgan and Fayetteville, was dedicated in the autumn of 1940. It was built at a total cost of $698,564.77, the largest outlay of WPA and state funds for a city building during the Great Depression in North Carolina.* (DAH)

Top: *The Municipal Building and City Auditorium burned on the night of October 24, 1930, during the Negro State Fair Marshall's Ball. Raleigh firemen saved the city offices, but the auditorium was completely destroyed.* (DAH)

Above: *Named to honor the city's war dead, the Raleigh Memorial Auditorium, completed in 1932, was built to replace the City Auditorium on Davie Street that had burned two years earlier.* (DAH)

additional $523,564.77 destroying the old structure known for many years as the Branson House and erecting the new Justice Building, which Governor Clyde R. Hoey dedicated on September 4, 1940.

Although the facilities of the Rex Hospital on Salisbury Street were never totally adequate, trustees continued there until government funds made the construction of new facilities possible. On November 15, 1935, the cornerstone was laid for a new WPA-assisted $250,000 building on St. Mary's Street. While the building was under construction, women active in welfare work had formed the Rex Guild in 1936 to assist patients financially, physically, and emotionally.

Presidential candidate Al Smith (seated, far left) ate dinner with Governor O. Max Gardner (seated, third from the right) at the Executive Mansion during Smith's campaign trip to Raleigh in September 1928. (DAH)

Below: *Humorist Will Rogers began his visit to Raleigh by meeting Mrs. Josephus Daniels (second from right) and friends at the airport on October 28, 1932. (DAH)*

When the 174-bed unit was completed a year and a half later, all patients were moved from the old to the new hospital in a single day—May 30, 1937. Dr. Annie Louise Wilkerson, a Raleigh native, became the first female intern at Rex in the summer of 1938. Trustees sold the abandoned property to Wake County and used the money to help finance the $135,000 Daniels Nurses Home at the new hospital, named after Addie Worth Daniels, wife of *News and Observer* editor and owner Josephus Daniels.

(Rex Hospital would continue as a revered fixture in the community, but even the St. Mary's Street installation proved insufficient amid the post-World War II population explosion. In the 1970s, after much searching, trustees and governmental officials finally selected 4420 Lake Boone Trail as the site of the ultramodern, $41-million new Rex Hospital dedicated on September 21, 1980. The massive complex has over 1,400 rooms—386 for patients, seven floors of patient beds, 11 operating rooms, $3.2 million in equipment, and even a multichanneled, in-house television system, WREX. Once again all patients were transferred from the old to the new in a single day, but this time the move required the assistance of the National Guard, 15 area Emergency Medical Services ambulances, and all the Wake County school system's wheelchair buses.)

WPA funds also helped pay for Devereux Meadow Stadium in 1939, named for the Devereux family of Raleigh. The

stadium was the home of Raleigh's professional baseball teams. (When the last team folded in 1971, the stands were demolished to make way for the Raleigh Public Works Department headquarters, which now occupies the site.)

During the Depression years, Raleighites converted some of their WPA funds to artistic uses. Local directors in 1935 selected a gallery at 413 Fayetteville Street, located between a hotel and a Chinese laundry, to house the Raleigh Art Center. Hoping to present art to a wider audience, to stimulate artistic activity, and to educate children, the managers held nine exhibits during the six months of the program. Six federally paid employees hung the shows, delivered lectures, conducted

Raleigh's rising population and increasing crime rate kept the small police force busy. Elizabeth Waugh wrote in the August 11, 1974, News and Observer *that "until 1916 the officer worked a 12-hour shift seven days a week for $80 a month. Rookies got $60. And each of those seven days in the week he pounded out 10 to 12 miles in the course of his beat carrying a night stick, a heavy Smith and Wesson .32 or .38 and several pounds of gun belt, uniform and shoes." (DAH)*

tours, and held classes. After an average of 3,266 people per month had viewed the paintings and participated in the variety of activities, the directors considered the Raleigh Art Center a great success.

Following two earlier failures, Sadie Root, Sallie Lynn Wilder, Jimmie Thompson, and others tried in 1936 to bring the Raleigh Little Theatre back to life, this time with success. Eager to assist, Professor Frederick H. Koch brought some of the Playmakers from Chapel Hill to advise, instruct, and perform for those attending the organizational meeting. The Little Theatre went into production that year with *The Drunkard; or the Fallen Saved* and *Coquette,* the latter a murder-melodrama written in 1928 by Ann Preston Bridges of Raleigh. The group performed in several auditoriums before settling into the "Workshop" on the third floor of the Briggs Hardware Building. Meanwhile, they were preparing a 40-foot by 66-foot stage at the 2,500-seat Amphitheater located inside the racetrack at the old Fair Grounds.

During their formative months, Little Theatre members concentrated on opera, performing such difficult fare as *Cavalleria Rusticana, Tales of Hoffman, Il Trovatore, Faust,* and—for the initial operatic performance in the Ampitheater—*Martha.*

Money from the Federal Theatre Project paid the salaries for a director, an assistant director, stagehands, and a seamstress until July of 1939. Anticipating an end to those funds and seeking local revenue to increase WPA matching funds for a building of their own, in 1938 Little Theatre members and supporters began selling pasteboard bricks at one dollar each and soliciting donations. But in March 1940, their new facilities nearing completion, they ran out of money. They were saved, in an appropriately dramatic fashion, on March 25, when President Roosevelt personally approved a WPA allotment of $22,571 to complete construction and landscaping. When it was dedicated on September 12, 1940, the Raleigh Little Theatre had cost $118,000—of which approximately $31,000 had been raised and contributed by local sponsors.

Music Professor Lamar Stringfield began an institution in 1931 that would later become the most prestigious of the musical groups in Raleigh—and, indeed, the state. A dozen music students gathered under Stringfield's baton one evening as guests in the Chapel Hill home of Mrs. Johnsie Burnham. Forty-six years later, Mrs. Burnham could still vividly remember "all of them fiddling and tootling away and sounding as if all the evil spirits in hell had been turned loose. But at least they had sense enough to know it was bad. That was the beginning." Soon about 30 members were traveling to Raleigh, Durham, Winston-Salem, and other North Carolina cities to give concerts, and in 1932 the General Assembly became the first state legislature to enact a bill creating a state-supported symphony orchestra, the North Carolina Symphony Society, which has grown into the Raleigh-based North Carolina Symphony. It has played in New York, Washington,

Nursery school-aged children play at a Chavis Heights playground around 1941 (above). Before the 1940s, Raleigh's predominantly black Chavis Heights area was notorious for its substandard housing (left). (DAH)

D.C., and other large cities, and it has reaped critical acclaim near and far.

As in the past, however, and as in most other cities, some citizens in Raleigh insisted on pursuing pleasures that were unacceptable to their neighbors. Those pleasures periodically aroused efforts to "clean up" the city. Gambling is a case in point. The *News and Observer* frequently printed editorials on the matter, and T.K. Fountain based his 1939 campaign for reelection as Commissioner of Public Safety squarely on the gambling issue.

Fountain "conservatively" claimed in a handout that the per annum amount gambled in Raleigh in 1936 was at least $720,000. He put the figure in perspective. At prevailing prices, he claimed, $720,000 would pay for 250,000 visits to a doctor, 6,666 uncomplicated births, 3,333 appendectomies, 10,000 tonsillectomies, 100,000 days in a private hospital room, 14,286 weeks of private nursing care, or one million bottles of medicine. The $720,000 could also have purchased 63,330 tons of coal, "666,666 pairs of excellent hose for women," the services of 10,000 lawyers, "2,777,777 quarts of milk for hungry babies," 500 new or 1,500 used cars; and it would have been enough to pay for "Burying 2,500 people with exceptionally nice funerals."

Fountain credited himself, the police chief, and the city court prosecutor for reducing and keeping the level of gambling low, but he called for private citizens to join the battle: "GET BUSY, BUSINESS PEOPLE . . . let us be assured that

The first American ship to bear the name "Raleigh," this 131-foot three-masted frigate raided commercial British ships until the Royal Navy captured it off the coast of Maine in 1778. The (newly British) Raleigh was decommissioned at Portsmouth, England, in 1781. (DAH)

The cruiser USS Raleigh, was assigned to Admiral Dewey's Asiatic Fleet during the Spanish-American War. The ship— with its escort, the USS Baltimore—forced the surrender of the fortifications at the entrance of Manila Bay on May 1, 1898. (DAH)

According to Bill Womble, the motor lighter Raleigh was not "apparently" the property of the United States Navy. However, the U.S. government did use it as a fuel transport around Hong Kong. (DAH)

The third USS Raleigh (night cruiser) was hit twice during the Japanese attack on Pearl Harbor on December 7, 1941. None of the crew was killed, and the ship's antiaircraft gunners shot down five airplanes. The USS Raleigh went on to win three battle stars in the Pacific theater during World War II. (DAH)

this annual gambling amount will be spent for food and clothes for hungry women and children, and that it not go again into the hands of the gamblers." But, alas, when Josephus Daniels returned from Mexico, enough gamblers still remained active to spur him into a new editorial campaign to eradicate the evil.

The 20th century had been relatively peaceful and harmonious in terms of race relations. One attempt at reviving interest in the Klan in 1921 had proven a spectacular flop. Official segregation was, of course, the norm for the South and for the times, but Raleigh citizens appear to have placed an honest emphasis on facilities being as "equal" as they were "separate." On November 11, 1935, the city opened the Richard B. Harrison Public Library at 135 East Hargett Street, in a building constructed in the 1920s by black businessman Lemuel T. Delany. Mollie H. Lee, a graduate of Howard University and president of the Negro Library Association of North Carolina, was the first librarian. A year later she had accumulated 2,641 books and over 2,500 card-carrying patrons. By 1940 the library held over 6,000 volumes and was used by more than 5,300 borrowers.

When WPA revenues became available, the city reserved $88,431 in federal money and $24,976 in city resources to construct the John Chavis Memorial Park, named after the early 19th-century educator and dedicated on May 10, 1938. Nevertheless, Raleigh was a strictly segregated city, and in addition to the library and parks, blacks were required to patronize their own motion-picture theaters, churches, schools, newspapers, banks, shops, and institutions of higher education. Housing, too, was segregated, and Chavis Heights,

Antique vehicles, like this horse-drawn fire engine, were brought out for the Centennial Parade of Transportation. (DAH)

Raleigh commemorated the 100th anniversary of the completion of the state capitol and the Raleigh & Gaston Railroad with a series of events, including the Centennial Parade of Transportation, on May 21, 1940. According to the News and Observer *of the day, a special train brought 1,000 "free passengers" from surrounding areas for the celebration. (DAH)*

1840—1940

CENTENNIAL CELEBRATION

Raleigh, N. C.   **May 21, 1940**

Celebrating Completion of the North Carolina State Capitol and the Raleigh and Gaston Railroad

9:30 A.M.	Special Train Leaves Weldon, N. C.
12:15 P.M.	Special Train Arrives Union Station, Raleigh
12:30 P.M.	Celebration—State Capitol, East Side
	Speakers:
	Governor Clyde R. Hoey of North Carolina
	Governor Burnet R. Maybank of South Carolina
	Mr. W. L. Stanley, Seaboard Air Line Railway
	Hon. Thad Eure, Secretary of State of North Carolina
3:00 P.M.	Parade of Transportation
7:30 P.M.	Transportation Dinner, Hotel Sir Walter
9:00 P.M.	U. D. C. Reception for Dance Sponsors and Marshals. Hotel Sir Walter
10:00 P.M.	Script Dance—Auditorium. Tickets, $1.10 Per Couple

Window Displays Along Fayetteville Street

Transportation Equipment Display Union Station

Oberlin, and the Southside community were almost entirely black.

More than 70 years after the defeat that had theoretically destroyed racial inequality, Raleigh lost its last living tie to the great "Lost Cause." The General Assembly in 1891 had appropriated $3,000 to convert the old Pettigrew Hospital into a Confederate Soldiers Home, and hundreds of veterans had taken advantage of the haven. By 1935 death had decimated their ranks from more than 100 in 1925 to 40 in 1930 to only 15 in 1935. When the General Assembly approved a bill in March of 1937 allowing the Board of Directors to decide if they should continue the Home or farm out the remaining residents, the final six old soldiers wrote a letter to the legislators pleading that they not be forced to leave: "The end is in sight for each of us and we know that here we will receive tender care and heartfelt sympathy . . . we do not know how to appeal to you on this subject, but place yourself in our position."

The heart-wrenching prophecy of the old men was not long in coming to pass. In August 1938, Walter Barfield alone remained alive. If he left the Home, he would qualify for a one-dollar-per-day pension, but Barfield had no relatives. However, he found a "friend" in Wilson, North Carolina, and when he moved out the Home ceased to exist. In February 1939 the *News and Observer* carried a brief article announcing that Barfield had died.

As the state capital, Raleigh naturally attracted attention from beyond its borders, but Raleigh's sons and daughters in the 20th century have also left their mark on the outside world. Nell Battle Lewis offended some in her battles for enlightenment in North Carolina and Raleigh, but she gained widespread renown as a journalist in the process. In 1930 Josiah W. Bailey of Raleigh entered the U.S. Senate as a Democrat, but he assured himself a place in history as an unflinching opponent of the New Deal and President Roosevelt's efforts to "pack" the Supreme Court.

The Royster family had migrated to North Carolina from Virginia in the early 1800s, and Royster's Candy Store is still remembered in Raleigh. The family has garnered attention as well for an entirely different reason. Members formed the habit of giving their offspring state names so that cousins could easily distinguish each other, and the practice unquestionably contributed to the most unusual personal nomenclature in Raleigh. There was an Arkansas Delaware Royster, a Virginia Carolina, a Georgia Alabama, a Wisconsin Illinois, and in the way of a variation on a theme, a Nathaniel Confederate States Royster. In 1936 one of the Raleigh Roysters with an unusual name embarked on a distinguished career with the *Wall Street Journal*. Vermont Connecticut Royster left North Carolina happy to have landed a reporter's job; he returned more than 30 years later having risen to editor of the *Wall Street Journal* and later editor emeritus. He later became a William Rand Kenan, Jr., Professor of Journalism and Public Affairs at the University of North Carolina at Chapel Hill.

In 1938 the *Who's Who in America* listed 58 Raleigh citizens, including Dr. Robert P. Daniel, president of Shaw, the first capital black so honored. But Raleigh's most "visible" citizen remained Josephus Daniels, a longtime activist in the Democratic Party. His advice and support had contributed to Democratic victories. Consequently, Woodrow Wilson rewarded Daniels by appointing him Secretary of the Navy and acknowledged his administrative abilities by keeping him on for the duration of World War I and, in fact, for the entirety of both the Wilson administrations.

In 1928 he was a delegate to the Democratic National Convention in Houston, which the caustic H.L. Mencken covered for the Baltimore *Sun.* In his July 30 editorial, "Civil War in the Confederacy," Mencken attacked an old enemy: ". . . The new North Carolina is almost everything that Josephus is not. It is, in many respects, the most advanced of all the Southern States, and he is one of the hollowest and dumbest of Southern politicians. Even his make-up is grotesque: he still clings to the black string-tie and long-tailed coat of the professional Southerner of the last generation. It is highly improbable that he could be elected to any office of dignity in North Carolina today. But he was in Wilson's cabinet, and so he was sent to Houston, and there he disgraced the State with his maudlin bellowing about Prohibition."

Daniels won recognition for diverse reasons. As a teetotaler, he drew attention at social gatherings attended by career military men, and he abolished grog rations aboard ship, something that sailors still remember. He also had the Navy excellently prepared for World War I. Franklin Roosevelt was his assistant secretary, and later Daniels served from 1933 to 1941 as Roosevelt's ambassador to Mexico. He pleased the folks back home in 1920 by naming a cruiser the USS *Raleigh.*

One hundred years after the twin celebrations denoting the completion of the capitol and the Raleigh & Gaston Railroad, Raleigh citizens were again treated to gala festivities celebrating advancements in transportation. An estimated 40,000 persons attended the Century of Transportation Parade on May 21, 1940. Forty-six units were in the parade, and engines from the *Tornado* to the most up-to-date *Silver Meteor* were displayed. The star of the show was a miniature steam engine sent by the Norfolk & Southern Railroad. The *News and Observer* report evokes an excitement akin to that of the Register of long ago, reporting that the boiler "was steamed up to the point of bursting and the engineer bore down upon a whistle that threatened at any moment to destroy the tympanic membranes of all within earshot."

At the very moment the spectators were enjoying that parade, the world was becoming "steamed up to the point of bursting." During the ordeal that followed, Raleigh would undergo a sea of change, and it emerged from the turmoil so economically strong that for 40 years—and still counting—it would remain impervious to the devastating cycles that seem to have made instability a permanent condition for so many American cities.

W hen Raleigh residents opened their copies of the *News and Observer* Sunday morning, December 7, 1941, the headline read: "ROOSEVELT SENDS PERSONAL APPEAL FOR PEACE TO JAPANESE EMPEROR"; two front-page photos recorded Governor Melville Broughton's launching the day before of the 10,400-ton military freighter the USS *Zebulon B. Vance;* other headlines reported the beginning of the German retreat from Moscow and the declaration of war by Britain on Finland, Hungary, and Rumania. In mid-afternoon a crowd of 4,000 was filing out of the Memorial Auditorium after hearing a 234-voice chorus sing Handel's *Messiah* when the word of the Japanese attack on Pearl Harbor broke. The movie theaters halted programs to announce the news, and citizens clustered around radios and into small groups to appraise the future. The police, the highway patrol, and radio stations notified service personnel that they were to return to duty immediately, but, for the most part, calm prevailed.

VII

A MODERN CITY BLOSSOMS:

1940 - 1982

Secretary of State Thad Eure opined that the attack would totally unify America, an opinion also expressed in a December 8 *News and Observer* editorial. On the evening of December 8, Josephus Daniels spoke to a "patriotic mass meeting" of the Raleigh American Legion in the Memorial Auditorium. By then all Raleigh knew that Admiral David W. Bagley—formerly of Raleigh and the brother of Mrs. Daniels—was the commander of a battleship division of the Pacific Fleet, but no one at the time knew that 20-year-old Private Robert H. Westbrook, Jr., had died during the Japanese air raid on Hickam Field, the first Raleigh citizen to die in the war.

Raleigh quickly settled into a routine of blackouts and rationing, of salvaging programs and Victory Gardens—capital women in Home Demonstration Clubs and Wake County youth in 4-H Clubs guided efforts to produce the necessary food to "Win the War and Write the Peace." And on Tuesday, July 14, 1942, Raleigh was the location of a national "Win the War Mass Meeting" in the Memorial Auditorium.

When the international situation had begun to deteriorate irrevocably in 1939, the Marine Corps set up a recruiting station in the Post Office, from which Captain John M. Green and Sergeant Motte V. Griffin directed recruitment throughout North Carolina and in parts of South Carolina and Virginia. On December 9, 1941, over 500 men volunteered for enlistment—the Navy accepted 32, the Marines eight, and the Army six. The next day the three branches accepted 72 volunteers, and the Navy recruiting center was operating around the clock seven days a week. By the end of the war, the Raleigh Marine Corps station had inducted thousands, the local Army and Navy recruiters thousands more.

On September 9, 1941, 18 Raleigh volunteers agreed to serve as air wardens at a station in the Country Club Homes offices at Oberlin and Fairview roads. In October and November of the same year, Raleigh residents got a close look at the nation's military buildup when 400,000 troops participated in training exercises in Wake and nearby counties. Thousands of soldiers were housed in the capital, and hundreds of transports moved through its streets.

After the attack on Pearl Harbor, Mayor Graham H. Andrews named State University Professor Earl H. Hostetler as commander of the Raleigh Citizens' Defense Corps. Hostetler was responsible for drawing up and implementing procedures for clearing the streets during air raids, providing auxiliary police to direct medical per-

Fayetteville Street was still the domain of motorized transport when this photograph was taken from the roof of the capitol in 1972. Six years later it became a pedestrian thoroughfare, stretching from Union Square to Memorial Auditorium. (DAH)

To save gasoline and rubber for the military effort during World War II, Pine State Dairy relied on another form of horsepower to deliver products to customers. Fully motorized service was resumed in 1945. (DAH)

sonnel, directing nurses' aides to assist professionals, designating casualty stations, establishing a blood bank, rationing supplies, and restoring electrical power, telephone service, and traffic. W. Grimes Haywood was in charge of the control center, which he activated in March 1942 with 14 women volunteers initially and with plans to expand the unit to 72. All told, more than 4,500 Raleighites volunteered for civil defense assignments during the spring of 1942.

In a statement to the *News and Observer* on March 8, 1942, Billy Anderson warned his fellow citizens that Raleigh "must be prepared for the octopus arms of any enemy." He pointed to Raleigh's importance as a railhead, its symbolic significance as the state capital, and its proximity to Fort Bragg and Norfolk, but he also noted that "Raleigh is no high-geared industrial center which produces quantities of essential defense materials." Industry, which had all but disappeared in Raleigh during the 1930s, would be revived by the war, although not in time to produce much in the way of wartime materiel. But a few local companies did make contributions. In December of 1943, Peden Steel Company executives displayed a steel barge that their company had built for the U.S. Army Transportation Corps. The 104-foot craft could be broken apart for shipment and reassembled where needed; it was equipped to carry either gasoline or dry cargo.

Company president James M. Peden presided at the 1943 unveiling ceremony, and Mayor Graham H. Andrews and Josephus Daniels spoke. Daniels, declaring, "This is a day of achievement and big promise for North Carolina," also joked, "I am sure this barge has enough 'tar' on it to carry it wherever it may go." On October 26, 1944, Peden Steel received the

Army-Navy "E" pennant for superior wartime production for turning out 48 barges six weeks ahead of schedule even though steel had twice been diverted to jobs with higher priorities.

Not all activities during this period were war-related, however. Raleigh let down its guard long enough between April 26 and May 1 of 1942 to hold an elaborate Sesquicentennial celebration featuring parades, floats, and exhibits. James M. Landis, former dean of the Harvard Law School and current U.S. Director of Civilian Defense, spoke on "Victory Day," April 28; and Paul V. McNutt, U.S. Director of Health and Welfare Services, spoke on "Education Day." Local directors maintained a civil defense posture of readiness for the duration of the war, but anxiety decreased as the situation became more familiar and Raleigh's safety more assured. Meanwhile, many Raleigh citizens met danger abroad.

Among the many Raleigh men who fought on the battlefields of World War II were the four sons of Mr. and Mrs. Thomas R. Garner of 215 East Morgan Street. Willie C. Garner earned seven Battle Stars fighting in the Pacific, including the bloody campaign for Guadalcanal; Bennie R. Garner collected three Battle Stars in the Philippines; and Grover O. Garner received the Bronze Star Medal for bravery, the Bronze Arrowhead, and five Battle Stars in Europe. Thomas R. Garner won the Bronze Star Medal, the Bronze Arrowhead, and five Battle Stars—and died in action in Germany on February 23, 1945. Hundreds of their comrades fought as bravely, scores died as tragically.

As V-E Day approached, national and local officials appealed for calm and sober celebration, and the last days brought sobering news to Raleigh. Family and friends learned that Sergeant James C. Atkins had been killed on Okinawa on April 11 and that Captain John W. Sasser had died in a German prison camp hospital on May 6 from wounds received in a crash landing on September 12, 1944. When the long-expected news arrived on May 7, the reaction was one more of relief than of unrestrained joy, but V-J Day, August 14, was something else indeed.

Raleighites learned of the Japanese surrender at 7:02 p.m. Within minutes thousands of uninhibited celebrants had thronged Fayetteville Street, blowing horns, blasting trumpets, ringing cowbells, setting off fireworks, using any instruments of noise available, including lungs descended from those which had once made the rebel yell the most frightening sound on the continent. By 7:12 p.m. Fayetteville Street was hopelessly jammed with traffic, as sirens and horns created a deafening din. One car carried a three-piece band, with a drummer, and a hook-and-ladder firetruck inched its way along flying a banner proclaiming "Victory is Complete" until the crowd could give way no farther, in spite of the whining siren.

Beer and wine shops either closed voluntarily or at the request of the Military Police but liquor still flowed openly and freely. By 7:30 p.m. over 20,000 people crowded Fayetteville Street, but the extra constables Police Chief Ralph Hargrove had called to duty had little to do other than try to keep traffic moving. Three hours later only a few lingering diehards remained downtown following a celebration that the police said made the average New Year's Eve seem like a "Sunday School picnic."

The next morning, the *News and Observer* emblazoned the single word "PEACE!!" in six-inch-high letters over its masthead, and the citizens of Raleigh set about adjusting to peace. But 197 Wake County men had already made their "peace": 114 had died in action; 16 had died of wounds; 57 had met noncombat deaths; and 10 were officially declared dead. Hundreds of others had suffered wounds and harsh incarceration in prisoner-of-war camps.

Finally, in a repetition of the somber burials following the Civil War, bodies began to come home in a slow trickle, and Raleigh earth received the noble likes of PFC. Chester T. Daughtry, Pvt. Herman L. Harvey, and Second-Lieutenant Lawson E. Perry, Jr., long after the guns had fallen silent.

World War II changed Raleigh as it did so many cities across America. An April 26, 1942, *News and Observer* assessment points directly to the source of Raleigh's relative stability at the end of the Great Depression: "Since the conclusion of the World War and the outbreak of the current conflict the notable characteristic of Raleigh has been its tremendous growth in spite of the town's lack of great industry. The capital strictly is a center of education, government, and culture." The article also notes that the presence of state government had chiefly influenced the economy of Raleigh by greatly expanding the middle class: "Raleigh doesn't have any

Children usually save money for things like bicycles or college; William D. Beatty used his savings to buy a defense bond from Mr. Haynes of the Raleigh Industrial Bank in 1941. (DAH)

Left: A war bonds promotional booth was set up in the Boylan-Pearce department store on Fayetteville Street during World War II. Wyatt Taylor and Dallas Holleman hold the store's Retail Award pennant. (DAH)

millionaires nor is there a large poverty-stricken group." Only four years and one month later, the same newspaper spoke in a quite different tone: "Raleigh's market in business real estate, stimulated by a wartime flow of money seeking an investment medium, has boomed as never before in the city's 150 years of existence." The citizenry's traditional caution, if not exactly thrown to the wind, was sorely tested by the opportunities accompanying the postwar boom. Residents who had earlier been reluctant to risk savings now poured money into business ventures, and outside investors were entering the Raleigh market in unprecedented numbers. Raleigh would remain "a center of education, government, and culture," but on this firm foundation would be built a wider prosperity.

Just in time to handle the tens of thousands of soldiers soon to begin passing through the city, the new downtown Union Bus Station opened for business. Raleigh architect James M. Edwards, Jr., designed the terminal, the Raleigh general contracting firm of John W. Coffey & Son built it at a cost of $185,000, and Governor J. Melville Broughton, a Raleigh native, dedicated it in noon ceremonies on October 10, 1941. (By the mid-1960s, five bus companies ran 97 different routes through Raleigh, city residents had a choice of 15 taxi companies, and 3,500 commuters daily used the 35-vehicle mu-

nicipal bus fleet.) A second new transportation facility went into service on the evening of September 28, 1942. Passenger trains ceased using the old Union Depot and called instead at the new $200,000 Eugene C. Bagwell Station on Franklin Street. The first train to arrive and depart could not have been more appropriate for an old Confederate state capital—the *Robert E. Lee.*

The war years also witnessed cultural innovations in the capital. The Raleigh Little Theatre remained active, continued to expand its repertory, and in 1949 completed the new Children's Theatre in the basement of its Pogue Street headquarters. The Little Theatre also hosted performances other than the strictly dramatic fare. In 1941 St. Mary's Dean of Music Russell Broughton, Meredith's Dean of the Violin Department Edgar Alden, and about 20 others joined together to form the Raleigh Chamber Music Guild and began holding concerts in the Little Theatre. Beginning in 1947, operas would also be staged there, when the North Carolina Festival Association sponsored the Eastern Seaboard Regional Opera Festival. Assaying the title role in the festival production of Mendelssohn's *Elijah* was a Raleigh man named A.J. Fletcher.

The founder of the Capital Broadcasting Company, Fletcher carried his interest in opera beyond performing as a

Servicemen line up for refreshments at a YWCA dance, held in Raleigh in 1942. (DAH)

dilettante singer. In 1948 he provided the funds and the organizational impetus to start the Grass Roots Opera. Fletcher had three basic intentions: to acquaint children with opera, to give qualified singers a chance to perform, and to allow those "not qualified to go to the Met . . . a chance to get it out of their souls." Performing all operas in English, the Grass Roots Opera became the National Opera Company, and over the years it has performed before millions of schoolchildren and adult audiences in at least 37 states.

Governor Broughton led ceremonies for the opening of the Colony Theatre on Glenwood Avenue, which began entertaining moviegoers on April 1, 1942. The Colony cost $65,000 to build. It had 603 seats, used turnstiles to eliminate the need for ticket-takers, and charged an initial admission of 10 cents for children at all times and 15 cents for adults at matinee screenings and 20 cents at night. The opening night feature was *Four Jacks and a Jill,* starring Anne Shirley and Ray Bolger.

In 1943 Governor Broughton proposed the creation of a museum of art in Raleigh, which would be dedicated to North Carolinians who had served in World Wars I and II. The General Assembly delayed construction of the museum until after the war, but in 1947 it became the first state legislature in the nation to appropriate money—one million dollars—for art purchases. (In 1951 the legislature created the State Art Commission to oversee museum purchases, and the Samuel H. Kress Foundation promised to donate a collection equal in value to the 1947 appropriation. After celebrating at the biggest banquet ever held at the Sir Walter Hotel, hundreds of guests looked on at 9 p.m. on April 6, 1956, as Governor Luther Hodges cut the ribbon opening the East Morgan Street galleries, in the old Highway Building. By the time the state accepted the Kress donation, it had more than doubled in value. Currently, the North Carolina Museum of Art contains treasures from all periods, including masterpieces by Rembrandt, Rubens, Van Dyck, Jan Brueghel, Kinnaird, and works by many other artists old and new. The new museum on Blue Ridge Road has provided sufficient space to assure the North Carolina collection continued national prominence.)

The war years would have a positive effect as well on local businesses. Retail business rose sharply from $18 million in 1940 to $92 million in 1949. Wholesale figures were even more impressive, increasing from $22 million in 1940 to $200 million in 1949. Raleigh's population jumped from 46,879 in 1940 to 65,679 in 1950, an increase of 40 percent, but the city had also expanded 66.6 percent in area during the same period. To deal with the problems congruent to the rapidly expanding economy and population, the city adopted a council-manager form of government in 1947. Seven council members were elected at large for two-year terms. They selected a city manager and chose one member to be mayor.

Population growth, while welcome, brought attendant problems, which the new council-manager government had to address. Raleighites rushed into a post-World War II love

As a child, Joseph Melville Broughton (1888-1949) wanted to be a professional baseball player. Instead, he was the first Raleigh native to become governor of North Carolina, holding the office from 1941 to 1945. (DAH)

affair with the automobile, and the massive increase in traffic was anything but compatible with a street system designed for Depression-level concentrations. As early as 1946 city officials had tentatively approached the problem by preparing a "Master Transportation Plan," but they did not hope for immediate success. Relief arteries were the only feasible answer, but they "would call for moving many houses, stores and other buildings, changing hundreds of property lines and building new bridges and underpasses, and it is the opinion of city officials that it can't be undertaken any time soon—if ever."

A new plan in 1951 concentrated on providing additional routes to the north and west, constructing a belt line, and restricting truck traffic. A Chamber of Commerce study in 1953 concluded, "Raleigh traffic is a headache! It irritates everybody involved—motorists, merchants and traffic controllers." The study also found three distinct trends: the number of vehicles was increasing rapidly; commercial enterprises, industries, and residents were moving away from the downtown area; and passengers were shifting from public to private transportation. The study also offered three solutions: create more through streets, build a belt-line highway, and expand U.S. 1 to four lanes.

(The bold plan of 1946 is now a reality, and Raleigh traffic flows with amazing precision. But the "costs" have not been light. Hundreds of millions have gone into the effort, and the face of "Old Raleigh" has been altered beyond recognition.)

Urban sprawl intensified in the postwar years as new developments began to dot the map. As a striking example, the city limits were expanded every year between 1951 and 1962. Increased construction activity, including large apartment complexes and home developments, were the natural consequence. In 1940 County Club Homes Incorporated had purchased the 25-acre Horace W. Davis estate and spent $300,000 building 76 new homes. Other developers pushed Raleigh's residential areas ever outward during and following the war. But the first really big postwar impetus was centered on the old plantation of Duncan Cameron. Paul Cameron had inherited the estate in 1866 and, upon his own death, had left it to four daughters and to his granddaughter Annie Cameron Graham, who later married Robert Smallwood. The family sold off a 110-acre tract in 1910, which was developed into Cameron Park.

After the war, J.W. York of Raleigh and R.A. Bryan of Goldsboro purchased a 158-acre section from Mrs. Smallwood on which they built the Cameron Village Apartments and the Cameron Village Shopping Center. When completed in 1949, the residential complex consisted of 561 apartments and 100 private homes, and it won that year's esteemed National Association of Home Builders award for best neighborhood development. York Construction Company architect Leif Veland of Teaneck, New Jersey, designed all the original buildings and Seward H. Mott of the Urban Land Institute of Washington, D.C., was the planning engineer for the shopping center.

The Cameron Village Shopping Center was consciously patterned after the Country Club Plaza in Kansas City—the nation's first regional-type center. The democratization of automobile ownership vastly extended the area of its appeal. Sears opened a $1.5 million store in February 1951, and Cameron Village remained the ranking shopping center in its region for well over a decade. The Connecticut General Life Insurance Company, which purchased the shopping center in 1964 for $8.4 million—the largest sale then on record in Wake County—leased it back to J.W. York. He has continued innovative expansion, introducing the Village Subway in 1971, Thalhimers in 1972, and numerous specialty shops.

J.W. York was also responsible for the first large industrial park in postwar Raleigh. He opened the York Industrial Area in 1951, a 700-acre industrial park now occupied by

Carl Vernon Reynolds (1872-1963), state health officer from 1934 to 1948, enforced stricter inspection of restaurants and grocery stores. He also advocated a tougher anti-venereal disease program, surprising many with a campaign directed squarely at the public, at a time when the subject was rarely discussed openly. (DAH)

Westinghouse Electric, IBM, ITT, Kraft Foods, the Raleigh Farmers Market, and many other firms. Industrial activity throughout the Raleigh area had been revived by the war and continued to expand. Burlington Industries established a dyeing and finishing plant in 1948. Morris & Associates, Inc., began producing refrigerator equipment the following year. But the most important single development was the creation of the nearby Research Triangle Park. When Governor Luther Hodges announced plans for the park in 1958, Raleigh leaders acted quickly to take advantage of the new opportunity. Frank A. Daniels headed the Service for Newcomers Committee organized to entice RTP families to settle in Raleigh. The Committee agreed with their counterparts in Chapel Hill and Durham not to "knock" each other, and they obviously did a good job of selling Raleigh, in spite of their benign restrictions, since about 65 percent of all RTP employees have chosen to live in the capital. The welcome influx began in the spring of 1959 when Chemstrand moved 450 families into the area. Thanks, in part, to the new RTP employees, Raleigh had the distinction of appearing for the first time as a "metropolis" in the 1959 Rand-McNally *Commercial Atlas and Marketing Guide,* listed among other cities or suburbs topping 100,000 in population.

An additional factor in the capital's population increase was the continued growth of government. The number of state employees in Raleigh began an upward spiral in the 1940s, more than doubling from 2,213 in 1940 to 5,500 in 1950. (As late as the 1960-1970 period, state employment in Raleigh increased as much as 47 percent, and in 1978 more than 28 percent of all state employees, excluding teachers, lived in Wake County.)

The growth in state government renewed moves to enlarge or replace the capitol. The State Commission on Modernization of the Capitol recommended in 1947 that the state either build a new capitol and turn the old one into a combination hall of history and art gallery, or add two wings to the existing State House and reserve it solely for use by the General Assembly.

Instant opposition to the proposal came from the North Carolina Society for the Preservation of Antiquities, the Caswell-Nash chapter of the Daughters of the American Revolution, and C.A. Cannon of Cannon Mills, Inc. Opponents grew to include the North Carolina chapter of the American Institute of Architects, the State Art Society, the executive board of the Needham Broughton High School PTA, the Twentieth Century Book Club of Raleigh, and many more individuals and organizations. For this and other reasons, no action regarding the capitol was taken, except to clean the exterior in 1952, until the early 1960s.

City government also expanded during this period and the need for a new city hall could not be similarly delayed. The city council accepted $400,000 to purchase property for a new city hall in July 1956, but finding a site was no easy chore. Members first voted to buy the property now occupied by the

Above: *President Harry S Truman was in Raleigh for the dedication of the* Three Presidents *statue on Union Square, October, 19, 1948. Shown with him on the*

reviewing stand are Secretary of the Army Kenneth Royal (center) and Governor R. Gregg Cherry (right). (DAH)

Right: *Hurricane Hazel passed through Raleigh in October 1954, leaving many area homes and businesses without electricity. Unable to use their kitchen appliances, Mrs. Joe Phillips, Charlie Pullen, and his son Charlie, Jr., make breakfast in the Pullens' backyard. (DAH)*

The emphasis on progress in the business community did little, however, to alter the basic conservatism of many Raleighites in the 1950s. The Blue Law issue, for instance, came to another climax in 1954. Golf and baseball were permissible on Sundays, but promoters and participants in other games were subject to a $10 fine. When Arthur Ingram requested permission to conduct a bowling tournament at his Man Mur Bowling Alley, the city council and city ministers became bitterly divided. The Raleigh Ministerial Association expressed outrage over the "growing commercialization" of the Sabbath. Temple Baptist Church minister G.W. Bullard suggested a compromise by restricting commercial entertainment to the hours of 1:30 to 6:30 p.m. on Sundays. In the end, the council approved Ingram's request four to three. Now, of course, in pragmatic terms Blue Laws have all but vanished.

But other signs of change, especially the rise of the radio and television media, were accepted with enthusiasm by large numbers of people in Raleigh and the surrounding area. NBC had created a furor in eastern North Carolina in October 1938 when it announced that it would exercise an option to buy WPTF from Durham Life for $210,000. The following January the North Carolina secretary of state hurriedly chartered the North Carolina Radio Corporation, made up of 33 businessmen and professionals who were prepared to buy WPTF in order to keep its operation in the state. Realizing the degree of attachment North Carolinians felt toward the station, NBC withdrew its bid in April, and Durham Life has continued to retain control of the station.

WPTF drew a national spotlight to Raleigh in February 1956 when producers of the NBC network programs "Monitor" and "Weekday" chose the capital as the first in a new "Great City of the Week" series. WPTF announcers Jim Reid, Sam Beard, and Carl Goerch kicked off the event with half-hour programs at 10:30 a.m. and noon on Sunday, February 19. NBC announcers took over the WPTF booth from 2:30 until 5 p.m., broadcasting interviews and commentary from and about Raleigh to the nation. "Monitor" producer Al Capitoff said that NBC had picked Raleigh because "it is the best example in the nation of an old city, with a historic past, that has modern 'get-up-and-go.' " "Weekday" programs originated from Raleigh until February 29.

WPTF first encountered what has proven to be its most formidable competition when A.J. Fletcher organized the Capital Broadcasting Company in 1937 and put WRAL on the air in 1939. Capital Broadcasting expanded WRAL's audience by forming the Tobacco Network, which linked several eastern North Carolina stations via telephone lines to broadcast simultaneously programs originating at WRAL. Capital added WRAL-FM in 1946 and WRAL-TV in 1956. WRAL-TV broadcast for six years as an NBC affiliate before switching to ABC. Durham Life took over the vacated NBC affiliation with WPTF-TV, and the independent WLFL-TV went on the air in early 1982.

Museum of History, but they could not close a deal. Then they agreed on a lot on Hillsborough Street between Dawson and McDowell, but that prospect also evaporated. Next a plan to build in the 200 block of New Bern Avenue fell through. Finally, in April of 1958, they agreed on the plot facing Nash Square, upon which the municipal building now stands.

Governor Luther Hodges' announcement, on June 20, 1958, that Kellogg Switchboard and Supply Company, a division of ITT, would locate in the Research Triangle Park was considered the most momentous business news of the 1950s for Raleigh—it demonstrated that major companies would indeed be willing to move to central North Carolina. But major companies had, in fact, flowed into Raleigh throughout the entire decade: Montgomery Green in 1950, Pepcom Industries (Pepsi Cola) in 1952, IT&T in 1954, Oscar Miller Contractor in 1958, Carolina Steel Corporation and Atlas Steel Products in 1959.

Left: *Senator Jesse Helms, holding his eight-month-old grandson Mike Stuart, waves to the crowd at a press conference in November 1978. Courtesy,* The News and Observer, *photo by Jim Strickland*

Right: *Suntanned Senator John Fitzgerald Kennedy, Democratic party Presidential nominee, greets well-wishers at the Executive Mansion. He visited Raleigh during a campaign tour of the South in September 1960.* (DAH)

TV broadcasting also provided the springboard into national politics for Raleigh's most controversial citizen of the postwar years—Senator Jesse Helms. Born the son of the chief of police of Monroe, North Carolina, Helms worked as a dishwasher and a laborer while attending Wingate and Wake Forest colleges. He served in the Navy from 1942 to 1945, when he settled in Raleigh. Helms became city editor of the *Raleigh Times* and, in 1950, established himself as another in the line of editors with considerable political savvy.

J. Melville Broughton had won a U.S. Senate seat in 1948, but he died on March 6, 1949. Governor Kerr Scott had appointed Frank Porter Graham to fill Broughton's position, and Graham had polled more than 49 percent of the vote in the Democratic primary of 1950. Jesse Helms and others persuaded the second-place finisher, Willis Smith of Raleigh, to call for a runoff, and Helms directed Smith's campaign in which he upset Graham.

Jesse Helms served two terms on the Raleigh city council in the late 1950s. In 1960 he joined WRAL-TV and the Tobacco Radio Network as a commentator and as an executive. He soon became a household name as one controversy after another revolved around his commentaries, especially over WRAL-TV. His involvement in political and social issues won him many enemies, but it also won him many friends, as became evident to the surprise of many when he defeated Democrat Nick Galifanikis to become a U.S. Senator in 1972.

In the 1960s the trends in population growth and commercial expansion continued. The decade also witnessed significant changes in the look of the city, especially in the downtown area. Raleigh's population grew from 93,931 in 1960 to 122,830 in 1970, an increase of more than 30 percent that was only partly explained by further annexation. The number of jobs related to manufacturing rose considerably in the 1960s, although Raleigh still lagged behind the state in that category. In 1960 manufacturing jobs accounted for 9.3 percent of Raleigh employment and 31.7 percent statewide; by 1970 the figures were 11.4 percent and 35.5 percent respectively.

A study of new residents who moved to Raleigh between 1960 and 1970 showed that 51 percent had come from elsewhere in North Carolina, 25 percent from other Southern states, 12 percent from the Northeast, and 12 percent from the Midwest and West. Some 28 percent of the new arrivals worked in various levels of government, 6 percent were self-employed, and 66 percent took jobs in private industry.

The newcomers blended in smoothly, the quality of life improved, and impartial judges began to recognize Raleigh as a pleasant, progressive city. Longtime residents were also, on the whole, pleased by the many changes. Downtown construction and remodeling in the private sector redefined the commercial district. In the fall of 1963, Governor Sanford broke ground for the $5-million, 16-story Branch Banking and Trust at Fayetteville and Davie. He viewed the modern glass-and-steel edifice as being "symbolic of the progress of the capital city." The *News and Observer* built a new shipping department on West Martin Street on a spot steeped in history; the Capitol Theatre, the Nash Hotel, and several taverns had previously occupied the space. As established downtown hotels began to falter, motels rushed in—the Downtowner on Hillsborough Street, the Raleigh Cabana on South Salisbury, and that instant landmark, the circular Holiday Inn at Hillsborough and Dawson.

Other concerns were rebuilding or altering existing structures. First Federal rebuilt on the old Academy Building site on South Salisbury, Wachovia rebuilt on the old Montgomery Ward site on Fayetteville, Hudson Belk expanded next to the old city hall site on Fayetteville, and the Raleigh Savings and Loan extensively renovated its existing quarters at Fayetteville and Exchange. Businessmen and city officials wanted to convert Fayetteville Street into a pedestrian mall and, for a while in 1960, the Citizens Central Business District Committee seemed to have come up with a convincing concept. On July 25 Committee representatives presented city council members with detailed plans prepared by architect Donald E. Jackson. Jackson envisioned a bricked-over Fayetteville Street relieved by a sprinkling of fountains, canopied businesses, and walkways connecting Fayetteville to Wilmington and Salisbury. But the plan came to no avail due to a shortage of cash. The

mall that now graces the area resulted only when city, county, and state resources became available and when downtown property owners agreed to a surcharge of 12 cents per $100 valuation to help finance the project. Outside the downtown area, E.N. Richards continued to master the art of cultivating shopping centers by raising the huge North Hills Fashion Mall in 1963 and Eastgate in 1964.

In 1961 the Olivia Raney Library Trust purchased the old S.H. Kress building in the first block of Fayetteville Street for $450,000 and set workmen to refurbishing it in preparation to receive the overly confined Olivia Raney Library collection. Jonathan Daniels led the dedication ceremonies in the new quarters on January 3, 1963. Two years later, the Raney and the Richard B. Harrison libraries joined to form the Wake County Library System, and the completion in 1967 of the new $300,000 Harrison Branch Library at 1313 New Bern Avenue gave librarians the additional space they had long requested.

In 1962 the legislature finally moved out of the capitol and into quarters that raised the eyebrows of a few. Governor Luther Hodges and Governor-Elect Terry Sanford broke ground for the Legislative Building on December 29, 1960. Holloway-Reeves & Associates of Raleigh, together with internationally known Edward D. Stone of New York, designed the 200,000-square-foot structure, which includes legislative chambers, committee rooms, offices, public galleries, television- and audio-recording facilities, fountains, and a Great Seal of North Carolina measuring 28 feet in diameter. Planned at $4.5 million, the final costs ran to $6.2 million for a "monument" that some loved and others deplored. Detractors referred to it as "Baghdad-on-the-Neuse" and the "Taj MaHodges." North Carolina State Senator Edward O. McCue told the Richmond legislature in January 1964 that it was "a big museum that belongs in the World's Fair."

Beloved or hated, the new capitol is the focal point in the State Mall that includes all the property bordered by Person, Peace, Edenton, and the Downtown Boulevard. During the 1960s, too, the state added the Archives and History-State Library Building, the Administration Building, and the Albemarle Building. In 1967 the General Assembly approved funds for a replica of Canova's statue of Washington and instituted the Capital Police Force to patrol Capitol Square and other state property in Raleigh.

If the capitol received something less than universal acclaim, the Dorton Arena inspired the admiration of residents and visitors alike. The most immediately conspicuous of all Raleigh's public buildings, it was dedicated in October of 1961. Architect Matthew Nowicki had designed an arena for the State Fair Grounds before he was killed in a plane crash in 1950. After many delays and some revisions to the Nowicki plan, state officials erected the saddle-roofed coliseum and named it after J.S. Dorton, State Fair manager from 1937 until his death in 1961 during construction of the arena. In 1967 the *Centennial Publication of the American Institute of Architects* named Dorton Arena as one of the 10 buildings of the 20th century most likely to influence future architects.

The decade's biggest sensation on the industrial front came when Governor Dan K. Moore, former Governor Luther Hodges, and IBM executives called a press conference in Raleigh on April 14, 1965, to announce that IBM would move into the Research Triangle Park. While IBM was definitely the most important arrival of the 1960s, the flow of manufacturing concerns into Raleigh was at its crest, including Exide, Aerotron, Corning Glass, Action Corporation, Athey Products, Duraw Manufacturing, Mallinckrodt, Litho Industries, Crown Zellerback, and Inco Electro Energy.

But when the city completed a new water treatment plant on the Neuse River eight miles north of town in 1968, the availability of water drew development in that direction at a rate that alarmed many. Mrs. R.R. Doak, president of the League of Women Voters, cited figures in 1971 showing that the population in the northern region was growing at over 5,800 per year, and she proposed a moratorium on growth to allow for a period of adjustment. Too much was at stake, however, to slow expansion for long.

The only area of business to suffer significant losses during this period, in fact, has been traditionally among Raleigh's strongest: the hotel trade. The status of the Sir Walter Hotel, the latest "third house of the legislature," began to slip somewhat in the postwar decades. Arthur Buddenhagen managed the Sir Walter Hotel for 20 years, beginning in 1947, and for well over a decade he could count on a minimum level of business from state government officials. The legislators, in particular, were short of conference space, and Buddenhagen was able to fill their needs in the large Virginia Dare Ballroom and in five other banquet halls. The owners of the Sir Walter had leased the hotel to the Meyer Investment Company in 1935, and the Meyer Company bought the property in 1956 for $2.5 million. Business continued as usual for several years, but the Sir Walter received a double blow in 1962-1963. The new Legislative Building gave legislators ample space, and J.W. York's Velvet Cloak Inn began to compete as a social mecca. Th Hilton Inn, the Royal Villa, and now the Radisson have

A new Archives and History and State Library building was completed early in 1969 at 109 East Jones Street. As director of the Division of Archives and History from 1968 to 1973, Dr. H.G. Jones "developed what has been called the largest and most comprehensive records program in the United States," according to the March 8, 1974, issue of The Chapel Hill Newspaper. *(DAH)*

The State Legislative Building dominates this view of State Government Mall. Other structures shown are (clockwise from Jones Street) the Seaboard building behind the legislature, Dobbs building left of the Seaboard, Archdale building towering over the mall (completed in 1977), and the Bath building. This photograph was taken shortly before the Seaboard building was moved to Salisbury Street. (DAH)

continued to disperse the "third house" function as never before.

In 1964 the Meyer Company sold the hotel for a reported $1,015,889 to a corporation organized by E.N. Richards and John A. Williams, a member of the auditing firm of Williams, Urquhart, and Ficklin (soon to merge with Peat, Marwick, Mitchell). Williams bought out his partners, and in September 1967 he donated the Sir Walter to the state at a time when it was operating at a profit and valued at $2 million.

Then, in 1969, the Sir Walter changed hands twice in one day. The state sold it to Plaza Associates, who combined the hotel with other downtown properties and traded the package to Kidd Brewer for the land used to develop the Crabtree Valley Shopping Center. Currently the Sir Walter serves as subsidized housing.

Other downtown hotels declined and fell. Built in 1928-1929, the Carolina Hotel at Dawson and Hargett was sold in 1934 by Gillette and Company of Baltimore to Robert I. Lee

and four others. Over the years the Carolina developed its own reputation for political activity, being used as a headquarters by Kerr Scott, William Umstead, Robert Scott, Richardson Preyer, James Gardner, Terry Sanford, and many others. In 1952, Mr. and Mrs. Joseph McKinley Bryan of Greensboro purchased the Carolina for approximately a million dollars. The hotel prospered for a while, but in the 1960s it began to succumb to the same pressures as the Sir Walter. Mr. and Mrs. Bryan gave the hotel, appraised at $625,000, to the city of Raleigh in 1973 for the payment of debts not to exceed $125,000 and for use as office space. A third downtown hotel became defunct in 1975 when the Andrew Johnson Hotel at Salisbury and Morgan was padlocked. It was too expensive to operate, and no buyer was willing to risk investing in it.

Raleigh had a long history of fairly good racial relations when civil rights emerged as the dominant social movement of the 1960s. However, it took the resources of many elements within the community to reach a satisfying resolution when events forced a crisis in the summer of 1963. Bishop Vincent S. Waters of the Raleigh Diocese had responded to the 1954 Supreme Court ruling in *Brown* v. *Topeka* by ordering all Catholic schools integrated, and the downtown Cathedral Latin High School accepted eight black students in 1955 with little upheaval, although all student social functions were dropped for the year. However, integration was slower in the public schools, and nonexistent in a wide range of private and public facilities.

Blacks had formed the Raleigh Citizens Association to promote voter registration and to upgrade black employment. NAACP and CORE chapters had been organized. Then in May of 1963, black students at Shaw and St. Augustine's, supported by white students at State University and other area institutions of higher education, conducted sit-in demonstrations against segregation at the S&W Cafeteria, the Sir Walter, the Ambassador Theatre, Gino's Restaurant, and the Statehouse dining room.

On Wednesday and Thursday, May 8 and 9, over 150 demonstrators were arrested and 106 jailed—taxing confinement facilities beyond their limits. On Thursday, City Court Judge Pretlow Winborne told those not yet booked that they were free to leave. They refused and remained in place until another conference with Judge Winborne the following afternoon, when they dispersed.

That evening, May 10, about 500 black residents marched to the governor's mansion, where Governor Terry Sanford and guests were being entertained by a North Carolina Symphony concert. Sanford promised to meet black representatives in his office, but he refused to discuss the issue then and there. After the demonstrators had sung hymns for 20 minutes, Sanford thanked them, renewing his invitation for discussions while insisting, "You have not come to me with any request."

Leaders in both the black and the white communities set about trying to resolve the situation peacefully. Charles A. Lyons, ex-secretary of the Raleigh-based North Carolina Teachers Association, headed a group of black leaders desirous of finding a solution. Mayor W.G. Enloe worked desperately to set up negotiations between black representatives and businessmen, saying "Something has got to be done or our city is going to be embarrassed nationwide." He appointed a Committee of One Hundred to discover "What, if anything, can be done to avoid another Birmingham."

Victor E. Bell chaired the Committee, which met with delegations from each side. Restaurant, motel, and hotel proprietors agreed to integrate; blacks agreed to cease their demonstrations. Dr. Lyons and Dr. James Boyd of St. Augustine's headed the biracial Mechanics Committee to oversee gradual desegregation.

On July 26, 1963, Mayor Enloe appointed still another committee—the 15-member Community Relations Committee—to implement gradual integration of city facilities.

When the Yarborough House burned in 1928, the Hotel Sir Walter supplanted it as the "third house of the legislature." By July 1979 the building became the Sir Walter Apartments, which provide housing for the elderly, disabled, and handicapped. (DAH)

Raleigh attorney W.C. Harris was chairman, and Dr. Lyons was vice-chairman. The committee issued a "Statement of Purpose," which emphasized the basic good will of Raleigh citizens but which warned that full membership in the community is possible only when each person is able to participate equally in the decision-making process and to enjoy services and freedoms.

The Community Relations Committee brought as many groups as possible into the effort via subcommittee appointment. After significant progress, the Community Relations Committee joined the Raleigh Ministerial Association in planning "Community Relations Week" for the second week of June 1964.

By the time June 1964 arrived, the success of Mayor Enloe's initiative was readily apparent. All downtown lunch counters, all theaters, both major hotels, schools, city recreation facilities, sales forces in variety and grocery stores, the Chamber of Commerce, and the Merchants Association had all integrated. Racial tensions have occasionally flared since 1963, but never to dangerous proportions or for extended periods; thanks to the dedication of black and white men and women of good will, another Birmingham was avoided.

Raleigh life in the 1970s continued much as usual. The state completed the Bath Building and the Archdale Building. J.W. York built the Mission Valley Shopping Center. The Crabtree Valley Shopping Center developed by Seby Jones opened. E.N. Richards built two shopping centers, Lake Boone and Tower, and started a third, North Ridge. New industries arrived routinely: Carolina Components; the Peavey Company; Chloride, Inc.; EMA, Inc.; Georgia Box Company; Ajinomoto, Inc. But problems surfaced as well.

The Miller Brewing Company chose to establish a major brewery in Eden rather than Raleigh to avoid conflicts with businessmen and public officials opposed to the entry of a union-shop operation. In 1974 North Carolina labor leader Wilbur Hobby charged the Raleigh Chamber of Commerce and state officials with willfully thwarting a planned move into Raleigh by the Xerox Corporation, which would have brought 1,500 jobs. The State Industrial Resources Director denied any state effort to discourage Xerox officers, but he conceded that the Chamber of Commerce opposed Xerox paying $5 per hour to union workers at a time when the average wage in Raleigh was $3.74. Chamber of Commerce industrial development director Stephen E. Kelley readily admitted, "We discouraged them from bringing in a union contract." As corporations continue to migrate into the Sun Belt, followed by employees accustomed to working under union contracts, the issue of the open versus closed shop will surely arise again.

In the 1970s the capitol received another complete face-lifting. The General Assembly authorized $500,000 in 1971 for renovation and alterations designed to return the capitol as nearly as practical to its original state. State Department of Archives and History officials and architect William W. Dodge III oversaw the work between 1972 and 1975. Governor Robert Scott used offices in the State Administration Building while workmen—under the immediate supervision of Fred Senter—took out bathrooms on the second floor, replaced plaster frieze work exposed when the bathrooms were removed, stripped accumulated paint, removed carpets and desk platforms in the old legislative chambers, and exposed the original fireplaces, discovering an ornate grate, a log, and a poker. Senter also had crews refurbish the rotunda, steam clean the stone work, and replace the copper on the dome.

The State House, then, was in the best of condition on June 2, 1975, when Governor James Holshouser and Lieutenant Governor James Hunt presided over a ceremony designating

Governor Terry Sanford faced civil-rights demonstrators who marched on the Executive Mansion in May 1963 and interrupted the annual North Carolina Symphony Ball. (DAH)

In May 1963 about 500 people demonstrated at the Executive Mansion. Governor Sanford was with the crowd for almost 20 minutes while the protesters sang hymns. When Sanford urged black leaders to discuss their grievances with him in his office at the capitol, the demonstrators dispersed. (DAH)

the capitol a National Historic Landmark. When James Hunt became governor, he moved the governor's office back into the historic state capitol. Oakwood, the oldest surviving downtown neighborhood, was named Raleigh's first Historic District on June 3, 1975. The next year Capitol Square and Blount Street were named Raleigh Historic Districts.

The ranks of the preservationists swelled quite suddenly in 1971 when the General Assembly moved to erect a new governor's mansion and to use the old only for state social events. The mansion had been a source of controversy and discontent from the day Governor Daniel G. Fowle moved into his unfinished official residence. Plumbing was installed during the administration of Governor Elias Carr (1893-1897), but the General Assembly had refused to appropriate money for electric lights when it was requested by Governor Locke Craig (1913-1917), leaving that convenience to be enjoyed first by Governor Thomas W. Bickett (1917-1921). In 1925 newly elected Governor Angus McLean refused to move in because he considered the mansion unsanitary. A health department inspector agreed, and the legislature granted money to place plumbing and heating pipes inside walls and to remove dirty insulation from the floors. For the next generation, routine maintenance sufficed. Then Governor Kerr Scott (1949-1953) had the exterior steam cleaned and an elevator installed, and Mrs. Dan K. Moore purchased new furnishings and objets d'art in the 1960s.

When the General Assembly brought up the issue of a new mansion, reaction was immediate and largely negative. The Executive Residence Building Commission had Bill Dodge of Dodge & Beckwith Architects design plans for a replacement, which called for a 21-room residence with no public rooms. Architects, led by Dean Emeritus of the State University School of Design Henry Kamphoefner, condemned the design for being old-fashioned, "French Country," and more appropriate for a middle-level executive than for the governor of North Carolina. Former first ladies Mrs. Melville Broughton, Mrs. Terry Sanford, and Mrs. Dan K. Moore voiced emphatic opposition, and 1972 gubernatorial candidates Hargrove "Skipper" Bowles and James Holshouser both disapproved. The legislature shelved the plans for a new mansion, approving instead a $575,000 renovation in 1975. Walls were repainted, rotting supports replaced, the sagging roof rebraced. Layer upon layer of paint was removed from the carved heart-pine central stairway and sterling silver fixtures. A new heating and air-conditioning system, a fire escape, and a second-floor family kitchen were all added, and when work ended, the governor's family and guests had access to seven modern bathrooms.

The controversy over plans for a new governor's mansion and the proposal's decisive defeat indicated the growing power of Raleigh preservationists, which had begun to emerge much earlier. For a period after World War II, Raleighites had concentrated almost totally on economic progress. As an extreme example of official acceptance of the primacy of development,

in January of 1950 the city council voted six to one to use a portion of Moore Square for parking. The Mayor's Advisory Committee even presented plans calling for 180 parking spaces, but the city needed General Assembly approval since the property belonged to the state. The Raleigh Council of Architects responded negatively, opposition built, the city allowed the project to die, and preservationists were heartened.

That same year the Order of Masons purchased Josephus Daniels' old home at Glenwood and Caswell from the Daniels

During the mid-1960s and early 1970s, people on college campuses across the country protested the United States' involvement in the war in Vietnam. Students at North Carolina State University, pictured expressing their sentiments on campus, were no exception. Courtesy, North Carolina State University Archives, Raleigh

J.R. Tisdale fastens another sheet of new copper to the dome of the capitol in the summer of 1972 during the building's restoration. (DAH)

family for $65,000. The Masons spent the next nine years renovating Wakestone, named for its stone quarried in Wake County, and in April 1960 they dedicated it as a Masonic Temple—ensuring continued existence for the house that had been visited by Franklin Delano Roosevelt, Paderewski, Will Rogers, and others of note.

Mayor W.G. Enloe appointed the 10-member Historic Sites Commission to preserve historic structures in Raleigh in December of 1961, with Mrs. Edward Waugh as its first chairman. Two years later the city council approved a Sites Commission plan to preserve the Richard B. Haywood house at 127 East Edenton as an historic site. In July 1966 Walter Muir Whitehall, director of the Boston Athenaeum, studied the downtown area and suggested that the Sites Commission seek, in descending order of preference, to 1) save old buildings by using them as they were originally intended, 2) preserve them as memorials, 3) convert them to other uses (citing the old water tower as a prime example), or 4) move them to vacant lots.

The North Carolina National Bank applied Whitehead's primary dictum to the old State Bank a short time later. Christ Church had used the State Bank as a rectory between 1873 and 1951, and after 1951 for other purposes. In the mid-1960s, churchwardens decided to move the old building to make way for a new one, but several members of the congregation objected. Church officers then offered it to the state, provided the state move it. The state declined. But in 1968 NCNB saved the day. NCNB purchased the building, spent $250,000 restoring it, moved it 77 feet east and 21 feet nearer to New Bern Avenue, and operated it as a branch. The old State Bank is now used as an office and bank of the State Employees' Credit Union.

The most ambitious preservation project in recent years involved the work of many individuals and organizations and has resulted in the creation of Mordecai Historic Park. The Junior League of Raleigh helped the Raleigh Historic Sites

Top: After its renovation was completed in 1976, the Executive Mansion boasted new timbers, updated heating and air conditioning, a second-floor family kitchen, and restored woodwork and sterling silver fixtures. (DAH)

Above: According to the Mordecai Square Historical Society, Mordecai house is important because of "its 18th and 19th-century architecture, its furnishings, portraits and books from its original collection (extremely rare for an historic house), and its use as both house museum and center for historical activities and study." (DAH)

This aerial view of North Carolina State University, taken in 1968, includes Harrelson Hall (designed by Edward Walter Waugh), the first circular classroom building ever to grace a university campus in the United States. Courtesy, North Carolina State University Archives, Raleigh

Commission raise enough money to purchase the Mordecai house in 1968 and all the original furniture in succeeding years. The house, the centerpiece in the Historic Park, had been built in 1785 by Joel Lane for his son Henry. Moses Mordecai had lived in the original part of the house after marrying Henry Lane's daughter Margaret. He provided in his will for enlarging the structure, which was done in 1826. The Historic Sites Commission obtained a Department of Housing and Urban Development grant of $29,750 in 1970 to restore the house, which was opened to the public in 1972.

In 1972 the Mordecai Square Historical Society, Inc., grew out of the Raleigh Historic Sites Commission and took over management of Mordecai Park. Members opened reconstructed gardens to the public on April 16, 1972, and over the years they have brought to the park the Andrew Johnson birthplace, the Badger-Iredell law office, a small chapel, and other small structures of historic interest. The president of Mordecai Square Historical Society, Mrs. A.C. Menius, credits the generosity of the Raleigh business community for making much of the Society's work possible.

In April 1982 two more old houses were moved to another preservation area on New Bern Avenue that has long contained the White-Holman house, built in 1798, and State Treasurer John Haywood's 1799 home. The Mordecai Square Society oversaw the relocation of the house that Supreme Court Justice Walter A. Montgomery had built in 1906, and the private Historic Preservation Fund of North Carolina moved the 1890s Bretsch house, which it intends to use for its home office.

Private organizations do not have a monopoly on downtown preservation efforts, however. In March 1982 the city council approved the Downtown East/Downtown East Side redevelopment plan. City Planner George Chapman and Mayor C. Smedes York hope the program will create an influx of residents into the area bordered by Wilmington, Lenoir, New Bern, and South East Street. The program restricts new structures to a scale compatible with the existing historic buildings, and the Mayor has committed his office to providing any assistance possible to private developers.

In 1975, after Arthur M. Louis had ranked the nation's 50 largest cities by their desirability as places to live for an article in *Fortune,* the *News and Observer* commissioned him to rank Raleigh. After studying relevant data, he placed Raleigh fifth—below San Diego, Seattle, San Jose, and Tulsa, and ahead of cities such as Honolulu, Portland, and Denver. Louis gave Raleigh high grades for its low crime rate, its health-care facilities, and its lack of pollution, but low marks for its nightlife.

That same year Mayor Clarence E. Lightner, League of Women Voters President Mrs. Betty Ann Knudsen, and others traveled to San Diego to present Raleigh's case for being selected an "All America City" by the National Municipal League. The League agreed and so designated Raleigh, citing among its reasons the "citizen revolution" that had led to district representation on the city council and to the creation of the Citizens Advisory Council, made up of the chairmen of 18 community groups representing every sector of the city. Mayor Lightner compared Raleigh's achievement to that of David Thompson of State University, who had recently won All-American honors in basketball for the third successive year, adding, however, that "Unlike David Thompson's jersey . . . Raleigh's All-American honors will not be retired."

The *News and Observer* assessment of 1942, which pointed to Raleigh's relative stability at the end of the Great Depression, had singled out state employment as a major stabilizing force. The public institutions located in the capital still provide reliable employment as is evidenced by recent experiences. During the recession of 1975, when state

David Thompson shoots for two points against the University of North Carolina. The Wolfpack basketball star holds nine collegiate athletic records, including most points scored in a single game (57), most scored in a season (838), and most career points (2309). Holder of 16 other major awards (including AP Player of the Year, 1973 and 1974, and UPI Player of the Year, 1975), Thompson scored 23 points against UCLA and 21 points against Marquette to help lead N.C. State to the national title in 1974. Courtesy, North Carolina State University Department of Athletics, Office of Sports Information

Tommy Burleson of N.C. State moves past UCLA's Bill Walton during the semifinal game of the 1974 NCAA Basketball Championship. State won, 80-77, and defeated Marquette 76-64 to become national champions. Burleson, an All-America player in 1973 and 1974, was the first-round draft choice for the Seattle Supersonics after his senior year. Courtesy, North Carolina State University Department of Athletics, Office of Sports Information

unemployment rose to 10.8 percent and national figures to 8.5 percent, no more than 4 to 5 percent of Raleigh workers were jobless at any one time. In the deeper recession of 1981-1982, Raleigh again maintained a jobless rate about half that of the state's, despite the fact that city population had risen to some 154,000 by 1978.

The continued presence of state government and educational institutions, the steady growth of business and commerce, and the increased importance of the Research Triangle Park have all combined to enhance Raleigh's stability and ensure bright prospects for the future. The vigilance of preservation groups, with their desire to couple historical continuity with economic progress, promises to keep the City of Oaks a pleasant place to live, no less in coming years than in its fascinating past.

Members of a wedding party linger in the WRAL Gardens shortly before sunset. Capitol Broadcasting Company founder A.J. Fletcher planted the five-acre gardens on Western Boulevard in 1959. Open year-round to the public, the park has also been the scene of many social functions.

Although the carnival aspect of the fair has gained in popularity over the years, ornamental plasterwork on the wall surrounding the North Carolina State Fair Grounds offers a subtle reminder that the annual event is to showcase North Carolina's farm produce, material handiwork, and industry.

Previous page: A view of Raleigh's capitol building and Confederate monument is attributed to N. James Littlejohn (Jacques) Busbee (1870-1947), artist, writer, and lecturer. In 1907 the North Carolina Historical Commission sent Busbee to study and record the historical monuments on Roanoke Island. He and his wife Juliana later rediscovered the pottery district of northwestern Moore County, whose residents were descendants of the English Staffordshire potters. Busbee opened a pottery shop in the area calling it "Jugtown," and the artists' colony that cropped up around it retained the same name. Busbee left his painting career to revive and promote Jugtown pottery. Courtesy, North Carolina Museum of Art

The Meredith College skyline changed in August 1982 with the completion of the Christina Brown and Seby Brown Jones Chapel. Founded in 1891 as Baptist Female University and opened eight years later, by 1904 the school's name had been changed to Baptist University for Women. The school acquired its current cognomen — honoring Thomas Meredith, founder of the Biblical Recorder *and advocate of higher education for women — in 1909. Classes were moved in 1926 from the original turreted building at Blount and Edenton streets to Meredith's current location on Hillsborough Street.*

Top: *Pullen Park has provided a setting for the rest and recreation of city residents since 1887, when R. Stanhope Pullen donated 60 acres to the city for use as a public park.*

Above: *These girls await their chance to perform in the Capitol Square Arts Festival. The state Department of Public Instruction sponsors the event each spring, giving student groups from North Carolina public schools an opportunity to display their skills in art, music, drama, and dance.*

G.S.H. Appleget designed the Andrews-Duncan house, 407 North Blount Street, for railroad baron Alexander Boyd Andrews. The symmetrical Italianate home was completed around 1872.

Smedes Hall was constructed around 1839 at St. Mary's College and named for founder Aldert Smedes. The Greek Revival building houses major campus organizations.

Incorporated in 1869, Oakwood Cemetery includes some interesting examples of 19th-century stonecutter's art among its gravestones. This final resting place for many city residents eventually expanded to include the Confederate and Hebrew cemeteries, established in 1867 and 1870, respectively. A turn-of-the-century monument in the form of an angel marks a child's grave in the cemetery.

The North Carolina Veterinary Medical Association initiated the movement to construct a school in 1967, and students were first admitted to the new North Carolina State University School of Veterinary Medicine for the 1981-1982 academic year. The $32 million, 300,000-square-foot learning center, designed by Fereby and Walters, occupies 160 acres near Blue Ridge Road.

In 1938 the Raleigh Little Theatre, the City of Raleigh, and the WPA pooled resources to turn "the old mud hole" off Pogue Street into a drama center. The amphitheater shown here was completed during the summer of 1939.

Mrs. Frances P. Pugh has owned the 100-acre Tara Farm on Newton Road since 1961. The farm specializes in the breeding of Morgan horses, one of which, Apollo's Reflection, won the 1981 World Grand National title in Oklahoma.

A Morgan mare and colt graze at Tara Farm.

Presently undergoing renovation for use as a community cultural center, Estey Hall was erected between 1874 and 1880 on the Shaw University campus. The edifice contained the country's first college for black women.

The four-story Briggs building, hailed as the city's first skyscraper when constructed in 1874, has kept its 19th-century appearance. Descendants of founder Thomas H. Briggs still own the original hardware business and the structure in which it has been housed for more than a century.

Joel Lane built Wakefield during the 1760s. Now located at 728 West Hargett Street, the farmhouse with its gambrel roof (whose shingles have rounded edges to prevent weather-induced curling) was the focal point of a large plantation. Lane sold 1,000 acres of land to the State of North Carolina in 1792, providing the site for the capital.

Above: *Elmwood, 16 North Boylan Avenue, was built by John Louis Taylor, first chief justice of the state supreme court. The house, completed in 1810, was owned by two other supreme court justices, William Gaston and Thomas Ruffin, and by editor-historian Samuel A' Court Ashe.*

Right: *This 1912 postcard shows how Hillsborough Street appeared in the early 20th century. From the Postcard Collection, Manuscript Department, Perkins Library. Courtesy, Duke University, Durham*

Top: *Before its building was completed, the first offerings of the Raleigh Little Theatre were outdoor performances at the amphitheater. The new building was dedicated on September 12, 1940. Raleigh residents still enjoy Little Theatre productions.*

Above: *Apart from its performances, the Raleigh Little Theatre is also known for its rose garden.*

Although a large wooden drum no longer adorns the top, the water tower at 155 West Morgan Street appears much as it did in 1887. W.H. Deitrick bought the tower in 1938 and transformed it into an office building, which presently serves as headquarters for the state chapter of the American Institute of Architects.

The home of Walter
Montgomery, Confederate
cavalry officer and North
Carolina supreme court
justice, was moved from its
original site at 124 East
Edenton Street to a city-
owned lot at 212 New Bern
Avenue in 1982, Christ
Church having donated the
house to the Mordecai Square
Historical Society. Its relocation demonstrates the commitment of a growing number
of city residents to preserving
their past.

New York sculptor Bruno
Lucchesi designed the statue
of Sir Walter Raleigh, which
mingles with visitors to Bicentennial Plaza. The Sir Walter
Raleigh Commission of the
state Department of Cultural
Resources directed the creation
and placement of the 11-foot
monument in the park located
across from the State Legislative Building.

When the congregation of Christ Church outgrew its 1829 wooden frame structure at 120 East Edenton Street, it commissioned New Yorker Richard Upjohn, founder of the American Institute of Architects, to design something larger and more substantial to occupy the site. The granite church Upjohn envisioned was consecrated in 1854; its unusual stone steeple-tower was added in 1861. At the right acolytes and choir are shown preparing for the Sunday processional.

Ancient Greek design motifs are evident in the senate chamber of the capitol. According to a Division of Archives and History publication, "the capitol has been less changed in appearance, inside and out, than any other major American civic building of its era. The stonework, the ornamental plaster and ironwork, the furniture of the legislative chambers, and all but one of the marble mantels. . . are original, not restorations or reproductions."

Busts of John M. Morehead (left) and M.W. Ransom (right) flank the 1970 reproduction of the Canova statue of George Washington that stands in the capitol rotunda. The original likeness of the general was unveiled on December 24, 1821, and destroyed in the State House fire 12 years later.

Left: *Charles Duncan McIver (1860-1906) founded the State Normal and Industrial School, now the University of North Carolina at Greensboro. A statue of him (by Ruckstuhl) was placed on Union Square in 1911.*

Above: *People who are accustomed to neatly shelved books and carefully filed papers are often shocked at the sight of the capitol library, restored to appear as it did during a typical legislative working day in the mid-1850s. Both state lawmakers and the general public had access to the room; one wonders how anybody found anything amid such chaos.*

Right: *Fayetteville Street has undergone many changes; buildings came and went, horses gave way to trolleys, and the automobile replaced them both. However, on January 7, 1976, the street was closed to motorized traffic. By November 3, 1977, the first three blocks of a pedestrian mall had been dedicated.*

Below: *Charles Keck's bronze statue,* Presidents North Carolina Gave the Nation *was dedicated on Union Square in October 1948, with Harry S Truman present. The three leaders are Andrew Jackson (on horseback), 7th President of the United States, James Knox Polk, 11th (left), and Andrew Johnson, 17th (right).*

Above: *Atlanta architect P. Thornton Marye, designer of the 1911 Municipal Building and the Memorial Auditorium, also drew the plans for the Commercial National Bank building. Intended to be the tallest structure in the city, the 10-story, late Gothic Revival office building was completed in 1912. First Citizens Bank assumed ownership of the building in the mid-1930s.*

Top right: *The Cafe Promenade in the Radisson Plaza Raleigh Hotel, provides a congenial atmosphere for luncheons and other social activities. The 362-room hotel on the 400 block of Fayetteville Street Mall was dedicated on May 20, 1982.*

William Christmas provided for five urban parks in his 1792 plan of Raleigh, only three of which remain: Union, Moore, and Nash squares. The latter, shown here, provides a lone senior citizen a few minutes' peace before nightfall.

When the first edition of *Raleigh: City of Oaks* appeared in late 1982, one Raleigh fixture was in the process of putting a wrenching new beginning behind it in preparation for what has become a splendid presence, and another was in the midst of early days of glory that would give way to personal and institutional gloom.

When Governor Dan Moore named the State Art Museum Building Commission in 1967 to construct a new, permanent home for the state art collection, the Capitol Area Planning Commission wanted the facility built on Heritage Square in downtown Raleigh. Building Commission members, desiring a site that would allow for growth, won approval from the legislature in 1969 to make its own decision and in 1972 selected a state-owned 157-acre plot on Blue Ridge Road. Supported by editorials in the *N&O* and the *Raleigh Times*, opponents to the Blue Ridge site initiated a lawsuit and urged efforts in the legislature to keep the museum downtown. Continuing its initiative while the lawsuit rose to the state supreme court, the Building Commission obtained ownership of the desired land and selected from 43 design proposals a plan devised under a joint venture combining Edward Durell Stone Associates of New York City and Holloway-Reeves Associated Architects of Raleigh, the team that had designed the Legislative Building.

VIII

HEADING TOWARD THE 21ST CENTURY:

1983-1997

The original plan called for a 395,000-sq. ft. white-marble pile with two wings graced by roof gardens and a reflecting pool carrying an estimated price tag of $28.3 million. The lawsuit eventually ended in favor of the Building Commission. However, a sharp jump in construction costs and a shortage of money combined to force a scaling back of the grand design. By June 1977 when the Middlesex Construction Company submitted the winning bid of $5.7 million, a far more modest plan called for a 181,000 sq. ft., four-level brick structure sans the two wings, the aerial gardens and the reflecting pool.

A private fund-drive raised $5 million to support construction, but problems continued, and the October 10, 1980, completion date passed amid growing concerns over substandard construction. Nevertheless, determined museum officials dedicated the incomplete building on May 28, 1981. Six months later, the Building Commission terminated the contract and Middlesex sued the state. Inland Construction Company completed the project, including costly remedial work, and in April 1983 the museum finally opened—28 months late at a final cost of $15.75 million.

Problems still continued. Naming Holloway-Reeves as a third party as insurance in case it lost the suit, the state filed a countersuit against Middlesex in 1985. The lawsuits progressed to the state supreme court three times before being tried in superior court from May to August 1987. A ruling by Judge Giles R. Clark on March 21, 1988, exonerated the state and Holloway-Reeves, producing a judgment against Middlesex of $373,603. Architect Ralph Reeves died in 1984 during the drawn-out ordeal that had affected his partner John Holloway so emotionally that he had never entered the state showpiece his firm had designed.

As the construction calamity was evolving, museum director Moussa M. Domit was progressively angering his assistants and volunteer groups with what they termed an "abrasive" management style, creating another heavily headlined controversy that ended only when Domit announced in March 1980 that he was resigning. Edgar Peters Bowron was appointed permanent director on May 1, 1981, in time to oversee the transfer of 6,000 works of art valued at $50 million into their new home. Bowron generated his own

Facing page: Fayetteville Street, a longtime center of commerce for Raleigh, is featured in this 1910 postcard view, looking toward the capitol. From the Postcard Collection, Manuscript Department, Perkins Library. Courtesy, Duke University, Durham

When this architects' model of the new State Museum of Natural Sciences becomes reality in June 1999, the major new exhibits will include North Carolina's Natural Treasures, a show-case of the natural resources of the state; Mountains to the Sea, a walk-through diorama with a water-fall and live animals; Marine Hall, holding the popular whale skeletons; Fossil Hall, recreating the clash of the plates that created North Carolina; Tropical Conserv-atory and Tropical Connec-tions, containing a dry trop-ical forest with living insects and flying, crawling and swim-ming animals; and the Arthro-pod Zoo, a utopia for ants, honey bees, spiders and water fleas. Courtesy, North Carolina State Museum of Natural Sciences

controversies by discarding the Collectors Gallery that had sold works by North Carolina artists and by rescheduling what had been an annual exhibit of North Carolina artists to occur only once every three years.

However, the story has a pretty ending. Attendance soon quin-tupled from the 52,306 visitors to the downtown gallery the previous year; the museum is now one of the most respected in the nation; and current director Lawrence J. Wheeler has over-seen recent developments that widened the appeal and the audience of the museum.

Stimulated by a gift of $600,000 from its namesake, the $2.5 million Joseph M. Bryan Jr. Museum Park Theater was ready for dedication in the fall of 1996 when Hurricane Fran blew past at 2 a.m. on September 6, leaving only minor damage to the mu-seum but uprooting dozens of trees and delaying the ceremony. Dedicated belatedly on April 19 and 20, 1997, with the world premiere of *Night Falls on Manhattan*, a film by Durham producer Thom Mount of *Bull Durham* fame, the theater has a performance stage, a 60' X 30' outdoor screen, a 500-seat amphitheater with lawn seating for 2,000, and an outdoor sculpture of 80' letters created from concrete, wood, sand, boulders and plants that spell "PICTURE THIS" to observers who have vivid imaginations or the advantage of being airborne.

To celebrate the fiftieth anniversary of the museum, 45 of the state's most well known writers responded to their favorite works

Below: Stephen Acai and John Saputo headed the committee that erected the North Carolina Vietnam Veterans Memorial on Capitol Square in 1987. Sculptor Abbe Gowdin of Colfax, NC, designed and created the memorial, financed

in a grassroots effort aided by significant contributions from WPTF, Capital Broadcast-ing, 18 distributors of Adolph Coors Brewing Co., and the General Assembly. Courtesy, Stephen A. Acai, IV

An April 10, 1997, aerial view of the North Carolina Museum of Art clearly depicts the massive outdoor sculpture "PICTURE THIS," with the "T," "H," and "I" of "THIS" incorporated in the recently opened Joseph M. Bryan, Jr., Theater in the Museum Park. Courtesy, The N.C. Museum of Art

in the collection in *The Store of Joys: Writers Celebrate the North Carolina Museum of Arts' Fiftieth Anniversary*—a collection of poems, short stories, and essays by Daphne Athas, Doris Betts, Fred Chappell, Wilma Dykeman, Clyde Edgerton, Jill McCorkle, Tim McLaurin, Reynolds Price, Lee Smith and three dozen more poets and writers of fiction.

With the exception of writers attached to the NCSU English Department, the literary arts have hardly flourished in Raleigh during the past decade and a half.

Within that English Department, Lee Smith of Chapel Hill left on a leave of absence after winning a $105,000 Reader's Digest grant in December 1994. The Sir Walter Raleigh Award and O. Henry Award winner was preparing a final draft for her 11th book, *Saving Grace*, which followed a long list of popular novels. Tim McLaurin resides in the woods of Chatham County, collects snakes, and builds an increasing national reputation for his novels including 1997s *The Last Great Snake Show*. John Kessell writes scientific fiction, the latest being *Corrupting Dr. Night*.

While she was polishing her craft, Raleighite Kaye Gibbons worked as a waitress at MacGregor Downs Country Club, the type of job she bid farewell to permanently in 1993 when her fourth novel, *Charms for the Easy Life*, hit the New York Times bestseller list. Luke Whisnant, whose novel *Watching TV with the Red Chi-*

nese focuses on three Chinese students adjusting to American ways against the background of the Reagan-Carter election and the assassination of John Lennon, lives in Raleigh and commutes to his professorial duties in the English Department at East Carolina University. In the summer of 1997 Charles Frazier garnered reams of favorable reviews and enjoyed the view from atop the New York *Times* fiction best-sellers list for his first novel, *Cold Mountain*, in which the wounded Confederate soldier Inman leaves a Raleigh military hospital in the fall of 1864 for a hazardous trek back home to Cold Mountain west of Asheville for a tragic reunion with his cherished Ada.

In addition to the Museum of Art, public-supported art in the Capitol flourished in the 1980s with the formation of the Raleigh Area Flute Association, the North Carolina Theatre (NCT) joining local actors with visiting professionals in performances in

Distinguished by its fountains, pedestrian walkways, courtyards and sitting areas, the nine-level Moore Square Station contains 725 parking spaces convenient to Fayetteville Street Mall and acts as the transfer center for the metropolitan and regional bus systems. Courtesy, Wilbur Smith Associates.

Memorial Auditorium, the Capital Area Community Chorus presenting light classical and Broadway productions, the City Gallery of Contemporary Art on South Blount Street exhibiting regional and national contemporary art. Artsplosure began in 1980, sponsoring the New Year's Eve First Night alcohol-free celebrations, which attract as many as 45,000 party goers prior to the descent of the gigantic acorn in Moore Square at the advent of the new year, and features arts events throughout the year, highlighted by a 10-day spring festival of arts exhibits, outdoor concerts and theatrical performances. Artspace on East Davie Street created 44 artist studios, viewer galleries, and the UpFront Sales Gallery in an old automobile dealership next to the City Market.

The drive for public support of the arts intensified in 1990 when the Capital Area Arts Foundation merged with the Wake County Arts Council to form the United Arts Council of Raleigh and Wake County, charged with raising money for the arts from local governments, businesses, and other private contributions. The Council was soon assisting more than 60 groups—including within the city the Raleigh Little Theatre, the City Gallery of Contemporary Art, Artspace, Artsplosure, The Raleigh Symphony Orchestra and Boyschoir—and delivering block grants in the county to Apex, Cary, Fuquay-Varina, Garner, Holly Springs, Knightsdale, Morrisville, Rolesville, Wake Forest, Wendall and Zebulon.

In the summer of 1997, the A.J. Fletcher Foundation and Preservation North Carolina gave new life to the 123-year-old Briggs Hardware building on Fayetteville Mall, which had sat vacant for two years after Briggs Hardware moved to North Raleigh. The Fletcher Foundation devoted the 5,000-sq. ft. street level space to art exhibits, public performances and educational programs and rented upstairs space to non-profit organizations.

Compared to the problems in building the Museum of Art, the construction of the new Museum of History progressed with the smoothness of a contractor's promise. In 1978, museum director John D. Ellington urged Raleighite Eve Ragland Williamson to take the post of executive director of the 900-member NC Museum of History Associates, a volunteer group devoted to supporting the museum. Within 10 years, Williamson had boosted membership to more than 13,000, had raised $5.9 million, and was eagerly awaiting the beginning of construction on the new building in 1989.

The dedication on April 23, 1994, included the opening of four new exhibits on women, sports, folklife, and North Carolina history plus more adequate space for the collection of 250,000 artifacts. A party of Lumbee Indians, Richard Petty on a Pontiac, and a contingent of Highway Patrol troopers in vintage autos led a 50-unit parade prior to the ribbon-cutting. Doc Watson and the Surrey County String Band performed; poet Maya Angelou spoke; and governors Terry Sanford, Robert Scott, James Holshouser, Jim Martin and Jim Hunt participated in extended festivities marred only by the sudden illness of four-time UNC All-American Charlie "Choo Choo" Justice, who had just finished telling tall tales of gridiron clashes and who recovered to tell them again.

The Archdale Building looms over a Travel and Tourism Division's Tourism Works for America celebration on the Government Mall. Discontent with Artist Bill Fontana's $142,250 "Spiraling Sound Axis" (a "sound sculpture" broadcasting pounding surf, croaking frogs and other sounds of North Carolina) in the new Revenue Building to the right helped to prompt the General Assembly to abolish the NC Arts Council's Art-works for State Buildings program, created in 1988 to require .5% of construction costs of state buildings to be spent on artworks. Courtesy, NC Department of Commerce

Located on Bicentennial Mall between the Capitol and the Legislative Building, the new Museum of History edifies with delight in exhibitions ranging from a replica of the Wright brothers' plane above the entrance to Andy Griffith chronicling the state's past on video to one of Richard Petty's blue #43 NASCAR racers to the wardrobe of Thomas Wolfe's mother Julia to dozens of other exhibits assembled from more than a quarter of a million historical keepsakes. Courtesy, NC Museum of History

Texan James C. McNutt succeeded John Ellington as director in February 1995 and foresaw a productive future with the support of the growing Museum Associates, whom he labeled "without a doubt the strongest support group for any state museum in the country." In recognition of her work, the NC Council of Women honored Eve Williamson with the Distinguished Women of North Carolina Award in March 1997.

While the Art Museum approached its uneasy opening in the winter of 1982-1983, the basketball program at N.C. State was in the mediocre beginning of what would end as the most dramatically exciting season for any team in hoop history.

When coach Norm Sloan moved on to Florida in the spring of 1980, NCSU athletic director Willis Casey selected as his replacement brash New Yorker Jim Valvano, who had taken over a 4-19 Iona College team in 1975 and led it to the NCAA tournament in 1979 and 1980. In his first news conference after arriving at NCSU, Valvano made two prophetic pronouncements: one tragically ironic, the other spectacularly confirmed. When asked about UNC's Dean Smith, he quipped, "I don't intend to live in anybody's shadow. And besides, I'm going to outlive him."

In explaining his success at Iona he pledged, "In three years, I intend to do it again, but this time I will not settle for anything less than a national championship. In fact, I guarantee it."

A first year record of 14-13 in a schedule peppered with weak non-conference opponents offered scant promise of fulfilling the bold guarantee, but a 22-10 posting the following year and a trip to the NCAA tournament began to draw attention to the braggadocio coach and his "Cardiac Pack."

Valvano knew in the spring of 1983 that he had to win the ACC tournament to have a solid shot at entry into the NCAA tournament. Starters Derreck Whittenberg, Cozell McQueen, Lorenzo Charles, Thurl Bailey, and Sidney Lowe, and sixth man

Terry Gannon captured the tournament with three upsets—beating Wake Forest by a single point, taking UNC in overtime, and topping Virginia and Ralph Sampson 81-78. In Corvalis, Oregon, NCSU battled Pepperdine University to win in double overtime: then after trailing UNLV by 12 well into the second half they were again victorious. In Ogden, Utah, for the second round, State beat Utah by 19 then came from behind in the final seconds to squeeze past Virginia 63-62. In Albuquerque for the Final Four, State's 67-60 win over Georgia prompted little national notice, since experts concluded that Houston's victory over Louisville amounted to the de facto national championship, with the remaining Houston-State match-up serving as nothing more than Houston's formal introduction to the officials who would pass out the NCAA trophies.

State led at the half, but the hopes of Pack fans flagged early in the second-half when a Houston run built a 42-35 lead that seemed to confirm the obvious. But Houston burned the clock, failing to use the talents of Akeem Olajuwon and Clyde Drexler. State resorted to fouling, and a combination of poor Houston free-throw shooting and State's hitting six of seven from the field in the final minutes led to a tie with 44 seconds left. After a missed Houston shot, State rebounded, called a time-out, and then waited for a final shot. Pressure defense by Houston forced Derreck Whittenberg to take a 30-foot jump shot, which was far short, but Lorenzo Charles caught the air-ball and dunked it for a 54-52 win and the national championship for the Team of Destiny—and Valvano ran wild on the court looking, he said later, for someone to hug.

Valvano and State's good fortunes on the court continued, advancing to the Final Eight in both 1985 and 1986, winning the ACC tournament in 1988, and tying for the ACC regular season championship in 1989. However, on January 7, 1989, the

On May 6, 1997, four-term governor Jim Hunt welcomes members of the Durham Bouncing Bulldogs Rope Skipping Demonstration Team for a performance on the Government Mall. In the background is the Education Building, known to distracters as The Pink Palace and the Taj Mahal, home of the severely reduced (from some 1,200 in 1989 to about 460 in 1996) Department of Public Instruction and the "canvas" for controversial government-funded artwork. Courtesy, NC Department of Commerce

The NCSU Centennial Campus off Western Boulevard came into being in 1984 when the state donated 780 acres for a collection of "related villages, neighborhoods and courtyards" that has became the home of the College of Textiles, which produces more than half of all textile graduates in the nation, and the location of research laboratories for the National Weather Service, the Mars Mission Research Center, Materials Science Engineering research and additional research labs and offices for students, faculty, staff, and corporate and government employees. Courtesy, NC State University News Services

national press published details from the dust jacket of *Personal Fouls*, a slash-and-burn attack on Valvano and the State basketball program by Peter Golenbock scheduled to be published by Pocket Books, Inc.; and Valvano's long, painful, inescapable downfall began.

Earlier, faculty and administrators at NCSU had complained that Valvano's players were receiving preferable treatment regarding easy class schedules, attendance, and inflated grades. Golenbock added accusations of players' having their grades fixed, taking drugs, and receiving large sums of cash as well as jewelry and automobiles. Valvano and Chancellor Bruce Poulton denied the charges and invited NCAA investigators, who arrived on campus before the end of January. UNC President C.D. Spangler initiated a separate investigation, which received highly publicized assistance from the State Bureau of Investigation. On February 22, Pocket Books announced that it would not publish *Personal Fouls*. However, on July 27, Carroll & Graf Publishers released Golenbock's "exposé," and it was indeed a greatly flawed book, filled with errors and omissions. Nevertheless, the publicity was reaping its toll. Chancellor Poulton resigned on August 21, even though the NCAA report released in November exonerated Valvano and his staff while finding the university guilty of violating eight relatively minor infractions.

The 1989-1990 season was underway when former player Charles Shackleford admitted he had accepted $65,000 in 1987-1988 from a sports agent. Then ABC News charged that the Pack had

In the last summer of his content, Jim Valvano poses with Branson Hatley of Asheboro during the coach's 1988 basketball camp on the State campus. Although his teams would be winners for the next two seasons, the remainder of Valvano's life was largely doleful. He could not professionally survive the torrent of charges to come nor could he humanly defeat the cancer that became apparent three summers later. He would have also been disappointed in young Hatley, who chose to attend UNC-Chapel Hill. Courtesy, Branson Hatley

shaved points in a game against an NCAA Division II team. (Valvano pointed out that games matching Division I and II teams do not have a gambling point-line.) The 18-11 season ended with a loss to Georgia Tech in the first round of the ACC tournament, and all that remained were the negotiations to buy out Valvano's contract, which ended on April 7 when he agreed to accept $613,000 from NCSU and the Wolfpack Club.

Valvano capitalized on his notoriety/celebrity to become a color analyst for ESPN and ABC, travel the nation giving motivational speeches at highly motivating $15,000 fees, pitch products on television, market Coach V sportswear, and with Curry Kirkpatrick defend his tenure at NCSU in *Valvano: They Gave Me a Lifetime Contract, and Then They Declared Me Dead*, a book that incorporated an impressive if somewhat tortured use of statistics to compare the academic achievements of basketball players favorably to students on the whole.

In June 1992, Valvano learned he had a deadly form of cancer, metastatic adenocarcinoma, which led to his death on March 28, 1993, at age 47, after winning the admiration of even his most relentless distracters in his whimperless rage against the dying of the light. The Valvano name lives nationally in the Jimmy V Coaches Against Cancer basketball tournament in the Meadowlands and a Warner Brothers made-for-tv movie, *Never Give Up: The Jimmy V. Story*, and locally in Jimmy V's Steakhouse in the MacGregor Village Shopping Mall, the Jimmy V Celebrity Golf Classic, and the Jimmy V Foundation to raise money for cancer research.

Memory of Valvano's tragic demise was still fresh in June 1993 when NCSU fans received a second jolt from football coach Dick Sheridan, who had turned the Wolfpack into a consistent top-20 team. Arriving in 1986 Sheridan compiled a seven-year record of 52-29-3 against tough opposition, with promise of greater triumphs to come. However, shaken by the death of his close friend Valvano and the heart problems suffered by soccer coach George Tarantini, Sheridan announced he was resigning after a 9-3-1 season, including a trip to the Gator Bowl.

Sports interest in Raleigh entered a new domain in May 1997 when Hartford Whalers owner Peter Karmanos announced he would move his National Hockey League franchise to Raleigh, where the capital's first major league franchise would play as the Carolina Hurricanes after two seasons in the Greensboro War Memorial Coliseum while awaiting the completion of the new arena next to Carter-Finley Stadium. The announcement provided a dramatic finish to a year of feverish activity. In May 1996 Carl Moore assumed leadership of a Centennial Authority committee charged with attracting a major league team to compete in the new arena. In August, Moore, Mayor Tom Fetzer and others met with NHL commissioner Gary Bettman. In October, Charlotte Hornets owner George Shinn briefly expressed interest in basing an NHL expansion team in Raleigh. Then Karmanos began a search for a new home for the Whalers, who had lost $45 million during the past three losing seasons in Hartford. After visiting Raleigh twice in April and balancing bids from Raleigh and Columbus, Ohio, he selected Raleigh.

Top: *The NCSU School of Veterinarian Science graduated the first students from its new Hillsborough Street-Blue Ridge Road campus in May 1985. More than 70 students majoring in dermatology, oncology, orthopedics and other specialties help treat some 17,000 patients per year in small and large animal clinics at the Veterinary Teaching Hospital, established in 1983. Courtesy, Greater Raleigh Chamber of Commerce.*

Above: *At a price tag of $51,000 the 40-ft. Time + Light Tower on Capital Boulevard amounted to only 0.0215% of Raleigh's $237,000,000 budget, but in 1995 it became the burning focus of contention between incumbent mayor Tom Fetzer, who ridiculed the Tower as "an oil derrick with mirrors," and challenger Mary Watson Nooe, who pressed to continue the current $3.63 per-resident spent on the arts. Courtesy, Greater Raleigh Chamber of Commerce.*

That arena had a long, contentious history in Raleigh politics. Early in his first term in 1984, Raleigh Mayor Avery Upchurch placed on the agenda the idea of an arena financed in part by the city when he named Steve Stroud to chair a committee to study the feasibility of building a basketball coliseum Downtown. Upchurch had served three years on the Raleigh Planning Commission and four years as a city councilman in 1983 before winning the first of five elections for mayor. Known as the "drive-in mayor" because he was always available for constituents at his service stations on Glenwood Avenue and Peace Street, Upchurch was consistently pro-development and won sometimes grudging recognition for the transformation of Raleigh from a governmental to a vivacious commercial/information/light-industrial center in which citizens rejoiced in their high quality of life. Upchurch ended his tenure as mayor on November 16, 1993. Two months later he learned he had esophageal cancer. Following his death on June 30, 1994, the city council voted to recognize his service to Raleigh by renaming the Municipal Building the Avery Upchurch Government Center.

The city council abandoned the arena idea after the Stroud committee found it impractical, and the concept languished until 1988 when the General Assembly and NCSU each contributed $1.5 million to finance planning for an NCSU Board of Trustees concept of a 23,000-seat arena projected to cost $58.5 million and to be located next to Carter-Finley Stadium. A Wolfpack Pride campaign raised more than $22 million to help meet construction costs.

By December 1996, the estimated cost of the arena had risen to $132 million, and Mayor Tom Fetzer objected to the number of tax dollars involved. Nevertheless, excitement over attracting an NHL team to Raleigh rallied interest; in early 1997 the Wake County commissioners and the Raleigh city council agreed to commit $48 million from local hotel taxes to the project; and on July 20, 1997, Governor Jim Hunt joined enthralled dignitaries in ground-breaking ceremonies.

Following the 1992 election in which Republicans lost the gubernatorial race handily and maintained their 53-117 minority in the General Assembly and their four-four split in the congressional delegation but won Terry Sanford's U.S. Senate seat, the *N&O* tearlessly announced, "North Carolina Republicans are still shaking off their first post-election hangover in 16 years." Consequently, when Tom Fetzer broke with tradition and entered the mayor's race openly as a Republican in 1993, his chances seemed slim indeed, but his 965-vote victory over Barlow Herget harbingered a hangover cure of epic effectiveness.

In November 1994, for the first time conservative Republicans gained control of Wake County's delegation to the General Assembly as well as the County Board of Commissioners. In a stupendous upset, Fred Heineman captured David Price's "safe" Fourth District Congressional seat. State Senator J.K. Sherron was the only Wake County Democrat with opposition to win.

The origin of the political revolution is evident in a word, the word in North Ridge, North Bend, Northcliff, Northglen, North Haven, North Hills, North Oaks, North Trail, Six Forks North, Towne North. When Ed Richards built North Hills Shopping Mall in the early 1970s, the northern boundary of Raleigh was pine forest and farm land with scattered residences and isolated neighborhoods. By 1994 North Raleigh contained an estimated 109,798 people living upscale lives in affluent subdivisions off mainline arteries lined with shopping centers. Median household income topped $40,000 compared to $26,647 for the state, some 8,500 North Raleigh residents worked in the Research Triangle Park, less than half were North Carolina natives. Every precinct in North Raleigh voted for Fetzer.

Fetzer fulfilled his promise to cut taxes and add policemen and easily won reelection in 1995. The political norm returned to a degree in 1996 when David Price easily recaptured his seat from an ailing Heineman.

In 1978 retired NFL All-Pro John Baker set a pattern for black politicians when he won election as sheriff of Wake County. Vernon Malone won election as the first black Wake County commissioner in 1984, and Republican Frank Turner was the first black to win a city-wide election when he gained an at-large city council seat in 1989.

The Wall Street Journal *proclaimed Tom Fetzer's 965-vote victory in the 1993 mayoral election an "impressive reform victory" for Republicans in the "liberal Democratic stronghold" of the Capitol. Although political opponents staunchly fought his drives to reduce taxes and cut public financing of the arts, Fetzer both pleased and widened his base, leading to his easy reelection in 1995. Courtesy, Mayor's Office, City of Raleigh*

Wake County Sheriff John Haywood Baker, Jr., became the first black sheriff in North Carolina since Reconstruction when he won election in 1978. An All-Pro defensive lineman and captain of the Pittsburgh Steelers in 1965, Baker created the setting for one of the most famous photographs in sports in September 1964. Following a hard sack by Baker that broke three ribs and ended his career, famed New York Giant quarterback Y.A. Tittle rests on a knee, addled, his bald pate streaming blood. Courtesy, Office of the Sheriff of Wake County

Shoppers look over the constant supply of fresh produce in the State Farmers Market, which moved to its new 75-acre location off Lake Wheeler Road in 1991. Operated by the North Carolina Department of Agriculture, Division of Marketing, the Farmers Market registers more than $90 million in sales annually to merchants, restaurateurs, wholesalers, and individuals. Courtesy, Charles D. Edward

Dan Blue, in his sixth term in the General Assembly representing East Raleigh, captured the most powerful position in North Carolina, in that time before the governor had veto power, when he was elected Speaker of the House in 1990, the first black in North Carolina to serve in that post and only the third in the nation. Blue graduated from North Carolina Central University in 1970, earned a law degree from Duke, practiced law in Raleigh first with Terry Sanford's law firm and later as a partner in Thigpen, Blue, Stephens & Fellows, and won election to the house in 1980.

With the population of Wake County having risen 20% from 426,300 in 1990 to 534,075 in 1996 and expected to top a million by 2030, the likelihood is feasible that the 12 municipalities that now incorporate 60% of the land in Wake County will soon absorb all the open space in the county except for parks and the area around the Shearon Harris Nuclear Plant.

While the rapid population and commercial growth associated with North Raleigh may have irked some long-term residents, others responded so positively in a poll that in 1993 *Fortune Magazine* listed the Triangle Area as the most favorable location in America to do business, and examples validating the magazine's selection abounded. Only three years old in 1993, the Walnut Creek Amphitheater ranked sixth in the nation in attendance among outdoor concert facilities. The Carolina Mudcats ranked #2 in the sale of minor-league baseball paraphernalia, trailing only the Durham Bulls in sales. Respondents to a *Money Magazine* subscribers' poll in 1994 flattered the Raleigh area even more, naming it the best place to live in the United States. Seemingly only Hurricane Fran on September 6, 1996, could upset Eden.

With sustained winds of 79-mph gusting frequently to 100-mph, Fran was the first hurricane since Hazel in 1954 to hit Raleigh and the state's most destructive hurricane ever, wreaking by far the greatest damage ever in Wake County—$900 million to homes,

$30 million to businesses, $25 million to agriculture, $20 million to timber. Raleigh experienced a virtual blackout while repair crews from more than a dozen states rushed to help CP&L and Duke Power crews repair downed lines. Soon a disposal site on US-70 was accepting 1,400 truckloads of debris daily.

Large-scale development in the city centered on North and Northeast Raleigh, a focus that will undoubtedly intensify with the completion of the 31-mile Outer Loop. After years of dealing with environmental matters, the 1.2 million sq. ft. Triangle Towne Center off Capital Boulevard and Old Wake Forest Road is ready for construction, the first new mall in Raleigh since 1972. Just north on 47 acres off Capital Boulevard, a 400,000-sq. ft. complex holding 10 movie screens, three restaurants and retail spaces is planned. Still farther north one-fourth mile from the Outer Loop route, the largest commercial project in the history of Wake County is underway. When completed, the 2,000-acre Wakefield complex will include retail stores, offices and 3,000 homes. Falls River Centre, another mix of shops and homes, is under development off Falls of the Neuse and Durant roads. North Hills Mall & Plaza has been under new management since January 1997 with plans to spend $50 million renovating the current "social center" of North Raleigh. Raleigh's other mall, Crabtree Valley, completed a 30% expansion in 1996.

On the other side of town in the State Fairgrounds, the Governor James B. Hunt, Jr., Horse Complex attracts multitudes of the horsey set for an annual show that was once coincident with the State Fair before it required extra days to award more than $100,000 in premiums. The facility has stalls for 2,500 horses, mules, and donkeys competing in divisions ranging from American Quarter Horse to Hackney to Coon Mule Jumping.

Raleigh's Fayetteville Street Mall remains as the single existing pedestrian mall in the state. When the Mall was still new, the

Former New York Yankee pitchers Allie Reynolds and Tommy Byrne chat with editor Bill Uzzle, conducting an interview for an article in the February 27, 1993, issue of his sporadically published Raleigh Reporter. *Known as "The Wild Irish Rose," Byrne five times led his league in hit batsmen and once walked 13 in one game while accumulating a lifetime 85-69 record, including a 16-5 1955 season in which he was named comeback player of the year. After retiring in 1957, Byrne served as mayor of Wake Forest and contributed the column "Baseball Memories" to the* Raleigh Reporter. Courtesy, Michael Lewis Photography

Chapel Hill developer Joe Haken purchased the City Market in June 1995 and quickly transformed it into a busy center for dining with a thriving night life that is helping to stimulate after-five activity in Downtown. Courtesy, Greater Raleigh Chamber of Commerce.

N&O's Guy Munger lauded its beauty and conceded, "But at night, the mall is downright spooky. The pools of inky blackness between the cones of illumination from streetlights are frightening, prone to conjuring up images of muggers and other terrors of the night."

A New Raddison Hotel at the foot of the mall in the early 1980s helped to dim those images. When the 29-story First Union Capital Center in the 100 block and the 29-story BB&T/Two Hannover Square Towers in the 400 block opened in 1991, the national recession slowed leasing agreements momentarily, but soon Raleigh's economy surged upward and thousands of new downtown employees gave the Mall a daytime bustle that carried over into decidedly upbeat after-five activity.

Revitalization of downtown reached a new stride in June 1995 when Chapel Hill developer Joe Hakan and his son Michael purchased the set of financially troubled shops and restaurants in historic City Market for just over $1 million. The first innovation to create an active night life in the area failed when Big Ed Watkins' experiment in keeping Big Ed's City Market Restaurant open until 9 p.m. on Thursday through Saturday proved to be unprofitable. The Hakans confidently continued to upgrade the old market, hiring muralist Michael Brown to cover a wall fronting the parking lot with a cornucopia of vegetables containing faces associated with the market: Big Ed Watkins, City Market manager Smedes York, Angelo Liatos of Angelo's Restaurant, Brass

Key owner Ann Raynor, American Indian Shop owner Chris Bowman, Agriculture Commissioner Jim Graham, and Mayor Tom Fetzer—peering out of a cantaloupe. They opened apartments and offices in second story floors, brought in new businesses, and soon the City Market became the nightspot the Hakans envisioned, with the popular Black Dog Cafe and Greenshields Brewery & Pub picking up significant competition in December 1996 when proprietors T. Scott Bain and Richard McIssac and chef Pete Dougherty opened T.S. Elliott's City Market Bistro, bringing the number of City Market restaurants to eight, intermingled among more than a dozen specialty shops, a travel agency and a comedy club.

Hakan, who designed Crabtree Valley Mall, is also working with McLaurin Management Associates on another project to enliven downtown by converting the former Hudson Belk building into a collection of shops, restaurants, nightspots and sixty condominiums. Former mayor and City Market manager G. Smedes York continues to be active as a developer in Raleigh and Chapel Hill, as the manager of the renovated Cameron Village Shopping Center, and as a major regional player in the residential and commercial brokerage business.

Renovation on and around Capitol Square peaked after the 1990-1991 recession. In its first major improvement in more than 80 years, the 1859 neo-Gothic First Baptist Church spent $500,000 installing a sprinkler system, cleaning and restoring stained glass windows, repairing plaster, painting the interior, laying new floors and carpeting, and installing a new organ console and air conditioning. Christ Church ran scaffolding to the top of its 96-foot bell tower as masons replaced crumbling red sandstone and completely re-mortared the structure.

The state committed tens of millions to renovating the old Education and Revenue buildings and the Ruffin Building on Fayetteville Mall, but the renovation of the Capitol is the eye catcher. Capitol historian Raymond Beck suspected that the monochromatic "Grey Poupon" interior did not match the original color scheme, and research by George T. Fore revealed that during a 1920s restoration architect Philip Schwartz had removed the original white, pearl gray, and sky blue so thoroughly that in 1970 painters mistook a yellow sealant for the original and applied the uniform coat of "Grey Poupon." Plasterer Brian Ewing repaired injuries of time and previous workers to the patterned cornices.

A few hundred feet down Fayetteville Mall, the once majestic "third house of the legislature," the Sir Walter Hotel, stabilized in its decline, providing housing for the elderly and space for Diversified Senior Services, a franchise restaurant, a beauty shop and a bail bond businesses. The Virginia Dare Ballroom, where debutantes once danced and legislators paid a glad ear to lobbyists, sits vacant, evoking melancholic memories of its haughty yesteryears.

A landmark of another sort changed little in appearance though its transformation was as complete as it was unexpected.

In 1894 when Josephus Daniels convinced 100 Democrats they would serve their party well by investing $100 each to allow him to purchase the bankrupt *News & Observer*, he initiated a venture

In a converted automobile dealership on East Davie Street adjacent to the City Market, Artspace maintains working studios for practicing artists and exhibition galleries, all open to the public. Debby Jacobs, who teachers art at Underwood GT Magnet Elementary School, directs a child in print making during one of the dozens of summer arts classes Artspace conducts for children aged four upward. Courtesy, Nancy Novell

that rapidly evolved into a seemingly immutable institution in his town and in his state. Consequently, most Raleighites reacted in genuine amazement when they learned on August 1, 1995, that the Daniels family—who had been sole owners of *N&O* stock since 1915—had sold the adored *News & Observer* and reviled *Nuisance Disturber* for a reported $373 million to McClatchy Newspapers, Inc., which had purchased five South Carolina newspapers from The News & Observer Publishing Company in 1990. McClatchy publishes several West Coast papers, including its flagship, the Sacramento, California, *Bee*. Frank Daniels, Jr., remained as editor, and the quote from Josephus Daniels' will—wishing that his legacy always "devote itself to the policies of equality and justice to the underprivileged"—continued to run on the editorial page, but within a year the new owners were leaving their own stamp on the region.

In June 1996, McClatchy purchased *The Village Advocate*, a Chapel Hill free advertiser, and modified it to become an insert in the *Chapel Hill News*, which had been purchased by the *N&O* in 1993. Chairman of the Board Erwin Potts, a graduate of the

UNC School of Journalism and a member of the N.C. Journalism Hall of Fame, acted as a good neighbor and a devoted alumnus when McClatchy donated $200,000 to his alma mater to establish the McClatchy Newspapers Center for Newspaper Reporting.

Prior to the sale, the *N&O* ceased publication of the afternoon *Raleigh Times* with the November 30, 1989, issue. The *Times'* lineage dated back more than a century to Charles A. Brown and William M. Utley's *Evening Visitor*. John A. Park purchased the afternoon *Times* in 1911 for $25,000 in $20 gold coins and competed with the morning *N&O* until he sold out to the opposition in 1955. A national decline of interest in afternoon newspapers followed, and by the end of the 1980s, the *Times* ceased to be profitable and folded.

A final landmark took a battering when historical research cast a slur on the very name "Raleigh."

In the year of the 200th anniversary of the General Assembly's establishment of a city government in the Capitol in 1795, unsettling information concerning the flamboyant cavalier-poet for

The York Hannover Towers dominate the skyline of Raleigh from this southern perspective. Courtesy, Greater Raleigh Chamber of Commerce.

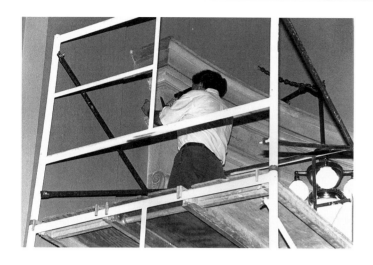

During the end-of-century restoration of the North Carolina Capitol, George T. Fore used a binocular microscopy and a surgical scalpel to examine paint layers one by one to determine original colors. In his research Capitol historian Raymond Beck learned that architect David Paton incorporated suggestions from The Laws of Harmonious Colouring as Applied to Home Painting, *written in 1828 by David Ramsay Hay, with whom Paton had worked in his native Scotland. Courtesy, State Capitol, N.C. Division of Archives and History*

whom the city was named came from Cambridge University archivist Mark Nicholls, who in searching the records of Sir Walter Raleigh's 1603 trial for treason discovered documents in the Bodleian Library at Oxford University that had remained untouched for some 250 years. When Sir Walter's patron and protector Queen Elizabeth died in March 1603, Sir Walter's enemies convinced James I that Sir Walter had committed treason by conspiring to murder the new king and his family, to install Arabella Stuart on the throne of England, to incite rebellion, and to encourage Spain to invade England—for pay. After Henry Brooke (Lord Cobham) named Sir Walter in confessing to the conspiracy in July 1603, Raleigh was arrested and committed to the Tower, convicted of treason in November, and sentenced to be beheaded on December 11. However, James granted a stay of execution on December 10, and the courier remained in the Tower with his family for 13 years, passing the time by writing poetry and the *History of the World*. Freed in 1616 to guide an English expedition searching for a Spanish gold mine in South America, he reneged on a promise not to attack Spanish possessions, and on his return to England the justices of the King's Bench revoked the stay of execution and had Sir Walter beheaded on October 29, 1618. Conceding that the precise degree of Sir Walter's treasonous activity remains questionable, Nicholls concludes, "What we cannot do is argue with any conviction that Ralegh was innocent at law." So far no movement has risen in Raleigh, NC, to cast off the sullied patronymic.

Raleigh entered the nineteenth century hardly more than a village, hoping to become the center of political power in North Carolina in fact as it was in name. It succeeded to the full measure. It entered the twentieth century a commercially stagnated town, hoping above all else to match Durham in the tobacco and textile industries. Fortunately, it failed utterly. It enters the twentieth-first century the prosperous metropolis of one of the most rapidly developing regions on the globe, content that *Money* magazine is right, it is the best place to live in America.

Dr. H.G. Jones, retired curator of the North Carolina Collection at the University of North Carolina at Chapel Hill, took advantage of new revelations concerning Sir Walter Raleigh's betrayal of England to correct the myth that Raleigh never spelled his name with an "i." Jones placed in evidence this December 4, 1583, contract from the NC Collection in which Sir Walter's name appears "Raleigh" throughout, including the signature "W. Raleigh" created by a steel stamp. Skeptics contend Sir Walter neither wrote the document nor provided the signature for the stamp. Courtesy, NC Collection, UNC-Chapel Hill

IX
CHRONICLES OF LEADERSHIP

The "City of Oaks" began as a planned state capital characterized by wide boulevards, wooded parks, an "immigrant" population, and a small commercial center dominated by the proximity of the institutions of state government.

A small coterie of industrious businessmen, planters, politicians, and newspapermen guided Raleigh through an initial three decades of mild "boom"; but the ravages of drought, exhausted farmland, and a general westward migration combined to drain Raleigh of over a third of its citizens in the 1820s, effectively removing the base essential for continued economic development.

Although railways provided connections to distant markets in the 1840s and 1850s, and although population steadily increased, the Wake County economy remained essentially limited to government, agriculture, noncommercial domestic manufacturing, and small enterprises such as hotels, retail stores, printing presses, blacksmith shops, a paper factory, and a regional market for produce and meats.

With the coming of the Civil War and the establishment of the Northern blockade, capital citizens joined the rest of the South in turning to their own resources to manufacture military and domestic products. Raleigh became a center for treating wounded Confederate soldiers, and area manufacturers produced uniforms, socks, gun powder, guncaps, cartridges, matches, and harnesses to supply the Southern armies.

The privation following war, defeat, Reconstruction, and bank closures was more severe in Raleigh than in most areas of the South, and the capital began its economic renaissance relatively late. Nevertheless, the city soon enjoyed paved streets, a telephone exchange in 1879, electric lights in 1884, a streetcar system by 1891, a new depot in 1892, 15 daily and weekly newspapers by 1892, and several textile mills before the end of the century.

Raleigh followed the nation through the prosperity of the early 20th century, the devastation of the 1930s, and the economic revival of the 1940s—a revival that has yet to abate in Wake County.

Simultaneously with a dramatic growth in transportation, distribution, and government activities, Raleigh has become a center in the production of electrical and electronic equipment, nonelectrical machinery, processed food, apparel, printing, fabricated metals, textiles and synthetic materials, wood products, chemicals, and premolded materials. The city is a consistent state leader in retail sales, wholesale trade, and commercial bank deposits.

In the following pages you will meet many of the corporations and individuals who share a large portion of the responsibility for Raleigh's recent prosperity. They have done well here, but they have done far more than simply enrich themselves financially. Their contributions have enhanced the quality of life for their neighbors economically, aesthetically, and socially; and their generosity in making this publication possible attests to their abiding concern for their community.

Built in 1932, and named to honor World War I veterans from North Carolina, the Raleigh Memorial Auditorium became the BTI Center for the Performing Arts in early 1997 when the telecommunications company pledged a $3.1 million addition to the $12.1 million available from Wake County room-and-meal taxes set aside to expand the facility by building performance halls on both sides of the existing auditorium. Courtesy, Greater Raleigh Chamber of Commerce.

Asea Brown Boveri (ABB)

ABB is an outstanding world leader in manufacturing and developing equipment and software used for power generation, transmission and distribution, transportation systems, and industrial and building systems. The company currently employs over 215,000 people in 140 countries with revenues of over $34 billion. In the United States, ABB has revenues of over $5.4 billion and employs over 20,000 people.

ABB has a large presence in the Raleigh area. The ABB Power T&D Company Inc., a subsidiary of ABB Inc., is headquartered on the N.C. State University Centennial Campus and shares facilities with the Electric Transmission Institute (ETI), ABB's premier research and development site for the electric utility industry. The T&D Company offers a complete range of systems and products for power transmission networks, and local distribution and control of electrical power.

ABB's other operations in Raleigh include the Information Systems Division, located in east Raleigh with additional operations in Santa Clara, California. ISD provides hardware and software solutions to the electric utility industry and commercial/industrial markets in the areas of electric metering, metering systems, distribution information systems, energy planning, energy trading, and energy management systems (SCADA / EMS). Raleigh is also ABB's "Center of Excellence" for electric metering worldwide which means that metering technology and the expansion of global metering operations is directed from Raleigh.

Although ABB is a fairly new name in the U.S., the electric metering operation has been a solid part of the Raleigh business community for over 40 years. The products being manufactured in Raleigh by ABB are found in the home, in power stations and factories, in stores, schools and office buildings. Most familiar to the majority of people is the electromechanical meter like that on the sides of homes everywhere—meters that measure the amount of electric energy being used by the residents.

Today, newer technologies in electronic metering, automated meter reading, and metering systems are being merged with other information systems solutions to provide new and better ways to measure and control the transmission and distribution of electricity. As the

ABB's Information Systems, Raleigh headquarters.

regulatory environment of the electric utility industry continues to evolve, ABB will maintain a strong leadership position and will be positioned for continued growth and profitability. They expect to be a strong and valued member of the Raleigh business community for a long, long time.

The ABB Alpha electronic meter.

Bolton Corp.

In 1923, William E Bolton, Sr., came to Raleigh to oversee construction of the heating systems for the Sir Walter Hotel. At completion of the project he remained in Raleigh to start the W. E. Bolton Co., which installed and serviced residential coal fired boilers. By the late 1920s the company had expanded to include the sale and installation of commercial refrigeration equipment at local dairies and meat packing companies.

The company's steady growth through the early 1930s required a move to an office and shop building on the corner of West Martin and Harrington streets, where they remained until the outbreak of World War II. Shortages caused by the war reduced sales and forced Bolton to operate his business out of his home.

In the spring of 1945 his son, William E. Bolton, Jr., returned home from serving six years on the USS Yorktown to complete his studies at North Carolina State College and to join the family business. With only three other employees, they opened a new office at 519 West North Street in 1946 and became an active part of Raleigh's phenomenal postwar growth. They continued serving their residential heating customers while seeking an ever-greater share of the commercial air conditioning and heating market.

By 1956 the newly named Bolton Air Conditioning and Heating Company had outgrown its North Street offices. Construction of a 10,000 square-foot office facility at 919 West Morgan Street was completed and occupied in 1957, and is the firm's present home.

William E. Bolton, Sr. (wearing bow tie), at the 519 West North Street office in 1955 receiving the company's first group insurance certificate from a representative of Blue Cross and Blue Shield.

In 1963 the company received its single largest project to that date: the contract for heating and cooling the new State Legislative Building. Work on that project coincided with the initiation of a decade-long move to broaden operations to include all mechanical trades (plumbing, heating, air conditioning, refrigeration ventilation, industrial piping, utility, and electrical construction). A few of Bolton's other projects during this period included the Martin County Hospital in Williamston, the North Carolina Archives and History Building, the North Carolina Department of Administration Building, the Century Station Post Office Renovations, and the D. H. Hill Library at North Carolina State University. This diversification of trades and projects prompted a change in the company name to Bolton Corp. in 1970.

During the 1970s the younger Bolton's three sons joined the firm on a full time basis. This marked another period of expansion of the size, scope and complexity of projects undertaken. Projects completed during this period are now Raleigh landmarks, including Rex Hospital, the School of Veterinary Medicine at NCSU, the Radisson Hotel, The Raleigh Civic Center renovation, the One Hanover Square office, UCB Plaza, and the American Airlines Hub at RDU.

Over the past 7 decades, Bolton Corp. has grown from a post-World War II service business of 5 employees, to almost 500 apprentices, craftsmen, technicians. engineers, and support staff presently employed in Raleigh, Asheville, Morehead City, and Wilmington. The scope of services now provided also include: data network installations for schools, banks, and utility companies; complete design/build services; and custom metal fabrication of stainless steel products that have a worldwide distribution. As the fourth generation of the Bolton family joins the firm, they are proudest of all to point out that some of the 25,000 regular service customers that depend on Bolton Corp. for their home service needs, were original customers of their great-grandfather.

Conservative growth, professional management, skilled tradesmen and women, and an eye to the future have marked the success of Bolton Corp. and its growth in North Carolina.

Bolton Corp.'s main office at 919 West Morgan.

Clancy & Theys Construction Company

In 1949, brothers-in-law E.I. Clancy and J.C. Theys began building homes in house-hungry, postwar Raleigh. The first three were on Edmund Street in Capitol Heights. The two entrepreneurs worked hard, staying on the job until 10 or 11 at night, even selling the houses themselves to make a profit. They turned to commercial construction, and, in 1952, they won the contract to build Raleigh's downtown Fire Station No.1. E.I. Clancy later recalled, "We didn't make a penny on it, but we learned a lot."

They learned much more in the years ahead, including the value of an "extended family" of skilled employees. The men worked hard to keep everyone busy—not always easy in the construction business. A tradition began of taking on tough jobs, including renovation projects many companies found too demanding. Though difficult, the work helped spread Clancy & Theys' reputation, and led to more new jobs.

The portfolio grew: public contracts, many for the area's colleges and universities, were later joined by work for blue-chip corporations locating in Research Triangle Park. Office, research, and manufacturing projects followed.

Clancy & Theys' success in Raleigh helped the company move into new markets. It first moved in 1984 to Wilmington, N.C., and later to Newport News, Va., Orlando, Fla., and Charlotte, N.C. In 1986, J.C. Theys and son Jeff sold their shares of the company to the Clancys. E.I. Clancy became chairman, son Tim Clancy president, and his brother Tick executive vice president—the leadership that took the company into the 1990s.

Today, it would be difficult to drive through Raleigh without passing by something Clancy & Theys built, renovated, or landscaped. Landmark projects dot Raleigh's scene, many of which called upon the company's renovation expertise. The North Carolina Governor's Mansion restoration, for instance, was perhaps the State's first cost-plus construction contract when Clancy & Theys was hand-picked to do the job in 1975. Other notable renovations include the North Carolina

State Capitol, Raleigh Memorial Auditorium, Tucker Carriage House, and Oakwood Mordecai Meeting House.

Founders Clancy and Theys have a special love for the land that led naturally to landscape work. The company left its mark on numerous city parks, including several projects at Pullen and Chavis parks, and its own skilled workers have helped reshape downtown Raleigh with the Streetscapes projects.

Clancy & Theys' new construction work covers nearly every category. The company has built public and private schools, as well as buildings for North Carolina State University, the University of North Carolina, Shaw University, and Meredith, Peace, St. Augustine's, and Wake Technical colleges. C&T has built dozens of churches; several million square feet of office, warehouse, and retail space; research centers; health care facilities; country clubs; and sports and recreation facilities. The company's other Divisions have led the way in new project types, including hotels, restaurants, apartments, resort condominiums, nursing homes, elder care centers, and large manufacturing plants.

Raleigh Memorial Auditorium addition and renovation.

Clancy & Theys—even after nearly 50 years in business—still has an entrepreneurial spirit, a fact that was recognized in 1992 when the company received the Greater Raleigh Entrepreneurial Company Award. C&T is Raleigh's (and North Carolina's) largest home-grown and independently-owned general contractor. Clancy & Theys perennially numbers among the nation's Top 400 contractors, but its growth and expansion have changed neither its commitment to building and improving its home town, nor the company's deep sense of pride in its Raleigh roots.

North Carolina Governor's Mansion restoration.

College Foundation Inc.

In 1955, few people could imagine making loans to college students; such a concept was radical in that era. Yet, when private, nonprofit College Foundation, Inc. (CFI) was chartered on November 29, 1955, by Governor Luther Hodges as a foundation for scholarships for North Carolina students, the seedlings of the North Carolina student loan program were planted. Little did the Raleigh community know that the humble Foundation, housed in leased office space of the downtown First Citizens Bank, would develop into an organization that would serve as the central loan originator and servicer for North Carolina's student loan program in the years to come.

Several North Carolina banks and other companies such as the well-known R.J. Reynolds Tobacco Company contributed funds totalling $89,000 to the first scholarship fund. However, as Trustee President J. Gregory Poole indicated in the early years of operation, the amount of scholarship funding was never sufficient to meet the growing demands of the college-bound population; some even suggested that the faltering Foundation should be dissolved after its first few years.

When Governor Terry Sanford (a former CFI Board member) took office in 1961, he made it clear that higher education—and education funding—were top priorities, crucial to the growth and economic well-being of the state. His efforts to "save" the faltering CFI included appointing Raleigh banker Victor E. Bell, Jr., as Chairman of the Board of Trustees in 1962 (Bell remained in this position for 30 years, retiring in 1992). When a reconstituted Board convened in 1962, the Trustees determined that the primary aim of the Foundation would be to operate a student loan program, funded by banks and centrally administered by College Foundation. Bell then personally visited banks all across the state, successfully recruiting the funding support of 97 banks.

On December 4, 1962, Governor Sanford announced the full support of

Raleigh banker Victor E. Bell, Jr. was appointed Chairman of the Board of Trustees in 1962, a position he held for 30 years.

his office and the North Carolina Bankers Association for the newly-established North Carolina Bankers Student Loan Plan to be administered by College Foundation. This program preceded the nationwide Guaranteed Student Loan Program, with its first student loans made during the 1963-64 year. In 1966, after the Congress established the Guaranteed Student Loan Program as a part of the Higher Education Act of '65, the Foundation's charter was amended to conform to the provisions of the new Act. Since 1966, CFI has administered North Carolina's student loan program (now known as the Federal Family Education Loan Program). Loans made through this program are insured by the N.C. State Education Assistance Authority (N.C. SEAA) and funded primarily through the N.C. SEAA and banks in North Carolina.

College Foundation has benefited tremendously from the historically long, dedicated service of its upper management and Board of Trustees. For example, Duffy Paul, former Financial Aid Director at High Point College, served as President of CFI for nearly 30 years (1964-1993). Current President Gwen Davis, former bookkeeper and chief accountant at Meredith College, first joined CFI in 1971. During the tenure of Mr. Paul and Mrs. Davis, the Foundation grew and moved from its second office space in the Ruark Building on St. Mary's Street (1969-1973), to the Methodist Building on Glenwood Avenue (1973-1988), to its current, fully-owned building on Yonkers Road. The Foundation has grown from 2 to 140 employees.

In his book detailing the history of College Foundation and the North Carolina student loan program—*The Will & The Way*—T. Harry Gatton quoted a comment by Victor Bell, Jr., at the groundbreaking for the current CFI building: "Our business is investing in the future—in young people, in students. We wish to make better opportunities for them and for the state." By mid 1997, the Foundation had lent about $1.6 billion to 316,000 students.

York Construction Company completed College Foundation's present building—named the Victor E. Bell, Jr. Building—on March 21, 1988.

David Allen Company

David G. Allen founded the David Allen Company in 1920 as a tile, marble, and masonry contractor. He soon established a reputation as a skilled craftsman that has endured in the ornamental, decorative, and artistic work he left behind in numerous Raleigh area buildings and homes. He also influenced many local masons who learned their trade under his guidance. Along with high standards of craftsmanship, Allen imbued his firm with a sound moral and ethical reputation which the company takes pride in continuing.

Allen, a recognized leader in the tile, marble, and terrazzo industry, was a strong influence in the industry's standards of quality and innovative installation methods. In the early '20s terrazzo was added to the firm's list of specialties. That industry, having its origin and rich artistic background in Italy, was dominated in this country by Italians. In order to maintain his quality reputation in the new terrazzo department, Allen arranged through industry friends in Italy to have several Italian craftsmen brought into this country and become the nucleus of

The David Allen Company in the 1930s, located on North West Street facing the street car garage.

The current home office of the David Allen Company of Raleigh

his terrazzo crews. After a short period of adjustment, a combination of English, Italian, hand illustrations, and demonstrations allowed the frustrated customers, supervisors, and fellow employees to communicate with the non-English speaking employees. Having overcome that and many other obstacles, the Allen Company progressed to its present industry position as the nation's largest tile, marble, and terrazzo contractor.

Robert Roberson was employed by Allen in 1957 with accounting and administrative responsibilities. He sustained his permanence less than two years later when he became manager. In 1967 he purchased controlling interest in the company, was named president, and acquired the remaining equity following Allen's death in 1977. Under Roberson's leadership, the company has become a nationally recognized leader in the tile, marble, and terrazzo industry.

The firm's contracts are in the Southeast and include such notable installations as the recently completed Washington National Airport which displays nearly half a million square feet of David Allen Company terrazzo and tile.

Roberson, with 40 years as head of the Allen organization, has established himself as an innovative national industry leader. With the help of talented management personnel and close to 300 field employees, this complex national organization has branch offices in Washington, DC, Columbia, SC and Norfolk, VA., and is guided by Roberson as president; Donald Scott, executive vice president; David Roberson, vice president; and Arthur Odom, vice president.

Although secure as an industry leader, the management team of David Allen Company recognizes that continued success and growth will be accomplished only by remaining committed to meeting the requirements of the customers they serve.

Golden Corral Corporation

When co-founders James Maynard and Bill Carl conceived the idea of Golden Corral in 1971, they set out on a journey to improve family dining in America. The mission was simple: "Making Pleasurable Dining Affordable." With start-up capital of only $50,000, the two young entrepreneurs with no prior restaurant experience, relied on the basics of good food and good service to create an environment in which Golden Corral customers could dine and feel as if they were guests in their homes. Two years later, in 1973, the first Golden Corral restaurant opened in Fayetteville, NC. The second restaurant opened in Raleigh within a few months.

From the beginning, growth has been a constant for Golden Corral Corporation. Only five years after opening the first restaurant, the company reached its first million dollars in net profits. Today, there are over 450 restaurants in 39 states and Mexico. Approximately 265 of the restaurants are franchised, and the remainder are company owned and operated. Last year, the company reported record annual sales of over $711 million. Golden

Corral has set an aggressive expansion plan for the next several years with a vision to exceed $1 billion in systemwide sales by the year 2000.

Golden Corral Corporation, the largest chain of privately held family steak houses in the United States, has approximately 20,000 employees systemwide, including about 250 who are employed at the corporate headquarters located in Raleigh, NC. The company's parent company, Investors Management Corporation (IMC), a privately-held holding company of food service and service industry companies, also located in Raleigh, is led by Golden Corral co-founder and Chairman James Maynard, who is Chairman and Chief Executive Officer of IMC.

One of the company's beliefs is to never stop striving to improve. In 1982, Ted Fowler was appointed President and in 1989 he was named President and CEO of Golden Corral Corporation. He has led the highly successful evolution of Golden Corral from a family steak house into a diverse family concept featuring steaks, buffet and a bakery.

Today, nearly 25 years and a quarter of a billion pounds of beef later, Golden Corral continues to serve only USDA Choice steaks cut fresh daily. In addition to steaks, Golden Corral offers entrees of chicken and seafood. The Golden Choice Buffet™ features "made from scratch salads" and a hot vegetable and meat bar with carved meats served daily. The Brass Bell Bakery® offers fresh, hot cookies, muffins, and yeast rolls and homemade pizza fresh out of the oven every 15 minutes. The Sweet Spot features homestyle cobblers, pies, ice cream and yogurt with toppings to make your own sundae. During the weekend, the "Start Your Day Breakfast Buffet" features a wide variety of breakfast items, including made-to-order omelettes and Golden Corral's signature Cin-A-Gold Cinnamon Rolls.™ Although the restaurants and the menu have expanded, since 1973, the company's focus remains on "Making Pleasurable Dining Affordable."

Golden Corral Metro GC-10 restaurants have annual sales of about $3 million.

Newcomb and Company

When Charles A. "Bo" Newcomb founded Newcomb and Company in 1954 as a mechanical contracting firm specializing in air conditioning and heating, he began in a 1,500-square-foot building on a single lot on Pershing Road. Today the company has grown to cover eleven lots and to include ten-fold the original square footage of space.

The true strength of the firm, however, relates more to growth in personnel than in physical property. Now home to 125 HVAC-skilled professionals, Newcomb and Company is a full service mechanical contractor covering the residential, commercial and industrial fields. Today the company is in the second Newcomb generation and is managed by Robert T. "Robbo" Newcomb. He has emulated his father's commitment to quality, integrity, and expertise and constantly works to serve his customers more efficiently and economically.

The quality of indoor air environment is a major factor in the productivity and happiness of the personnel in a commercial building and equally so within a residence. Newcomb and

Vice Presidents Tom Ellison, Paul Whit Howard and Alan Davis with founder and Chairman Charles A. "Bo" Newcomb.

Company is not only committed to the improvement of air quality through its design and installation of systems but also to providing a "quick response" team of service personnel to keep those systems maintained for their ultimate performance. The service division and the controls division combine to provide the maximum comfort level at the peak point of efficiency for all their many customers.

In the company's time span, its experts have been integral participants in the

Executive Vice President Mike Penick, and Treasurer Paul Thomas with Robert Newcomb, President of Newcomb and Company.

vast changes in their industry. In 1954, air conditioning was essentially limited to banks and theaters; now it is a component part of almost every commercial and residential structure. By ensuring that its staff maintains consistent expertise in air quality, the firm has grown from installation of simple residential systems to complex computer actuated heating and cooling systems for office buildings, shopping centers, clean rooms and high tech laboratories for industry.

While serving its customers and its industry, Newcomb and Company has always remembered the need to serve its employees. This is reflected by the fact that its 125 employees represent 1,049 years of service at the company. Newcomb's list of professionals includes eight with over thirty years of service and twenty two with over fifteen years. Experience is the best teacher, and employees average 8.6 years of service at Newcomb and Company.

It has been a pleasant journey for all at Newcomb and Company, and they have never failed to remember that the needs of the customer are foremost.

The News & Observer

When McClatchy Newspapers Inc. purchased *The News & Observer* in 1995, the California-based chain became the latest owner of a paper associated throughout the 20th century with the family of Josephus Daniels.

But the paper actually began publication Sept. 12, 1880, as a consolidation of the *Raleigh News*, edited by Peter M. Hale and Leonidas L. Polk, and *The Observer*, edited by Capt. Samuel A. Ashe. Ashe became founding editor of *The N & O*.

In July 1894, Daniels bought *The N & O* at auction for $6,810. More than a century later, McClatchy purchased the paper, six weekly newspapers, two sister publications and NandoNet, an online information service, for $373 million. Between those two sales came 101 years of Daniels family ownership.

Josephus Daniels was born in Washington, N.C. in May 1862. He was the son of a Confederate ship-builder later killed in the Civil War. His mother, Mary Cleaves Daniels, moved her three sons to Wilson where the young Josephus worked in a printing office at age 12, published the amateur paper *Cornucopia* at 16, attended Wilson Collegiate Institute, edited the *Wilson Advance* at 18, and developed into a staunch Democrat.

He bought the weekly *Advance* and turned it into a profit-maker; then he and a brother established the *Kinston Free Press* in 1882. Shortly thereafter he became editor of the Raleigh weeklies *Farmer and Mechanic* and *The State Chronicle*, matriculated at the University Law School in Chapel Hill, was chosen State Printer in 1887, and married Addie Worth Bagley on May 2, 1888. In 1891, *The Chronicle* merged with the *Daily Call* to become the *Daily Chronicle* and a morning competitor to *The N & O*.

Daniels became editor of the weekly *The North Carolinian* when the *Daily Chronicle* merged with The *N & O* in 1892, a merger that led to bankruptcy in 1894. He then convinced 100 interested Democrats to purchase 100 shares each at $100 per share to raise money to buy the paper, offering a lifetime subscription in lieu of dividends. His first editions of *The N & O* had a circulation of about 1,800 in a city of 12,678. He had become the chief clerk of the Department of the Interior and had moved to Washington, D.C., and he sent the majority of his $2,750 annual salary to support the fledgling newspaper. He went on to become the Secretary of the Navy throughout the Wilson administration, ambassador to Mexico from 1933 to 1941 and the author of many volumes, including *Our Navy at War* (1922), *The Life of Woodrow Wilson* (1924), *Tar Heel Editor* (1939), *Editor in Politics* (1941), *The Wilson Era* (1944) and *Shirt Sleeve Diplomat* (1947).

Josephus Daniels, a dedicated newspaper man his entire life.

Although he spent long periods away from Raleigh, Daniels maintained personal control over the paper until his death in 1948.

In 1955, the Daniels family bought the afternoon *Raleigh Times*, and within a year daily circulation had leaped from 14,983 to more than 22,000. But by 1989 the two papers had merged.

Upon the retirement of Frank Daniels Jr. at the end of 1996, Fred Crisp, who had headed day-to-day business operations at *The N & O* since 1990, was named publisher. The past few years also have seen the installation of new printing presses and an aggressive move into electronic publishing on the Internet.

In 1996, *The N & O* was awarded the Pulitzer Prize for Public Service for "Boss Hog: North Carolina's Pork Revolution," a five-part series that described the impact of corporate hog farms on the enviromnent of Eastern North Carolina.

The N & O now employs about 1,400 full-time and part-time employees, with a circulation of 172,000 daily and more than 200,000 on Sundays.

The News & Observer building

R. L. Dresser, Inc.

This family owned business was begun in the early 1920s by Raymond Losee Dresser. Born in Rochester, New York in 1894, he moved to Connecticut in about 1913 and then to Wilson, North Carolina in 1917.

In 1914 he married Anna Marie Berry in New Haven, CT. Dresser had always installed wood floors, mainly parquet, in New York and Connecticut. When the company he worked for sent him to lay a parquet wood floor in a residence in Wilson, NC., he realized that there was a big demand for wood floor installers in North Carolina.

Dresser decided that he and his wife would move to North Carolina in 1917 to start a business, relocating first to Wilson and then to Raleigh where he opened his first "office" on Sunset Drive. Their home had a separate garage with a small room above. Materials were stored in the garage and the office was upstairs. When the business outgrew the garage they moved to a larger home on Wake Forest Road at what is now named Dresser Court. Here he started hiring more and more field men and office personnel—eventually, estimators, salesmen, a secretary, bookkeeper, and warehouse manager

When Mr. Dresser had first come to North Carolina, he teamed up with Mr. James A. Davidson, who later

Above: Mr. Raymond L. Dresser, the original owner.

Left: House on Sunset Drive—the first office in his home.

co-founded Davidson & Jones Construction in 1917. Dresser rode with Mr. Davidson on the side car of his motorcycle. They would travel to different places soliciting their work. Much of Raleigh and the surrounding areas were just dirt roads at that time.

In 1927, the Dressers' only child, Sara Jane, was born. Their daughter helped in the office on Wake Forest Road doing payroll and secretarial duties as she grew older. On August 15, 1953, Sara Jane married Jimmy Edwards. Mr. Dresser hired Jimmy and trained him to, one day, take over the business.

In the late 1940s, Mr. Dresser started installing acoustical ceilings and eventually resilient flooring and wall base. The wood floor portion of the business began doing commercial work—in office buildings, colleges universities and installing gymnasium floors in schools. Jimmy encouraged Mr. Dresser to expand to the point where the company outgrew warehouse and office space on Wake Forest Road. Land was then purchased on Winton Road which is now known as Atlantic.

Construction was begun on a warehouse on Winton Road in 1969, but Mr. Dresser fell ill and passed away August 29, 1969. The business immediately was turned over to Sara Jane so that Jimmy could run it. He expanded the company, constructing a separate office building which was subsequently expanded twice. The expansion resulted in warehouse two for ceilings, and warehouse one for floors. Eventually two more warehouses were built to accomodate wood flooring in one and computer flooring in another. The business grew despite several recessions due to the reputation and respect Mr. Dresser had acquired over the decades because of his service and expertise. Many of his mechanics had worked for the company 20-30 years. The firm presently employs 80-100 people, many for over 20 years. Turn over is very low.

Some of the larger ceiling and floor jobs completed were the Crabtree Valley Mall in the early 70s which had 1,000,000 square feet of ceiling tile; the Vet school at NC State; the Legislature and Albemarle government buildings in downtown Raleigh; the Sheraton Imperial; Northern Telecom; and, the CP&L building downtown Raleigh. In the early days, the company installed wood floors in the Edgerton mansion on Oberlin Road; did work for Willie York when he built Cameron Village in 1948; Rex Hospital when it opened on Saint Mary's Street (and again when it moved to Blue Ridge Road); Raleigh Municipal Airport; Phillip Morris plant in Richmond, VA; and, numerous IBM buildings.

Above: Jimmy Edwards (son-in-law), to Mr. Dresser

Below: Reginald L. Edwards (Regge), grandson of Mr. Dresser, 3rd generation

The most publicized gym floor was the Dean Smith Center in Chapel Hill, NC and most recently, the gym at Univesity of Virginia at Charlottesville, and Duke University's Cameron Indoor Stadium.

Jimmy and Sara Jane's oldest child Regge Edwards graduated from NC State University in 1976 and started with the company in 1977, working on the jobsites at first and later in the office as an estimator. In early 1993, Jimmy retired due to failing health. At that time, Regge assumed the duties of the president and continues to run the business to this day.

After a long and courageous struggle with cancer, Jimmy Edwards passed away on September 25, 1994.

R. L. Dresser, Inc. is the franchisee for acoustical ceilings and resilient floors for Armstrong World Industries and also for the Robbins, Inc. franchise for sports surfaces. Their territory covers North and South Carolina, and Virginia for gymnasium, aerobic, stage, dance, and weight room floors.

When Mr. Dresser began the company, he covered much of the East Coast and went as far west as Arkansas.

Mr. Dresser incorporated the business in 1960, ceasing the residential work and continuing only the commercial. They undertake all size jobs, large or small.

All four of Mr. Dresser's grandchildren have worked for the business in some respect or another. The grandchildren are Reginald (Regge), Sherre, Bryan Edwards, and Tina (Edwards) Rowley.

All three generations have supported the Wolfpack Club at NC State University. Jimmy established a scholarship at NC State to help student athletes pay their tuition. The company has also supported other colleges and universities, including Peace, Meredith, UNC Chapel Hill, and Duke.

The firm has received numerous awards, including those from Armstrong and Robbins, Inc. for volume of sales of their products and were the number one subcontractor in the Southeastern region for eight years with Armstrong World Industries. In 1995 they received the Quarter Century Award from Armstrong.

Saint Augustine's College

Saint Augustine's College Chapel

According to its early beginning in 1867, Saint Augustine's College was established in Raleigh, North Carolina by the Freedmen's Commission of the Protestant Episcopal Church. History reveals that the institution functioned first as Saint Augustine's Normal and Collegiate Institute. Its purpose, printed on page 14 of the General Catalogue in 1882, was to "afford young men and women of the colored race, superior advantages for obtaining a thorough academic education, to train and equip teachers for efficient service, and to prepare young men for the Holy Ministry." At that time, preparation of teachers was determined to be a priority and normal training or teacher education was considered a shared responsibility of development that could be realized by help from the Episcopal Church.

Against this background, Saint Augustine's College grew out of a recognition of basic needs and among these were to provide funds, identify persons who seemed responsive to the calling, and to inspire these potentials to become teachers. Hence, the Episcopal Church and Saint Augustine's College came together to support this initiative. It has developed into an accredited four-year coeducational liberal arts institution which builds on the College's history to craft "A New Era of Excellence" that adds to its tradition and moves it forward in its thrust toward the twenty-first century.

In 1895, the cornerstone of the Chapel was laid. This edifice was built by students in the industrial arts department and faculty volunteers. The Chapel and Lich Gate were designed by Henry Beard Delany, who was an instructor of carpentry and masonry, chaplain, and superintendent of building projects. He later became Suffragan Bishop of the Episcopal Diocese of North Carolina and America, also serving as Assistant Principal of Saint Augustine's. Other construction work on the Chapel was done by three African American stone masons—William H. Haywood, Jerry Smith, and supervisor Washington Hayes, grandfather of Hubert Hayes, vestryman. The Chapel is a designated historic site and is listed on the National Register for Historic Places. The College maintains the Chapel for Episcopal, Anglican, ecumenical, and religious worship services as well as community activities. A font and pool are also maintained for baptismal upon request.

The Chapel program supports campus and community efforts which deal with issues in our world.

In 1896, Saint Agnes Hospital and Training School for Nurses was founded.

It provided medical services for the community. For a long time, this facility was the only hospital available to Raleigh's African Americans. Saint Agnes Building is also listed on the National Register for Historic Places.

The curriculum encourages intellectual inquiry and communicates the interconnectedness of disciplines, cultures, and time. Saint Augustine's College is committed to educating the whole person and to preparing students to make meaningful contributions to a challenging world. Therefore, the curriculum is innovative, interactive, interdisciplinary, and collaborative with emphasis placed on learning to think critically.

Nine heads of Saint Augustine's have provided leadership. Eight have served and one currently provides leadership to the institution. The first four principals were Episcopal clergymen. The first president, also a Caucasian, served as the fifth leader. The next leaders have the distinction of being African American laymen of the Episcopal Church. Their names and terms of offices are: The Rev. J. Brinton Smith, 1868-1872; The Rev. John Estes Cooke Smedes, 1873-1884; The Rev. Robert Bean Sutton, 18841891; The Rev. Aaron Burtes Hunter, 1881-1916; Dr. Edgar Henry Goold, 1917-1946; Dr. Harold L. Trigg, 1947-1954; Dr. James A. Boyer, 1954-1967; Dr. Prezell R. Robinson, 1967-1995; and Dr. Bernard W. Franklin, 1995-present.

Under the leadership of Dr. Bernard W. Franklin, ninth president, Saint Augustine's College looks toward his vision of a new era of excellence that is shaped by traditions, diverse visions, and technological and ethical challenges. The new era of excellence will require a synergy of individuals, community, and corporate partnerships to ensure real success and future growth. Crossing the threshold into the year 2000, Saint Augustine's will seek to attract global resources for the benefit of its students and the institution thereby enriching the local, state, and national community. Students will be taught to understand,

Dr. Bernard W, Franklin, President

interact with and build upon the computer based and information based technologies that will establish them as leaders in their academic and professional pursuits. His vision is a belief that a strong Saint Augustine's directly translates into a strong, stable community. By training young men and women to truly value the human contribution and spirit, the corporate community gains a more prepared, balanced, and capable employee. His vision is that Saint Augustine's growing reputation will bring outstanding students as well as distinguished faculty and staff.

Centers of excellence will be established for the twenty-first century.

There will be the Center of Excellence for Mathematics and Science; Center for Teaching Excellence; Center of Excellence for Management Science; Center of Excellence for Urban and International Studies; Center of Excellence for Visual and Performing Arts; and Center of Excellence for Technological Research.

In 1997, Saint Augustine's primary purpose is to ensure the students that they will receive the best education that will enable them to be well prepared to compete in the global society.

Shaw University

Talbert O. Shaw Living ◆ Learning Center

Shaw University, the oldest historically Black university in the South was founded in 1865 by New England missionary, Henry Martin Tupper. In 1866, the school was named the Raleigh Institute. It was renamed the Shaw Collegiate Institute in 1870 to honor its chief benefactor, Elijah Shaw of Wales, Massachusetts. In 1875, an Act of the North Carolina General Assembly chartered the school as The Shaw University. Originally, Shaw University was founded to teach freedmen theology and biblical interpretation. However, within 15 years of its founding, the institution began to broaden its curriculum.

Thirteen major departments constitute a variety of academic offerings that are geared toward today's employment market. The University offers 31 degree programs leading to the bachelor of arts or bachelor of science degree, and three degree programs leading to the associate of arts degree. The Center for Alternative Programs of Education (CAPE) allows students in nine cities across North Carolina the opportunity to pursue an academic degree through flexible course scheduling, independent study, and credit for prior learning experiences. Shaw University is accredited by the Southern Association of Colleges and Schools to award the associate and bachelor's degrees. Two of its academic programs also have national accreditation. The kinesiotherapy program is accredited by the American Kinesiotherapy Association and the teacher education program is accredited by the National Council for Accreditation of Teacher Education. The latter program is also approved by the North Carolina Department of Public Instruction.

Talbert Oscall Shaw, PhD, assumed the presidency of Shaw University in November 1987. Since President Shaw's tenure, student enrollment has increased from 1400 to an average of 2500. In 1993, under his leadership, the University made courses in ethics and values central to the general education of all its students in order to emphasize its commitment to high personal standards and citizenship in its graduates. This thrust challenges Shaw University students to ask questions about the social ills of the day and to seek answers to those questions.

University community service and outreach programs include a pre-college program sponsored by the US Environmental Protection Agency for 8th through 12th graders to enhance their skills in mathematics, English, science,

Leonard Medical Building

LEONARD MEDICAL BUILDING.

and computer science; and a community development project sponsored by US Housing and Urban Development to help small businesses.

Shaw University recently completed a $11,000,000 state-of-the-art complex that covers a half city block. The facility brings both economic and aesthetic contributions to the city of Raleigh. In November 1996 the University officially named the facility "The Talbert O. Shaw Living ◆ Learning Center" in honor of its current president.

Shaw University also has two buildings listed in the National Registry of Historic Places. Estey Hall, erected in 1873, was the nation's first dormitory to house women on a coeducational campus. The Leonard School of Medicine, founded in 1882, was the first four-year medical school in this country. It provided training for Black doctors and pharmacists in the South. The school closed in 1918, however, the historic building still stands and is currently under renovation.

Shaw University has implemented "Strides to Excellence: Why Not the Best?" as its administrative aim and motto as it prepares to meet the challenges of the new millennium.

York Properties, Inc.

York Properties, Inc., traces its history in the Triangle back to 1910 when C. V. York built Patterson Hall at North Carolina State University. Since then, the York name has been associated with local and state landmarks, from the familiar Bell Tower at North Carolina State University to Raleigh's Memorial Auditorium, home of the North Carolina Symphony.

Today, York's grandson, G. Smedes York, president of York Properties, continues his family's tradition of involvement and leadership in business and civic affairs having served as Raleigh Mayor, Raleigh-Durham Airport Authority Chairman, North Carolina Citizens for Business and Industry Chairman and President of the national Urban Land Institute.

York and his father, J. W. "Willie" York, moved the family's businesses in new directions in the 40 years following World War II. The construction company continues today as McDonald-York, formed in 1994 and one of the Triangle's premier builders. It is a division of Coleman and Wood Inc. of Rockville, Md.

York Properties is the locus of the family's enterprises today, and it encompasses a wide range of real estate services.

J. W. York, a member of the state's Business Hall of Fame, returned to Raleigh following World War II to launch in 1946 the construction of the first shopping center in the Southeastern United States, Cameron Village. The 606,000 sq. ft. shopping center and surrounding residential and office complex changed the city's business landscape. In 1992, Cameron Village began a $26 million renovation that has produced one of the Triangle's most popular and unique shopping centers. York also made history by building and managing some of the city's landmark hotels, including the Velvet Cloak Inn in 1963 and in 1973, the city's one-time largest hospitality complex, the Mission Valley Inn, now a part of NCSU. He also developed the York Industrial Center which became home to Westinghouse's Meter Plant in 1954 and

J. W. "Willie" York and son G. Smedes York, former mayor, who carried the Olympic torch in Raleigh in 1996.

IBM's first Triangle manufacturing plant in 1965.

To manage the family's growing number of properties, York Properties evolved in the 1960s as the successor to J.W. York Co. In 1997, York Properties managed eight shopping centers throughout the Triangle including Raleigh's historic City Market, Cary Village Square, Mission Valley Shopping Center, Durham's University Commons and the flagship Cameron Village as well as office buildings, apartments and homeowner associations.

Smedes York became president of York Properties in 1970 and established during the next two decades a complete and full-service real estate operation. Divisions in commercial and residential real estate were in place by 1984. York Commercial brokers, manages and develops commercial properties throughout the Triangle. York Residential is among the top four residential real estate companies with over 140 agents.

In 1987, York Ventures was established to help clients design, develop and coordinate new construction projects such as Raleigh's historic Murphey School conversion to apartments for older citizens. York Properties continues to evolve into an unmatched property management company, offering security, landscape, and maintenance services as well as homeowner association services and traditional management services.

A fourth generation of York leadership began in 1993 when Smedes York's son, George York, entered the business in property leasing. Says Smedes York, "Raleigh has had tremendous change during the past 90 years. Our challenge both as corporate and private citizens is to participate fully in this change. We can do our part in two distinct ways. First, we can strive to perform our business in a quality manner. Second, we can participate in the community, both in civic and governmental matters." It's a role that the York family has filled fully in the City of Oaks.

ACKNOWLEDGMENTS

I am thankful to have this opportunity to express my gratitude to Joan Pennell for her many kindnesses to me throughout my work on this history of her home city. I also thank Beth Crabtree for her early advice, and the remaining members of the Wake County Historical Society for providing me the opportunity to undertake what has been a pleasant task.

The staff of the North Carolina Room of the Wilson Library at the University of North Carolina at Chapel Hill have honored my hundreds of requests cheerfully, and they have voluntarily directed me to materials I would otherwise have missed. Jan Poff has passed on numerous tips he discovered while gathering historical photographs and illustrations, and Dixon Qualls has contributed far more than a few pages of color with his modern shots.

I especially want to thank Mr. Byron Freeman for sharing with me his memories of the Raleigh of his youth, in a time long ago, but in a setting still close to his heart.

James Vickers

I am deeply indebted to the following people and organizations for the illustrations that have been reproduced in *Raleigh: The City of Oaks:* Dick Lankford, at the Division of Archives and History, Raleigh; Jerry Cotton, of the North Carolina Collection, University of North Carolina, Chapel Hill; Maurice Toler, curator of the North Carolina State University Archives; Mike Finn, assistant sports information director, Department of Athletics at North Carolina State; Ellen Gartrell, assistant curator for Reader Services, and Patricia Webb, of the Manuscript Department, Perkins Library, Duke University, Durham; Sharon Broom, information officer for the North Carolina Museum of Art, Raleigh; Lany McDonald, librarian, and Betsy Marsh and Robbin Hyde, at the *News and Observer;* and Dixon Qualls, color photographer, who took the greatest care in the execution of his duties.

Although pictures may be worth thousands of words, they need captions, nevertheless. Dr. H.G. Jones, Alice Cotten, and the rest of the North Carolina Collection staff; Esther Presnell, at the Capital Area Visitor Center; Vicki Craft, of the Planning Department, City of Raleigh; Charles Murray, of the state Farmers Market; Bill Norton, Meredith College; Linda Harris, Mordecai Square Historical Society; Murray S. Downs, North Carolina State University; and Michael R. Hill, Alan C. Downs, John R. Detreville, and Connie Lael—among many others—deserve special mention for the advice and information they provided. I am also grateful to Mike Hill, Alan Downs, and Tim and Lori Farley for the unselfish manner in which they helped me deal with my personal transportation crisis.

My friend, William S. Powell, must take credit for introducing me to Jim Vickers. It was a pleasure working with him, and I wish him much success in future literary efforts.

Jan-Michael Poff

BIBLIOGRAPHY

Abernathy, Elizabeth Hill. *Historical Facts of Raleigh and Wake County.* Raleigh: Caswell-Nash Chapter of the North Carolina Daughters of the American Revolution, 1938.

Amis, Moses N. *Historical Raleigh from its Foundation in 1792.* Raleigh: Edwards and Broughton, 1902.

_____. *Historical Raleigh.* Raleigh: Commercial Printing Company, 1913.

An Architectual and Historical Inventory of Raleigh, North Carolina. Raleigh: The City of Raleigh and the Raleigh Historic Properties Commission in Cooperation with the North Carolina Division of Archives and History, 1978.

Ashe, Samuel A'Court. *Biographical History of North Carolina,* 8 Vols. Greensboro: Charles L. Van Noppen, 1905-1917.

Barbee, Mrs. James M. *Raleigh Public Schools, 1876-1914-1942.* Raleigh: Mitchell Printing Company, 1943.

Battle, Kemp P. *Early History of Raleigh, The Capital City of North Carolina, A Centennial Address, October 18, 1892.* Raleigh: Edwards and Broughton, 1893.

_____. *Raleigh and the Old Town of Bloomsbury.* Raleigh: Capital Printing Company, 1902.

_____. *Sketches of the Early History of the City of Raleigh, Centennial Adress, July 4, 1876.* Raleigh: Raleigh Job Printers, 1877.

Carroll, Grady Lee Ernest, Sr. *The City of Raleigh, North Carolina, and the Civil War Experience.* Raleigh: Privately Printed, 1979.

_____. *They Lived in Raleigh: Some Leading Personalities from 1792 to 1892, with Introduction and Appendices.* Raleigh: Southeastern Copy Center, n.d.

Centennial Ceremonies Held in Christ Church Parish, Raleigh, North Carolina, A.D. 1921. Raleigh: Bynum Printing Company, 1922.

Chamberlain, Hope Summerell. *History of Wake County.* Raleigh: Edwards and Broughton, 1922.

Clark, Walter. *History of the Raleigh and Gaston Railroad Company.* Raleigh: Raleigh News, 1877.

Coon, Charles L. *North Carolina Schools and Academies and the Beginnings of Public Education in North Carolina, A Documentary History, 1790-1840.* Raleigh: Edwards and Broughton, 1908.

Covington, Nina Holland. *Guide Book of Raleigh, North Carolina, Historical and Descriptive.* Raleigh: Capital Printing Company, 1924.

Daniels, Jonathan. *A Southerner Discovers the South.* New York: The Macmillan Company, 1938

_____. *Tar Heels, A Portrait of North Carolina.* New York: Dodd, Mead, and Company, 1941.

Daniels, Josephus. *Editor in Politics.* Chapel Hill: The University of North Carolina Press, 1941.

_____. *Tar Heel Editor.* Chapel Hill: The University of North Carolina Press, 1939.

Elliot, Robert Neal, Jr. *The Raleigh Register, 1799-1863.* Ph.D. Thesis, The University of North Carolina at Chapel Hill, 1953.

Gay, Dorothy Ann. *Crisis of Identity: The Negro Community in Raleigh, North Carolina, 1865-1900.* M.A. Thesis, The University of North Carolina at Chapel Hill, 1970.

Goerch, Carl. *Carolina Chats.* Raleigh: Edwards and Broughton, 1944.

Haywood, Marshall D. *Joel Lane, Pioneer and Patriot.* Raleigh: The Wake County Committee of the Colonial Dames of America, 1900.

Illustrated Raleigh, 1904. Raleigh: Chamber of Commerce, 1904.

Johnson, Guion Griffis. *Ante-Bellum North Carolina.* Chapel Hill: The University of North Carolina Press, 1937.

Lefler, Hugh T. and Newsome, Albert R. *The History of a Southern State: North Carolina.* 3rd ed. Chapel Hill: The University of North Carolina Press, 1973.

Lefler, Hugh T. *North Carolina History Told by Contemporaries.* Chapel Hill: The University of North Carolina Press, 1934.

Lemay, Thomas J. *An Address Delivered before Hiram Lodge No. 40, in the Masonic Hall, Raleigh, on the Twenty-Fourth June, 1846.* Grand Lodge Proceedings 1836-1851.

Mordecau, Ellen. *Gleanings from Long Ago.*

Savannah: Braid and Hutton, Inc., 1933.

Newsletter of the Wake County Historical Society beginning in 1963.

North Carolina Collection Clipping File Through 1975 for Wake County, 7 Vols. in the North Carolina Room of the Wilson Library at The University of North Carolina at Chapel Hill.

Olds, Fred A. "Story of the Surrender of Raleigh," *Orphans' Friend and Masonic Journal.* Vol. 50, no. 28. n.d.

Reid, Elizabeth. *From Raleigh's Past.* Raleigh: Branch Banking and Trust Company, 1965.

Salley, Katherine Batts. *Life at Saint Mary's.* Chapel Hill: The University of North Carolina Press, 1942.

Schumann, Marguerite E. *Strolling at State: A Walking Guide to North Carolina State University.* Raleigh: North Carolina State University Alumni Association, 1973.

Shaw, George C. *John Chavis.* Binghamton: Vail-Ballou Press, 1931.

Stolpen, Steve. *Raleigh: A Pictorial History.* Norfolk: Donning Company/Publishers, 1977.

Swain, David L. *Early Times in Raleigh.* Raleigh: Walters, Hughes and Company, 1867.

Waugh, Elizabeth Culbertson. *North Carolina's Capital, Raleigh.* Raleigh: Junior League of Raleigh and Raleigh Historic Sites Commission, 1967.

Wellons, Lee Douglas. *Historical Development of the Raleigh Public Schools.* M.A. Thesis, The University of North Carolina at Chapel Hill, 1942.

Williams, Alexa Carroll, ed. *Raleigh: A Guide to North Carolina's Capital.* Raleigh: The Raleigh Fine Arts Society, Inc., 1975.

Writer's Program of the Works Projects Administration in the State of North Carolina. *Raleigh: Capital of North Carolina.* New Bern: Owen G. Dunn Company, 1942.

Other Sources

Microfilm and/or clipping file articles from the following Raleigh newspapers: *Minerva, The North Carolinian, News and Observer, Register, Standard, Sentinel, Star, The State Chronicle,* and *Times.*